Activism and Women's NGOs in Turkey

Activism and Women's NGOs in Turkey

Civil Society, Feminism and Politics

Asuman Özgür Keysan

I.B. TAURIS
LONDON • NEW YORK • OXFORD • NEW DELHI • SYDNEY

I.B. TAURIS
Bloomsbury Publishing Plc
50 Bedford Square, London, WC1B 3DP, UK
1385 Broadway, New York, NY 10018, USA
29 Earlsfort Terrace, Dublin 2, Ireland

BLOOMSBURY, I.B. TAURIS and the Diana logo are trademarks
of Bloomsbury Publishing Plc

First published in Great Britain 2019
This paperback edition published in 2021

Cover design: Adriana Brioso
Cover image: Rally for International Women's Day on March 8, 2018 in Istanbul,
Turkey. (© Chris McGrath/Getty Images)

A catalogue record for this book is available from the British Library.

A catalog record for this book is available from the Library of Congress.

ISBN: 9-781-7883-1013-0
PB: 978-0-7556-4374-5
eISBN: 9-781-7867-2631-5
ePDF: 9-781-7867-3637-6

Series: Library of Modern Turkey

Typeset by Newgen KnowledgeWorks Pvt. Ltd., Chennai, India

To find out more about our authors and books visit www.bloomsbury.com
and sign up for our newsletters.

Contents

Tables

Acknowledgements

This book is based on research conducted for my PhD, awarded by the University of Strathclyde in 2015. I would like to express my deepest gratitude to my supervisor Dr Catherine Eschle for her invaluable guidance throughout all stages of my research. Without her guidance, ongoing support, criticism and encouragement this book would not have been possible. I am also indebted to Prof. Laura Cram, Dr Wolfgang Rudig and Dr Mark Shephard who sacrificed their valuable time for my research and gave me stimulating advice. I would like to include a special note of thanks to Prof. Nadje Al-Ali and Dr Sebastian Dellepiane Avellaneda for their valuable comments on my research.

This research was made possible by a Scottish Overseas Research Student Awards Scheme (SORSAS). I am grateful to the Scottish Funding Council (SFC) for the scholarship which enabled me to undertake this research at the University of Strathclyde, Glasgow.

I would like to express my sincere gratitude to the women I interviewed in Turkey and thank them for trusting me, showing willingness to share their experiences with me and making my fieldwork enjoyable. Without them, this book would not have been possible.

I would like to thank the editorial team of I.B. Tauris Publishers, especially Sophie Rudland for all of her assistance and confidence in my work. Also, the feedback from anonymous reviewers from I.B. Tauris Publishers was invaluable.

My friends, Dr Emel Uzun, Dr Feyza Bhatti, Dr Rosalind Greig, Dr Kirsty Henderson, Dr Kirtsy Alexander and Dr Andrew Judge, who accompanied me during my research, deserve all my love for their support. Their feedback on my work and their friendship were invaluable. A special word of gratitude is due to Dr Gökten Doğangün, Dr Zelal Özdemir, Dr Burcu Şentürk, Dr Özge Özkoç and my colleagues from the Office of Sponsored Projects at Middle East Technical University, who supported me in this process of book-writing.

Last but not least, I would like to thank my partner, Ozan Keysan, for his encouragement, love and belief in my success. I would also like to express my gratitude to my parents for their endless love and support.

Abbreviations

AGD	Anatolian Youth Association
AKP	Justice and Development Party
AKDER	Women's Rights Organization against Discrimination
AMARGİ	AMARGİ Association
ANAP	Motherland Party
AP	Justice Party
BDP	Peace and Democracy Party
BKP	Capital City Women's Platform Association
CEDAW	Convention on Elimination of all Forms of Discrimination against Women
CEE	Central and Eastern Europe
CSO	Civil society organization
CDA	Critical Discourse Analysis
CHP	Republican People's Party
ÇKD	Republican Women's Association
DEHAP	Democratic People's Party
DEP	Democracy Party
DİKASUM	Diyarbakır Research and Implementation Center for Women's Affairs
DİSK	The Confederation of Progressive Trade Unions of Turkey
DP	Democrat Party
DÖKH	Democratic Free Women's Movement
DMO	Democratic mass organization
DTP	Democratic Society Party
DYP	True Path Party
EU	European Union
FCDA	Feminist critical discourse analysis
FP	Virtue Party
HADEP	People's Democracy Party
HEP	People's Labour Party

KADEM	The Women and Democracy Association
KA-DER	Association for the Support and Training of Women Candidates
KAMER	Women's Centre
KCK	Kurdish Communities Union
KESK	Confederation of Public Workers' Union
Mazlumder	Association for Human Rights and Solidarity for the Oppressed
MEDA	Mediterranean Economic Development Area
MENA	Middle East and Northern Africa
MGK	National Security Council
MHP	National Movement Party
MNP	National Order Party
NGO	Nongovernmental organizations
Özgür-Der	The Association for Free Thought and Educational Rights
PDA	Poststructuralist discourse analysis
PKK	Kurdistan Worker's Party
RP	Welfare Party
SELİS	SELİS Women's Association
SFK	Socialist Feminist Collective
SIDA	Swedish International Development Cooperation Agency
TEMA	The Turkish Foundation for Combating Soil Erosion
TESK	Confederation of Turkish Tradesmen and Craftsmen
TİSK	Turkish Confederation of Employer Associations
TOBB	The Union of Chambers and Commodity Exchanges of Turkey
TSK	Turkish Armed Forces
TÜKD	Turkish Association of University Women
TÜRK-İŞ	Confederation of Turkish Trade Unions
TKB	Turkish Women's Union
UN	United Nations
US	Flying Broom
VAKAD	Van Women's Association
WB	World Bank
WTO	World Trade Organization

Civil society and women's NGOs:
Feminist reactions

This book critically examines the debate on the relationship between civil society and feminism and aims to identify to what extent and in what ways voices of women activists contribute to the meaning(s) of civil society and/or produce alternative understandings to the dominant neoliberal and gendered view of civil society. In order to throw light on this debate, this book particularly focuses on the empirical case of ten women's organizations in Turkey and discusses how women activists from these groups approach the concept and practices of civil society and whether and how they produce alternative ways of thinking to this dominant view.

This book is a response to two current political struggles over the theory and practice of civil society. The first has to do with the contemporary dominance of a neoliberal version and its contestation. Civil society has long been an ambiguous and contested term, as is evident in the existence of diverse traditions in the civil society literature – such as liberal, Marxist, Gramscian and Habermasian. However, since the global revival of the concept in the 1980s, the meaning of the concept has become more fixed. After the collapse of the Soviet Union, civil society was perceived by both scholars and policymakers as a way of overcoming a range of problems associated with authoritarianism and the crisis of the welfare state. Policymakers, scholars and NGO activists alike have interpreted the revival of civil society as 'a return to associational life, enabling engagement with the state and fostering solidarity in the public sphere' (Chandhoke, 2005), thereby facilitating the cultivation of 'trust, choice and virtues of democracy' (Young, 2000: 155). In this context, international institutions such as the European Union (EU), the United Nations (UN) and the World Bank (WB) have employed the notion of civil society as a policy tool for promoting democracy and development, including in the Middle East. The dominant approach of international organizations rests on a Western, liberal dichotomy between state and civil society, in which civil society is identified with associational life and control over the state. In this sense, civil society is construed as crucial to the functioning of liberal democracy and democratic governance an empowering force against the authoritarian state. However, civil society is also associated by international organizations with neoliberal policies intended to shrink the developmental and welfare state, bringing with it an emphasis on the delegation of key responsibilities to nongovernmental organizations (NGOs), including women's NGOs, in the areas of poverty, education, health and the like, a fact that has garnered significant critique.[1]

The second political struggle over civil society hinges on the gendered character of the theory and practice of civil society. Feminist thinkers and commentators locate the gendered bias of the term, particularly the liberal/neoliberal versions of civil society, in the reification of a public/private divide.[2] Put simply, liberals waver between two views of the public/private divide; in one view, civil society is squarely envisioned as part of a public, masculine sphere distinct from a private, feminine sphere, and in the other, it is private yet still distinguished from domestic life (Okin, 1998: 117; Squires, 2003: 132). In both views, civil society is associated with masculine traits and roles. Not only does this reveal the gendering of civil society as a concept, but it also calls attention to the historical exclusion of women from civil society and political life based on the desire to confine them to a private world. By exposing the reification of the liberal public/private dichotomy, feminist theorists highlight the interaction between civil society and both public and private spheres, and bring the family, considered as a part of the private or domestic sphere, back into political consideration (Benhabib and Cornell, 1987: 7).

The dominant neoliberal and gendered version of civil society is contested across different historical and institutional contexts in Central and Eastern Europe (CEE), Latin America, Southern Africa, South East Asia and the Middle East, including in Turkey. Particularly in the Middle East, where we observe many studies that criticize neoliberal civil society, there are scholars who seek to rethink civil society in the region by looking at women's position and activism. Such scholars indicate the gendered dimensions of civil society and the state, and the increasing significance of gender politics in challenging the state in the region.[3] To be sure, a number of studies have explored the history, trajectories and contemporary contexts of the women's movement, women's activism around state ideology and policies, NGOization, and the gendered dimensions of funding processes in the Middle East, including Turkey.[4] Particularly in Turkey, feminist scholars and activists have examined the understandings of women's groups and civil society organizations (CSOs) of the effects of the EU accession process on civil society organizations, especially women's organizations. They have critically researched the impacts of the EU and other international funding on the Turkish women's/feminist movements and women's organizations.[5] However, there is a limited research on NGO activists' articulation of civil society in the Middle East, which includes work by Abdelrahman (2004) and Pratt (2005) on the engagement of NGO activists with civil society and power in Egypt, and Kuzmanovic (2012)'s study on activists in Turkey. There has been even less attention given to women activists' articulations of civil society, with the exceptions of Doyle (2017a, 2017b), Çaha (2013) and Leyla Kuzu (2010).

This book builds upon and seeks to contribute to these critical interrogations of civil society in Turkey but takes as its starting point the question of how NGOs in general, and women's NGOs in particular, can contribute to the field of meaning around civil society, as this has not been widely discussed in the literature. As such, this book focuses on voices of women activists from ten different women's NGOs and their contributions to civil society in Turkey. Particularly, it seeks to identify how and in what ways voices of women activists in Turkey contribute to the meaning of civil society and/ or produce alternative understandings to the dominant view of civil society, which is gendered and neoliberal in character. Foregrounding women's voices and their experiences helps not only to engender the concept and practices of civil society but also to document the transformative potential of civil society activism for women.

Why Turkey?

The Turkish context offers a unique window of opportunity for analysing women's voices in the promotion and institutionalization of civil society.

Although Turkey cannot be regarded independently from the global revival of civil society, and particularly not from efforts to promote and institutionalize it across the Middle East, there are three reasons why the Turkish case is distinctive.

First, the Turkish modernization process has fuelled tensions between secularism and Islam that affect both civil society and women's organizing in distinctive ways. Turkey is unique among the other Middle Eastern countries with regards to its modernization process, led by the Kemalist elites who promoted secularism and Westernization. 'Turkey is often singled out as the only Muslim majority country with a secular Constitution and a Civil Code (adopted in 1926) that breaks with the *shar'ia*' (Kandiyoti, 2011b). The aspiration to be modern through Westernization and Europeanization dates back to the Tanzimat reforms of the Ottoman Empire in the nineteenth century, which intensified with the establishment of the Turkish Republic in 1923. Republican Kemalist elites sought to disengage with the Ottoman past, which they associated with Islamic traditions, through the top-down imposition of a secular state and secularist political culture, backed by military force (Arat, 2009; Göle, 1997; Tank, 2005: 6; Toprak, 2005). Their effort was only partially successful and a dichotomy emerged between the secular modernity of elites and urban centres, and Islamist values in rural areas and among the poor. Westernization by state-imposed reforms has predominantly been perceived as a reason for the subjugation of civil society by the Kemalist secular state in Turkey (Toprak, 1996). Tensions remain today as Islamic forces seek entry into civil society and Kemalists resist that move (Doyle, 2017a, 2017b, Ketola, 2011; Seçkinelgin, 2004; Şimşek, 2004).

The dichotomy between Western and Islamist values and the Turkish Republic's modernizing project have had crucial implications for women's organizing in Turkey (Kardam, 2005: 3). To begin with, Kemalism instrumentalized the women's movement. The struggle for women's rights in Turkey began in the Tanzimat period of the Ottoman modernization, and after the 1908 revolution 'women emerged as activists, forming their own associations and expanding the volume of their publications' (Kandiyoti, 1991: 43). However, in the early years of the Turkish Republic, as Al-Ali emphasizes (2003: 217), the women's movement in Turkey was induced by 'developmental and modernist aims' in contrast to colonized countries such as

Egypt, Algeria and Palestine; it was supported as pulling away from the Islamist roots of the Ottoman Empire and bolstering the secular ideology[6] that could justify 'the new state' (Arat, 1994: 71; see also Kardam, 2005: 39–40).[7] Since the 1980s the women's movement has been characterized by diversification, with the rise of feminist and Kurdish oppositional voices to Kemalism, as well as a conflict between Islamic organizing and Kemalism. In Kandiyoti's words (2011b), 'A new generation of post-1980s feminists were no longer content to be the grateful daughters of the republic.' Such women questioned 'the modernist gender discourse promoted by secular state elites', reconsidering women's position within society and challenging the public/private divide (Kardam, 2005: 43, 45).[8] But new divisions within the women's movement also emerged at this time (Diner and Toktaş, 2010: 42; Coşar and Onbaşı, 2008: 325; Landig, 2011), most obviously around sexuality (sexual orientation and gender identity), the headscarf issue, the Kurdish issue and class. Kurdish and Islamist women criticized Kemalists for 'being ethno-centric and exclusionary of other identities' (Diner and Toktaş, 2010: 47). In such ways, then, the dynamics of modernization and the tensions between secularism and Islam have played out in unique ways in Turkey and within its women's movement. What is more, it has been often framed that 'such divisions over different ideologies may prevent women's NGOs/NGOs from coordinating their efforts and may limit the effect of civil society in policy formulation' (Landig, 2011: 208), although issue-based coalitions and alliances have been formed to promote women's legal rights.

The second reason for focusing on Turkey is that, in contrast to other Middle Eastern countries, the development of civil society there was led by the EU – in ways that have had profound implications for women's organizing although this has been changing drastically in recent times. While other international institutions have had a role in the country, particularly as donors,[9] it is the candidacy of Turkey to the EU that has been fundamental to the way civil society has developed. EU influence has been widely debated among scholars and commentators, as has the extent to which this Muslim-dominated country could embrace concepts of civil society and democracy that originated in the West (Kubicek, 2005: 362). Nonetheless, Turkey has participated in Community Programmes for some time, having been granted candidate country status at the Helsinki Summit (1999). Since then, considerable political attention has been given to the reforms necessary to meet the political dimensions of the Copenhagen Criteria, which 'serve as a basis for the further democratization of the state–society relations' (Keyman and İçduygu, 2003: 224). 'The EU has explicitly directed its attention towards Turkish civil society as a partner/local agent with regard to bringing about social and political change and buttressing the development of a democratic policy' (Kuzmanovic, 2012: 14). More concretely, there has been since 2006 a programme of EU support allocated for the furtherance of the EU-Civil Society Dialogue in Turkey, with the specific aim of encouraging civil society engagement in the proposed accession of Turkey to EU membership. Thus Turkey has undergone an EU-led civil society development process.

The EU strongly encourages the participation of the women's movement in this process, as it makes clear in the Communication (EC, 2005: 9) that 'through close links between women's rights and equal opportunities organisations in the EU and in Turkey, the civil society dialogue will contribute to the objectives of strengthening the position and participation of women in all aspects of Turkish society'. Since 2006, EU funding has been offered to women's organizations in Turkey, which has consequently contributed to a shift in the focus of most of these organizations to projects enhancing 'civil society'. Certainly, 'gender equality, women's empowerment, gender mainstreaming and women's human rights' (Kardam, 2005: 1; see Landig, 2011) have become part of the agenda of civil society organizing, and women's organizations have become central to development programmes, taking on the provision of 'services to increase women's literacy, medical information as part of public health and population control programmes, development of women's skills and talents in order to increase their participation in the labour force, and shelters and legal consultancy to battered women' (Diner and Toktaş, 2010: 52). Such projects can be interpreted as part of the democratization process in Turkey (Gazioğlu, 2010) or criticized as precipitating the NGOization of the women's movement (Bora and Günal, 2002: 8–9; Hacıvelioğlu, 2009: 16–17) or it has been argued that although EU funding motivates and inspires women's NGOs, there is a lack of evaluation, monitoring and sustainability of projects (Landig, 2011: 211). Whichever interpretation is adopted, it is clear that EU-funded civil society programmes are a powerful force in reshaping women's organizing in Turkey. In parallel, women's organizations have contributed to key domestic legislative reforms, which are aimed at ensuring Turkey fulfils the requirements of the EU accession process.[10]

The third reason to focus on women's organizing in Turkey has to do with the fact that the country has recently become a laboratory for a unique government-led and conservative vision of civil society, with fraught implications for women. The victory of the Justice and Development Party (AKP) in the last four general elections (2002, 2007, 2011 and 2016), through an increase in votes, has enabled the party to set the agenda for Turkish politics during the 2000s and beyond. The rise of the AKP during this period invigorated the debate of secularism versus Islam because of its conflictual relationship with the Kemalist state and military elites. Nonetheless, it did to some extent succeed in inserting conservative and neoliberal values into civil society. The AKP supported the diversification of CSOs, a civil rather than military approach, a democratic opening for the Kurdish issue and EU-initiated reforms such as revisions of the Penal Code, Civil Code, Press Law and Anti-Terror Law. As an example, the laws regarding associations and foundations implemented in 2004 and 2008 under the AKP regime 'made it easier to establish organisations and harder for the state to monitor organisational activities' though 'there are still a number of legislative concerns in relation to securing full freedom of associations' (Kuzmanovic, 2012: 10). What is more, the first AKP government was in support of holding negotiations with civil society organizations, particularly women's CSOs[11] (Coşar and Onbaşı, 2008: 326) and its gender-sensitive policies included penal reform, 'the amendment to the Law on Municipalities (2005), which obliges municipalities with more than 50,000 inhabitants to open women's shelters, and the formation of the Parliamentary Commission for the Equality of Opportunity for Women and Men (2009)' (Coşar and Yeğenoğlu, 2011: 562), along with the 'nullification of the statement "man is the family chief" from its civic code' (Yılmaz, 2015: 157).

However, EU influence and, correspondingly, the AKP's commitment to democracy in Turkey began to lessen with the AKP's third term in office particularly beginning in 2011. Since then, the authoritarianism of the AKP has increased,[12] sparking protests from the women's movement in Turkey. Pursuing authoritarian gender policies, the AKP government has launched an ideological battle to control the female body and sexuality, promulgating several controversial laws and decrees.[13] Simultaneously, since the 2007 elections, the AKP government has negotiated more selectively with women's organizations (Coşar and Onbaşı, 2008: 326). In such ways, the AKP's support of civil society, and particularly of the role of women's organizations within it, has been limited and ideological; it has instrumentalized CSOs to legitimize its policies and 'acted selectively, excluding class-based and gender-based organisations deemed radical and/or marginal' (Coşar and Yücesan-Özdemir, 2012: 298). AKP has 'given five prominent Islamic charities the status of "public benefit organisations" which is very difficult to get and AKP's close relationship with a large body of charitable foundations (*Vakiflar*), which enables these organizations to claim tax exemption benefits on donations given to them' (Ketola, 2011: 7). The AKP government's 'active role in shaping the direction of civil society fuels discordant relations among NGOs' (Ketola, 2011: 7). Women activists are aware that the AKP government tries to find favour with some pro-government women's organizations – which have grown in number and influence during this period – by, for instance, inviting them to policy-making meetings, while marginalizing other groups, especially those with more radical views towards the body and sexuality. More concretely, as Doyle (2017a: 11) highlights, most of the women's organizations in her study articulate that AKP policies cause 'marginalization of voices that do not ascribe to the AKP's conservative ideology' and ' "state friendly" Islamic women's organisations were helping to fashion a more conservative society'. These women also indicated that 'the government's attempt to co-opt civil society by creating new women's organisations' and the 'objective of these organisations was to exclude and marginalize existing organisations that challenge the AKP' (12). Even though organized women have been 'questioning and challenging the prevalent gender relations in Turkish society and politics and pushing the Turkish government to make more gender-friendly policies' (Aksoy, 2015: 151–2), many women's organizations, apart from some of the Islamist organizations, are nowadays in the situation of hindering 'regressive change' instead of promoting 'progressive change' for women's rights in Turkey (Doyle, 2017b: 251).

While apparently embracing some of the core assumptions of the Western liberal understanding of civil society in AKP's first and partially second term in office, it leans increasingly towards supporting Islamist/conservative and/or pro-government organizations and muting the dissident and critical ones.

Particularly in the post-2011 period, the Gezi Park Protests which took place in 2013 due to the rising authoritarianism of Prime Minister Erdoğan (Bilgiç and Kafkaslı 2013: 8), the contestations afterwards with the Gülen Movement[14] (with which the AKP were previously in collaboration) and the trials of four AKP MPs for corruption have resulted in deepening tensions around AKP authoritarianism. What is more, the military coup attempt of 15 July 2016 has had drastic outcomes for the civil society in Turkey. Not only were the CSOs in line with the Gülen Movement closed but also the dissident voices were muted. This shows how the civil society terrain in Turkey is contested and continues to evolve, meriting close and continued research.

Defining terms: Civil Society in relation to democracy, democratization and development

Civil society is a term that has always juxtaposed to the notions of 'democracy', 'democratization' and 'development'. It is significant to elaborate on these often taken-for-granted terms in relation to civil society as they would take varying meanings. It is necessary to problematize these terms rather than use them in an uncritical way, since the main focus of this book is to identify to what extent and in what ways voices of women activists contribute to the meaning(s) of civil society through analysing whether there is any alternative vision of civil society to liberal civil society with its ideal and developmentalist approach to international organizations, states and NGOs, and how this is constructed.

Civil society is a historically variable and politically contested concept. While its neoliberal formulation may be dominant today, as disseminated through international organizations, this should not be treated as fixing the meaning of civil society once and for all, particularly in light of the many critical voices raised against the neoliberal view. In this book, the term civil society is approached as a discursive construction with the varying meanings it takes over time and space; that is, civil society is given meaning through discourses in historical and sociopolitical contexts. This book examines women activists' various articulations of civil society in terms of 'historical, social, political and cultural factors that shape the language [they] use' (Treleaven, 2004: 159). In this regard, it adopts a feminist perspective, one which is critical of the sidelining of women's voices on the problems of civil society in Turkey and which seeks to ensure that the full diversity of women's voices is given a platform.

Democracy is a broad and contested term that has been employed closely with the concept of civil society. The concept of democracy has been used as a key term in non-Western contexts, very often particularly after the rise of neoliberalism in the 1980s. What especially the international organizations, multilateral banks and donors look for in non-Western contexts is liberal democracy through democratization policies although there are various approaches to democracy.[15] For these actors, 'three core components of democracy building are support for free and fair elections, state institutions and civil society' and 'channeling technical and financial support to CSOs is therefore integrally linked to these broader aims of democratization' (Ketola, 2013: 17). Herein, NGOs are seen as 'functionaries of democracy, increasing citizen participation in activities that hold the state to account' (Ketola, 2009: 2). However, what is problematic here is that they 'see their aims to constitute a neutral, value free approach, forming a template ready for use in any context' (2). The suggested democratization policies should not be taken as a top-down recipe for achieving and maintaining democracy in those geographies as if there is only one ideal way of practicing it in every context. Feminist scholars also pay attention to the point that democractization should consider the nature and ways of doing politics in the non-Western contexts by taking into account 'socially diverse sections of the population including, but not limited to, women' (Pankhurst and Pearce, 1996: 2). At this point, this book cannot consider the concepts of democracy and democratization as unproblematic terms; thus, approach these terms with caution.

The civil society concept also links with the developmentalist approach of international organizations, states and NGOs. Civil society is regarded as significant for development processes in the Global South. Various actors, that is, multilateral banks, international development agencies, governments and some international NGOs perceive poverty and inequality as a global economic problem which can be fixed by a policy agenda set through a partnership of civil society, state and the market (Howell and Pearce, 2001: 17). This approach is criticized by Howell and Pearce as 'socially responsible capitalism', aiming to eliminate the risks that an individual market approach can create against social cohesion (17).

International donors start out with two implicit assumptions: namely, that 'democracy contributes positively toward development and that civil society is an important democratic check on the state' (Howell and Pearce, 2001: 40). The result is a system of financial assistance delivered through short-term projects to NGOs for development. In this approach, civil society is merely viewed as a 'negative liberty and protection against the state's encroachments' (40). As an alternative perspective to the developmentalist approach, grass-root movements and 'change-oriented NGOs' note 'the embedded power relationships and inequalities that make development an conflictual rather than consensual process' (17). Within the critical group, there is a strong transnational feminist movement, especially from the feminists of the Global South, against the developmentalist approach, who catch our attention to the lack of a gender perspective and so the necessity of the analysis of gendered implications of development processes (Rai, 2012). In other words, feminist views have been effective in challenging mainstream development theory and practices and they have made development actors pay attention to gender issues while formulating policies, even though they have 'been partial and uneven' (Craig, 2007: 121–2).

Third World scholars 'generally agreed on the need to focus on the poor, especially poor women; on the importance of global economic inequalities; and on the need to ground solutions to women's problems in the realities and experiences of women in the South' (Connely et al., 2000). In order to respond to this demand, new organizations were established for activism and research in the South, namely, the Association of African Women for Research and Development, the Gender and Development Unit of the Asian and Pacific Development Center and Development Alternatives with Women for a New Era (DAWN), which played a key role in these debates (Connely et al., 2000). Transnational arena has also been a great place of opportunity for these organizations and feminist activists, especially the United Nations World Conferences have made a great contribution to feminists in terms of expanding their area of activities in cooperation with other feminists around the world as well as getting aware of the importance of 'transnational resources and networks for feminism' (Ferree and Tripp, 2006: ix). In sum, particularly with the establishment of new NGOs, platforms and transnational networks, feminists get an opportunity to voice their concerns and to critique the developmentalist approach of civil society and NGOs.

Researching women in civil society: Methodology, method and sampling

Feminist critical discourse analytical approach and its application

In order to analyse the civil society discourses of women activists from various groups in Turkey and to uncover their gendered dimensions, this book adopts a methodological framework drawn from Critical Discourse Analysis (CDA), informed by Fairclough (1992, 1995) and Chouliaraki and Fairclough (1999), and developed in its feminist form by Lazar (2005, 2007). CDA is generally about exploring links between language and social practices and 'the role of discourse in social and cultural critique' (Wood and Kroger, 2000: 205).

The key focus of CDA is to show the relationship between language and power. Power is a key concept in CDA for analysing how and why the dominant discourse is reproduced and/or resisted. It often sees texts as 'sites of struggle in that they show traces of differing discourses and ideologies contending and struggling for dominance' as well as challenging and subverting power (Wodak and Meyer, 2009: 10; see also Fairclough, 2003). Although in CDA power is understood as structural and hierarchical, chiming with Marxist views, some CDA approaches, such as Fairclough's (1992; 2001: 233), argue that Foucault's post-structuralist approach to discourse is another useful theoretical reference point. There are, therefore, overlaps between CDA and post-structuralist discourse analysis. In the Foucauldian view, power is conceived as 'a force which creates subjects and agents – that is, as a productive force – rather than as a property possessed by individuals, which they exert over others' (Jorgensen and Philips, 2002: 63). In Foucault's words, 'power needs to be considered as a productive network which runs through the whole social body, much more than as a negative instance whose function is repression' (Foucault, 1984: 61). This approach to power claims that it is dangerous to see power as essentially unidirectional since, among other things, it can mean overlooking how domination is contested and negotiated and therefore seeks to illuminate sites of struggle over meaning between the powerful and the subordinated (Prinsloo, 2007). Indeed, the Foucauldian approach to power is very useful for identifying 'resistant discourses' because, in this view, power and resistance[16] are forever entwined. In the light of this discussion, in this book, 'power' is understood as manifesting in relations of domination, which can produce resistance as well as subordination.

Feminist Critical Discourse Analysis (FCDA) brings together CDA studies and feminist scholarship (Lazar, 2005: 1). According to Lazar (2005: 5), the close relationship between feminism and CDA offers a 'powerful critique for action'. In a feminist take on CDA, discourse[17] refers to 'a set of statements ... that produce and organise a particular order of reality and specific subject positions therein' (143). FCDA insists on the importance of gender as structuring power relations and 'adopts a critical feminist view of gender relations, motivated by the need to change the existing conditions of these relations' (3). In this sense, what FCDA adds to CDA is the necessity of analysing the 'oppressive nature of gender as an omni-relevant category in most social practices' (3). The central aim of the approach is to understand the 'complex, subtle ways in which taken-for-granted gendered assumptions and hegemonic power relations are discursively produced, sustained, negotiated and challenged in different contexts and communities' (Lazar, 2007: 142). In other words, FCDA seeks to 'demystify the interrelationship between gender, power and ideology' (Lazar, 2005: 5). Here, a reference point for ideology is Pecheux's (1982) approach to 'language in the ideological construction of subjects' by drawing on an Althusserrian notion of ideology (Fairclough, 2001: 233). Ideology manifests in 'rather hidden and latent types of everyday belief, which is often disguised as conceptual metaphors and analogies' (Wodak and Meyer, 2009: 8). The term hegemony refers to Gramsci's (1971) notions of hegemony, a combination of coercion and consent, to explain complex power relations. This underlines 'the idea of contested power' and enables us to 'look at audiences having oppositional readings to socially created forms of meaning or texts' (Prinsloo, 2007: 81).

By drawing on post-structuralist perspectives, feminist CDA also recognizes differences and diversity among women, which requires the researcher to undertake historically and culturally contingent analyses of gender in place of essentialist and universalist approaches (Lazar, 2005, 2007; Sunderland and Litosseliti, 2008: 4). Lazar emphasizes that gender intersects with other systems of power based on race/ethnicity, social class, sexual orientation, age, culture and geography, which means that 'gender oppression is neither materially experienced nor discursively enacted in the same way for women everywhere' (Lazar, 2007: 149). In this way, for FCDA, there is 'no universal category of woman/man' (141). That is to say, 'gender' in FCDA refers to both a set of power relations ('gender' as oppression, as related to patriarchy) and an identity category. In this book, I use gender in both senses where relevant. Additionally, approaching gender as a variable in my research means that it not only adds a 'gender' aspect to the analysis of interrelations among power, ideology and discourse but also seeks to challenge gendered hegemonic understandings and relationships.

I follow Lazar in turning to CDA because it provides 'a means of foregrounding for examination the taken-for-granted factors (historical, social, political and cultural) that shape the language people use' (Treleaven, 2004: 159). Rather than taking a structuralist or formalist approach to language and to the text, CDA and FCDA scholars underscore the importance of context in the construction of meanings. Thus, for my empirical research, I will focus on discourse as socially constitutive and constituted by social situations, institutions and structures, including gender. This will enable me to look at not only the content of the empirical material as texts but also the history and context that surround the production, dissemination and reception of the texts, 'thereby constructing different "realities"' (Philips and Hardy in Treleaven, 2004: 159).

Finally, since the aim of FCDA is to underscore in what ways power and dominance are discursively produced and/or (counter-)resisted (Lazar, 2005: 2, 149), this points me towards a focus on 'counter discourses'. Feminist discourse analysts underscore the importance of counter-hegemonic discourses from below, which challenge the naturalizing strategies and effects of dominant discourses (Sunderland and Litosseliti, 2002: 18). In this way, FCDA gives an active role to subjects who produce discourse, which means that it enables the researcher to see how women can actively create and change social situations, institutions and structures. This aspect is crucial for me to show the position of women activists from varying groups as active interpreters and producers of civil society discourses.

FCDA implies two broad steps to the research process: (1) the analysis of sociopolitical context and (2) textual analysis. Attending to the sociopolitical, economic and institutional factors within which the discourses are constructed is crucial for the FCDA methodology, as discourses constitute and are constituted by social structures (Lazar, 2005). In this regard, FCDA methodologically points me towards context analysis as prior to textual analysis, since the complex processes of discursive production cannot be interpreted independently from wider dynamics (Lazar, 2005: 1–2; Sunderland and Litoseliti, 2008: 5). The application of this approach to my own research question means that I must first establish the sociopolitical context in Turkey with regard to state-civil society relations, funding and gender as the precursor to the textual analysis. When I do this in the following chapter of this book, my goal will be to identify the official dominant views of civil society in Turkey and to analyse how it has been and is currently (re)produced. Only by doing this can I determine the extent to which women's civil society discourses are resistant to the hegemonic view and/or offer an alternative to it. The next step was the two-stage textual analysis. Initially, I conducted an 'in-depth textual analysis'. This is a close reading of the women's interviews and group documentation by using coding questions in order to identify the key civil society discourses and whether and how they refer to gendered dimensions of civil society. Specifically, in my coding of interview and organizational texts, I focused upon the following: the traits, qualities and roles attributed to civil society; what people, institutions and organizations are associated with civil society; the perceived relationship among civil society, the state and the market; the gendered dynamics of civil society and its role in (re)producing inequalities; and the value accorded to civil society, that is, if it is viewed as a positive, negative or neutral organizing space in the Turkish context. I then ran an 'interdiscursive analysis' to explore the interdiscursive encounters of women's discourses with the hegemonic civil society discourses in Turkey. This allowed me to analyse how the women activists treat those official hegemonic discourses circulated in Turkey and in what ways they reproduce and/or contest them.

Selection of sampling

The data used in this book consists of forty-one in-depth interviews conducted between May and August 2012 with Kemalist, Islamist,[18] Kurdish, feminist and anti-capitalist women activists from ten organizations located in four different cities in Turkey and the group documentation of these organizations. The names of these women's organizations are TKB (Turkish Women's Union), TÜKD (the Turkish Association of University Women), AKDER (Women's Rights Organization against Discrimination), BKP (Capital City Women's Platform Association), US (Flying Broom), KA-DER (Association for the Support and Training of Women Candidates), Women's Centre (KAMER), SELİS Women's Association (SELİS), AMARGİ Association (AMARGİ) and SFK (Socialist Feminist Collective).

With regard to the choice of women's organizations and interviewees for this book, I engaged in purposive sampling. In sampling women's organizations, I initially planned to select women's groups to interview based on three factors: geographical location, political position and relationship to EU funding. After conducting a set of thirteen pilot interviews[19] in December 2011, I revised and modified my sampling criteria on the basis of the positions I recorded from women's organizations in the field, re-categorizing these organizations in Turkey according to five criteria: political orientation, geographical location, relationship to EU funding, organizational structure, and framing of women's rights and feminism. This enabled me to capture a reasonable spread of views between and within each group. Thus, I spoke to women activists from a range of social backgrounds who were of varying ages, possessed varying degrees of political experience, had taken varying trajectories into women's rights activism and civil society, held varying positions in the group (e.g. the leaders of organizations and ordinary members), and had been employed in different industries and professions. In addition, I limited my sampling to advocacy and long-term women's organizations (ignoring non-advocacy groups such as service-oriented ones and those existing only to pursue particular short-term projects). The women's organizations in my study also vary in terms of the type of organizing, such as association, foundation and collective; the extent and type of their political ties with other women's groups; the degree of their involvement in platforms at the national and international level; and whether or not they carry out lobbying activities. Table 1.1 shows the list of women's organizations I interviewed during my fieldwork.

Table 1.1 List of Women's Organizations in the Sample

Women's Organization	Orientation	Geographical Location	Organizational Structure	EU Funding	Framing of Women's Rights/Feminism
TKB	Kemalist	Ankara	Voluntarism-based	Not funded	Equality
TÜKD	Kemalist	Ankara[a]	Voluntarism-based	Funded	Equality
AKDER	Islamist	İstanbul	Semi-professional	Not Funded	Justice-based equality
BKP	Islamist	Ankara	Voluntarism-based	Funded	Justice-based equality
KAMER	Kurdish- feminist[b]	Diyarbakır/ Batman[c]	Semi-professional	Funded	Empowerment
SELİS	Kurdish	Diyarbakır	Voluntarism-based	Funded[d]	Emancipation
KA-DER	Feminist	Istanbul	Semi-professional	Funded	Empowerment
US	Feminist	Ankara	Semi-professional	Funded	Empowerment
SFK	Anti-capitalist Feminist	Ankara	Voluntarism-based	Anti-funding	Emancipation
AMARGİ[e]	Anti-capitalist Feminist	Istanbul	Voluntarism-based	Funded	Liberation for all groups

Notes: [a] Although it would have been preferable to interview participants in Kemalist women's organizations in two different cities, such as İstanbul and Ankara, practical difficulties during my fieldwork meant that it was not feasible.

[b] Here I follow Arat and Altınay (2015) and Fisher Onar and Peker (2012) for calling KAMER as Kurdish-feminist differently from SELİS as while KAMER has prioritized its feminist identity and cover all women not only Kurdish but also Turkish, Arab, Sunni and Alevi, SELİS has emerged with its Kurdish identity and highlight that they are the representative of Kurdish women.

[c] I selected two women's organizations from South-eastern Turkey, particularly located in Diyarbakır and Batman, because it was much more important for me to make comparisons between the experiences of the women's organizations located geographically in the eastern and the western part of the Anatolia than to show the diversity and conflict within the eastern region.

[d] I am aware of the weakness that both women's groups in Diyarbakır are funded. However, although they are/were funded, their approach to the funding differs. For instance, in the SELİS an anti-project stance is dominant even though they received funding in the past. In contrast, the KAMER takes a pro-EU funding stance.

[e] The AMARGİ Group İstanbul decided in December 2012 to close AMARGİ after nine women decided to leave. This occurred after four months of fieldwork. These nine women expressed their reasons of leaving in a letter. They stated that their motto of "We are together with our differences (Farklılıklarımızla bir aradayız)" serves the ideology of liberalism. They also remark that AMARGİ disregarded opposing and/or advocacy (savunma) groups while declaring to be against all forms of violence (AMARGİ, 2012) (see the full letter in Turkish at http://goo.gl/hPdhb3).

Source: From author's date.

The dominant categorizations of women's groups in the literature[20] are political orientation-based, that is, Kemalist, Islamist, feminists and Kurdish[21] women's groups. For the first sampling criteria in my study, I followed this widely used ideology-based political categorization.[22] The relationship of women's organizations to EU funding is the second sampling criteria because of the prevalence and divisiveness of funding among women's organizations. I distinguished between groups that had received/were currently receiving funding, had not received/were not currently receiving funding, and that were against funding from the EU.

I consider geographical location to be one of the most important sampling criteria. I chose three major cities – İstanbul, Ankara and Diyarbakır – where the women's movement is politically effective and visibly active. Ankara, with a population of five million (TÜİK, 2013), is the capital of Turkey in the region of Central Anatolia. Notably, this is where the Turkish Grand National Assembly and government institutions are located. İstanbul is the largest city of Turkey with a population of fourteen million (TÜİK, 2013) and is situated in the Marmara region. Diyarbakir has a population of 1.6 million (TÜİK, 2013) and can be set apart from İstanbul and Ankara because of its eastern location, having one of the largest Kurdish populations in the region and the ongoing conflict between the Turkish government and the Kurdish people. Moreover, these cities are different from each other in terms of social, cultural and economic conditions, and this may reflect on women's organizing. In terms of the number of women's organizations, İstanbul has 123, Ankara has 101 and Diyarbakır has 35 (STGM, 2018). It is also fair to assume that the location of the women's groups in different cities may change their relationship with funding bodies, Turkish government institutions and ally organizations.

The organizational structure of the women's groups is another factor that could be influential on the civil society discourses of women coming from various women's organizations. Women's groups in Turkey vary when it comes to organizational structure, but I grouped them into two categories: primarily voluntary-based and semi-professional, with at least one professional employee who tends to lead and deliver projects with the help of volunteers. The framing of women's rights and feminism is the fifth criteria, closely linked to the first.

As a result of the Republican regime, state-sponsored feminism has emerged in Turkey (Kandiyoti, 1991: 42; Tekeli, 1986) and it, induced from above, has suppressed the evolution of a feminist consciousness (Kadıoğlu, 1994: 653). As Tekeli (1989: 36) indicates, before 1980 there was not any movement stating that the women are oppressed specifically due to being women. According to official political ideology, Kemalism, women's problems are solved by the state; for the dominant social ideology, Islam, women do not have a problem of oppression; and Marxist left ideology also supports the idea that women do not have a problem except capitalist exploitation (Tekeli, 1989: 36). However, it is evident that this is not the case. In spite of domestic repression and depoliticization engendered by the military intervention of September 1980, increasing association with the Western world let a second wave of feminism into the country (Arat, 2000: 112). In the 1980s, there were so many women who were subjected to economic, social and cultural subjugation and who, by their existence, created the material basis for a feminist ideology (Tekeli, 1990: 276). By the mid-1980s women began calling themselves feminist and organizing not only in small groups to discuss women's problems but also in public protests in Istanbul and Ankara (Arat, 1998: 119). They demanded substantive equality and 'expressed their needs to be in control of their own sexuality and protested domestic violence' (Arat, 2000: 113). Nowadays, feminism and the women's movement has become more diverse. In this context, women's organizations in Turkey have had multiple, sometimes conflicting, agendas such as violence against women, ethnic discrimination or the headscarf ban (Marshall, 2009: 373). In relation to this issue, the approaches of women's organizations to women's rights and feminism can be grouped under the following five headings: equality justice-based equality, empowerment, emancipation and liberation for all groups.

In terms of the interview format, open-ended and semi-structured interview technique were selected, which generally took approximately one and a half hours, but in some cases lasted two hours. While some respondents said that they were running short of time, others wished to speak at length as they were interested in my research. I had off-the-record chats with some women activists as I developed a close rapport with them. In the main, I met the participants at their organization's headquarters and sometimes at cafes or restaurants, which were decided by both sides, that is, participant and researcher. All the interviews were based on questions concerning demography, civil society and its relation to power, domination, their views on the relationship between civil society, state and gender, their evaluations of EU–Turkey relations and the EU's approach to civil society, feminism, information on their projects, their activism with their group, the organizational structure of their group and general questions on Turkey. Interviewing is a crucial method for feminist research as it 'gives voice' to those participating in the research (Sprague, 2005: 120); in my study, this meant giving a platform to women's perspectives and allowing their voices to be heard. In addition, I gathered documentation in the form of written sources and website materials produced by the women's groups. These documents included activity reports, by-laws of the organization (*dernek tüzüğü*), leaflets introducing the group's aims, activities, campaigns and projects, project outputs such as reports and publications, journals and books published by the group, and press statements.

In the research process, I was keen to form non-hierarchical and reciprocal relationships with the respondents, to be open and transparent with them, and to avoid taking a traditional approach to research which emphasizes 'objectivity, efficiency, separateness and distance' (Reinharz, 1992: 24; Ackerly and True, 2010; Oakley, 1981; Reinharz, 1992; Reinharz and Chase, 2003). Despite such intentions, I also recognized that it would not be possible to form a totally equal relationship between researcher and respondents. As Eschle and Maiguashca (2011: 9) caution, 'interview transcripts ... inescapably reflect certain power hierarchies involved in their production'. One of my respondent's sentences validates this statement: 'We cannot be totally equal in this setting because I am being asked questions by you.'

Identifying women's organizations

The interviews were conducted with a total of ten women's organizations: two Kemalist, two Islamist, two Kurdish-feminist, two feminist and two anti-capitalist. TKB and TÜKD follow the Kemalist ideology as they were both established in order to guard the secular pillar of the Republican establishment. Both follow secularist and nationalist programmes and regard women as citizens of the Turkish society and protectors of the Kemalist secular features of the state (Esim and Cindoğlu, 1999: 182). In line with this kind of political standpoint, the goals of the TKB are developing policies to promote equality and educating people on women's human rights and associative legal rights. In the same vein, TÜKD aims to 'protect the hard-won women's rights and other Atatürk's reforms such as secularism, and improve the educational, economic and social status of women throughout Turkey' (TÜKD, n.d.; TÜKD, 2012).

Since the 1990s, the Islamic movement, contesting the Republican interpretations of secularism, 'has served as a venue for the politicization of women in that women have actively taken part in the political parties of the religious conservative wing', and 'the fight against the ban on wearing headscarves at universities has also increased women's political participation' (Diner and Toktaş, 2010: 50–1). In this context, BKP and AKDER were established by religious women in 1995 and 1999 respectively. AKDER was set up to protest the headscarf ban, which was implemented in 1997, by students expelled from school and professionals denied employment because they chose to wear the headscarf (AKDER, n.d.). BKP was established to 'produce alternative views as well as theoretical and practical solutions so as to develop the ideological, political, legal, social and economic existence of women in Turkey', as well as to address the problems faced by religious women, which stem from established religious institutions that endorse patriarchy and from secularism (BKP, n.d.). It pursues such aims by challenging the traditional image of 'woman' in the interpretations of religious doctrines and discrimination against religious women in modern society. As Hatice Güler, women activist from BKP, underlines in the periodical titled 'From Yesterday to Today: Başkent Kadin Platformu', the headscarf issue has been important in the organization's agenda since it has provided safety for women in Ankara who were punished, exiled and/or removed from their offices for wearing the headscarf (Güler, 2007: 8). Thus, the headscarf ban has been their springboard for challenging the secularist Turkish state and its discriminatory policies against Muslim women at universities and in public institutions. What is more, both women's organizations aim to increase awareness about all forms of social discrimination and focus on the legal, economic, social and political empowerment of women, and issues such as domestic violence, honour crimes and sexual abuse of children (AKDER, n.d.1; BKP, n.d.).

Here it is vital to underscore two points. First, Islamist women's organizations are not a homogenous group. There are groups close to the government and other groups that are critical of the government. Both BKP and AKDER, to a certain extent, can be classified under the latter group. What is more, Marshall labels them as 'non-orthodox' or 'reformist' compared to other Islamist women's organizations in terms of their approach to the headscarf issue, women's problems and their role in society (Marshall, 2005). Within this group, AKDER differs from BKP. AKDER does not critique patriarchy in faith and does not develop a critical approach to veiling and gender dynamics in Islam (Aslan Akman, 2008: 79). BKP is unique in the sense that 'unlike other religious women's organisations, it is open to cooperation and dialogue with women rights organisations that are not organized around Islamic premises' (Coşar and Onbaşı, 2008: 332). Compared to AKDER, BKP focuses on more issues by being part of campaigns and protests against different types of discriminations rather than only fighting against the headscarf ban (Aslan Akman, 2008: 85).

The Kurdish movement has grown since the 1990s when it aimed to challenge Kemalist unitary and nationalistic understanding of the state. KAMER and SELİS grew out of the Kurdish women's movement; 'The majority of KAMER's founders are Kurdish women who suffered from the prevalence of violence in the regions populated mostly by Kurds' (Diner and Toktaş, 2010: 48). I follow Arat and Altınay (2015) and Fisher Onar and Peker (2012) for calling KAMER as Kurdish-feminist differently from SELİS since while KAMER has prioritized its feminist identity and cover all women not only Kurdish but also Turkish, Arab, Sunni and Alevi, SELİS has emerged with its Kurdish identity and highlighted that they are the representative of Kurdish women. What is more, whereas KAMER highlights its independence from all bodies in its publicity materials and its website, SELİS emphasizes that it is one of the components of the Kurdish women's movement[23] as a member of the Democratic Free Women's Movement (Demokratik Özgür Kadın Hareketi, DÖKH).[24] Nebahat Akkoç (2002: 12), one of the founders as well as the current president of KAMER, highlights, 'independence has been one of the most salient principles of KAMER since its establishment. As being an independent women's group we have started to work with women for women'. Moreover, 'the international links KAMER has developed and global networks that support KAMER initiatives' let the organization be autonomous from 'local political blocks' (Altınay and Arat, 2015: 15). Despite these key differences, the aims of the two groups converge. They both seek to 'develop methods to combat crimes committed against women under the disguise of honor' (KAMER, n.d.), campaign for violence against women, support women socially, economically and psychologically, and enhance women's cooperation and consciousness (Duman, 2010).

The US, KA-DER, AMARGİ and SFK are the feminist organizations in my study.[25] Whereas KA-DER and US are closer to liberal feminist approaches, AMARGİ and SFK take a leftist, explicitly anti-capitalist position. In this regard, KA-DER was established to 'defend equal representation of women and men in all fields of life' and targets equal representation in 'all elected and appointed decision making positions' (KA-DER, 2010). Since 2004, KA-DER has conducted various campaigns for gender quota, which 'requires all political parties to set aside a percentage of seats for women' (Negron-Gonzales, 2016: 203). One of the main principles of KA-DER is to keep equal distance from all political parties (Bora, 2002: 122). Yet, KA-DER members 'represent different ideological positions and some claim a non-ideological stance' (Coşar and Onbaşı 2008: 335). The US aims to empower women's organizations in Turkey by enhancing dialogue and establishing communication networks among them by using 'the media and all means of communication for increasing women's visibility and creating sensitivity and awareness pertaining to gender equality within the society' (Flying Broom, 2011). The US also claims a stance above party politics and acknowledges feminist engagements (Coşar and Onbaşı 2008: 332). Both KA-DER and US share the goal of challenging male dominance in and across a range of contexts such as party politics, policymaking, employment and family life, by employing tools such as lobbying, campaigns, training and projects.

Both SFK and AMARGİ are feminist grassroots organizations and all of the activist women in these organizations define themselves as feminist. Whereas most of the group members of SFK call themselves socialist feminist, the women from AMARGİ adopt different feminisms (SFK, 2008; AMARGİ, n.d.). For the women from AMARGİ, the women's struggle cannot be delimited to the oppression of women by men since women may exert power as well. In contrast, SFK maintains a socialist feminist approach that women as a group are oppressed by men, and emphasizes mostly class-based diversity and differences between women. Regarding the approach of both organizations to gender equality, SFK argues that the concept of gender equality conceals the subject; rather, it should be called 'women-men equality' in order to highlight the exploitation of women by men (SFK, 2008). For the women from AMARGİ, the notion of gender equality is seen to inhibit feminism and to reproduce categories central to heterosexism (AMARGİ, n.d.1).

The women's groups in my study also vary in terms of their legal status, for example, associations, foundations and collectives. Apart from SFK (collective) and KAMER (foundation), all of the women's groups are associations. In contrast to the other associations, TÜKD and TKB – the Kemalist women's organizations – had the status of social welfare association (*kamu yararına çalışan dernek*)[26] (Yalçın and Öz, 2011: 73), which was terminated for TKB after 2002 (TKB, 2015; TÜKD, 2012). SFK prefers to be a collective rather than an association or a foundation due to its rejection of the hierarchical presidential system that is dominant among the associations. It is not alone with regard to the challenge of selecting a chairperson. AMARGİ and the Kurdish women's groups – KAMER and SELİS – do not practise the chair system even though they are legally required to have one. In fact, the women's groups tend to prefer to be associations for financial and regulatory reasons. For instance, US was founded as a non-profit women's organization. The founding members chose the non-profit status to protect themselves from the audit and intervention of the Association Law. When the Association Law changed in 2004, it gave some flexibility to associations, and the US decided to change the organization's legal status to an association. In a similar way, AMARGİ changed its legal status from cooperative to association in order to ease the income tax burden and financial processes and to minimize state intervention. SELİS, established as an advisory centre in 2002, also changed to an association.

In terms of the year of establishment, TKB and TÜKD were established much earlier than the others, in 1924 and 1949 respectively. The rest of the groups were formed in the last twenty years, between the 1990s and 2000s. The membership size of the organizations and their means of accessing women differ as well. TKB, TÜKD and KA-DER have a broadly based membership and operate throughout Turkey. Although KAMER cannot legally have members due to having a foundation status, it has around 50,000 volunteers across its 23 branches. Lobbying, campaigning, demonstrating, consciousness-raising, training, media, law, projects, consultancy and welfare services are the instruments used by the women activists in Turkey for their struggle (Paker, Özoğuz and Baykan, 2008: 5). Except for SFK, all of the women's organizations in my study use lobbying. Additionally, none of them except SFK have an anti-funding stance. However, they differ in terms of their approach to funding: whereas a group of women in TKB and AMARGİ has a conditional approach to funding, the women activists from the other groups are open to international funding sources and they are funded[27] by several international funding agencies. The most common international funding institutions are the EU, UN and SIDA (Swedish International Development Cooperation Agency).

Profile of interviewees

Turning to the recruitment of individuals within the identified women's groups, I contacted key members from each and then used snowballing methods to expand the pool of participants. Most participants were very keen to be part of this research. I reached from six to ten women activists from each category of women's group and was therefore able to capture a diversity of views within each grouping. My respondents are mostly educated professionals from middle-class backgrounds. Almost all of the women had completed a university education. Out of forty-one, five of them had a high school education only. Six participants had received a masters degree and three of them had a PhD degree. Of those in education at the time of the research, I interviewed one undergraduate student, two MSc candidates and one PhD candidate. Most of the participants had high employment status, working in professional occupational positions such as lawyer, doctor, teacher, engineer, civil servant, performer, project officer and psychological advisor. Some participants were employees of the women's organization. Six participants were retired from positions such as instructor, engineer and civil servant. In terms of age, most participants were under 60 years. The smallest age group was women between the ages of 61 and 70 (four women in total). The two largest groups were those aged between 20 and 30 (young) and 41 and 50 (middle age), with eleven participants in each. Eight participants were aged 31–40, and seven were aged 51–60. Particularly, the age differences between the group members within and across groups catch my attention. On the one hand, the members of TKB and TÜKD that I interviewed were in their 50s and 60s, so they have the oldest membership of the organizations in my study. On the other hand, almost all of the women activists from AKDER, SELİS, AMARGİ and SFK have younger members than the other groups, with a high proportion of women in their 20s and 30s.

It is also important to explain my respondents' political experience and their trajectory into women's rights activism and civil society, and to show the variance within and between the organizations. The participants from the Islamist women's group AKDER decided to found the organization in response to the suffering and unjust treatment they experienced when they were university students due to the headscarf ban. In other words, AKDER was established by women who had to quit their university education or go abroad to be able to continue their education. Furthermore, two women from BKP were active in the area of civil society by being members of a civil society organization and a trade union before joining BKP. However, they decided to be part of BKP because of its non-hierarchical structure. As with the women from AKDER, those from BKP did not get a chance to obtain an academic position in a university due to their headscarf; for this reason they decided to organize into a women's group.

Three women from the Kemalist organizations TKB and TÜKD chose to be volunteers of these associations after they retired; that is, they did not have any previous experience in civil society and women's rights activism. There are also four women who were active in civil society and worked in the area of women's rights, including on national and international projects on women's issues. What is more, two of the TKB women indicated their membership in a political party. Among my respondents from the Kurdish organization KAMER, two women were politically organized and had a membership of a trade union and human rights organization before KAMER. The rest started to be part of a women's civil society organization when they came into contact with KAMER. Only one woman from SELİS had a women's movement background before becoming a volunteer with SELİS (Table 1.2).

Table 1.2 Age Range and Number of Participants

Age Range	20–30	31–40	41–50	51–60	61–70	Total
Number of Participants	11	8	11	7	4	41

Three women from the feminist organizations, US and KA-DER, were experienced in women's rights activism and civil society before they met their associations. In particular, one woman participant from US had close ties with the feminist movement in Turkey. Other respondents were not active in any women's groups and/or CSOs before joining US and KA-DER, although they stated that they were concerned with the issue of women's rights. Within my participants who identified as anti-capitalist feminist women, two from AMARGİ did not take part in any political activism; that is, they joined AMARGİ after an internship in the association. The rest of the women were either part of a political organization or the women's movement. Similarly, three women from SFK were members of a leftist political organization; however, they decided to quit from this organization and to struggle in a feminist group when they experienced gender discrimination and abasement because of their feminist identity.

There is also a variance within and between the individuals I interviewed in terms of their organizational positions. My interviewees include chair persons, general secretaries, members of executive committees, ordinary members and employees of the women's organizations. There was only one case – US – where I could not speak to the chair of the women's organization because of her unavailability.

Research questions and arguments

This book asks two main research questions of my case study. First, what are the main features of the civil society discourses articulated by women activists in Turkey and what are the key factors shaping their articulation? Second, in what ways and to what extent do these discourses reproduce and/or contest the hegemonic civil society discourses currently circulating in Turkey?

I will make four main arguments in response to these questions. To begin with, I will show that members of women's groups in Turkey produce multiple discourses of civil society, which I describe under the headings of voluntarism, autonomy, mediation, democratization, opposition, anti-hierarchy and co-optation. In this way, the women's movement in Turkey does not speak with one voice on civil society. Next, I claim that ideology is not the only factor that shapes which civil society discourse is articulated. The discourses circulate in complex and overlapping ways in that they do not map neatly onto ideological group identities; instead several discourses may coexist within the same group, and some cut across different ideological strands. It appears that factors such as location, funding, organizational structure and the framing of women's rights also play a role in shaping which discourse comes to the fore.

In addition, I will argue that the women's organizations do not passively reproduce dominant discourses of civil society but actively engage with and contest them. Most of the activist groups, to varying degrees, mirror hegemonic liberal pluralist, Western ideals of democracy and the role of civil society and retain a normative attachment to them. But all, also to varying degrees and in different ways, contest some components of the liberal-democratic civil society ideal and its institutionalization in Turkey. Finally, I will show that some of the activists, namely the anti-capitalist feminists, reject civil society as a normative ideal, seeking to resist it by foregrounding feminist agency and politics as the key vehicle for emancipation of women in civil society. When read in conjunction with more widespread critiques of and challenges to civil society among my interviewees, it would appear that there are important oppositional voices to dominant civil society norms in Turkey, which require more attention than they have thus far received.

Structure of the book

The book has seven chapters. Chapter 1 of this book focuses on the main goals, key research questions and the significance of the book and touches upon the methodology of the book. Chapter 2 turns to the relevant crucial literature on civil society and NGOs and its feminist critique. Chapter 3 addresses sociopolitical contexts in Turkey, evaluate the political, social, cultural and economic circumstances of Turkey over time with an aim of identifying the main dominant civil society discourses in circulation. Chapters 4 and 5 offer findings of the empirical research conducted with women from the Kemalist (TKB, TÜKD), Islamist (BKP, AKDER), Kurdish (KAMER, SELİS), feminist (KA-DER, US) and anti-capitalist (SFK, AMARGİ) women's organizations in Turkey. Identifying and mapping the civil society discourses articulated by women in these organizations laid the groundwork for Chapter 6 in which I explore the complex ways in which the women's civil society discourses reflect, critique and reject hegemonic narratives of civil society in Turkey. Chapter 7 concludes the book by summarizing the aims and arguments of the book, reflects on their implications for the wider debates about civil society and among feminists, and outlines a research agenda for further work on the concept and practices of civil society.

2

Civil society and NGOs: Theories, applications and feminist critique

This chapter touches upon the literature on women's activism and civil society in various regions with a particular focus on the Middle East. It aims to show the ways in which overgeneralization and stereotyping of civil society and NGOs in the Middle East and beyond should be avoided and highlights the feminist critique of the gendered exclusions of civil society and of the neoliberal limitations of women's organizing in the context of NGOization. It begins by examining the trajectory of the concept of civil society: its emergence in the West, the variety of views that have developed on it over time and its contested characteristics. This discussion highlights liberal and critical perspectives on the concept and also emphasizes the global dominance of the neoliberal understanding, paying particular attention to the Middle East and Turkey. The second and final part of this chapter centres on feminist debates about gender, civil society and women's NGOs, again paying particular attention to arguments about Turkey and the Middle East.

Revival of the concept of civil society: Dominance of neoliberal civil society and its contestations

Civil society as a contested concept

The concept of civil society can be traced back to political and philosophical developments in Europe and the United States during the Enlightenment (White, 1996: 142). It came to the fore in the context of the transition from absolutist monarchy to the modern state via industrialization and development, as a way of opposing the autocratic state (Kaviraj and Khilnani, 2001: 4). In other words, the emergence of civil society in the West coincided with the processes of 'capitalization, industrialization, urbanization, [and] citizenship' tied to the nation-state (Eddin Ibrahim, 1995: 28).

Throughout the seventeenth and eighteenth centuries, civil society was understood as equivalent to political society. This idea of civil society as political society was rooted in a social contract 'agreed upon by previously dispersed individuals' and was distinct from a 'state of nature' (Schippers, 2005: 344). Contract theorists viewed civil society as a driving force for the growth of civilization because the concept promoted a view of 'the civilized or political state of human beings' as opposed to 'the uncivilized or pre-political' (Kumar, 1993: 376–7).

However, by the early nineteenth century, civil society began to be conceptualized as distinct from the state (Keane, 1988: 35–6) and became an important term for the 'development of the public sphere' (Hagemann, 2008: 17). This was because the independence of civil society had become an important foundation for a democratic state (Ketola, 2010: 31), and civil society was conceptualized as an autonomous, self-generating and active force against despotism. In addition to such links to democracy, civil society came to be regarded as an important arena for the acquisition and protection of private property; indeed, 'the emergence of a distinct sphere of private property' as a result of 'the growth of capitalism and the development of the science of political economy' occurred in tandem with the independence of civil society from the state (Kumar, 1993: 377). In sum, civil society was initially formulated in, and performed a useful function for, emerging Western liberal societies.

After its initial emergence, a range of approaches to civil society appeared in the academic literature. Among these, liberal conceptions of civil society have dominated. In the liberal tradition, civil society is construed as a space of plurality beyond both family and state, first and most famously articulated in the works of Alexis de Tocqueville. According to de Tocqueville, because of the dangers of despotism and of 'a tyranny of the majority that might result from an electoral sweep in an era of populist politics' (Cox, 1999: 6), liberal societies should foster an active, plural and autonomous associational life as a mechanism to limit the interference of the state (Onbaşı, 2008). He thus defines civil society as a space for a network of voluntary associations (de Tocqueville, 1971: 126–33). De Tocqueville's idea continues to influence contemporary political thought, particularly in the work of Diamond (Onbaşı, 2008: 55). Diamond (1994: 5) approaches civil society as an area 'of organized social life that is voluntary, self-generating, (largely) self-supporting, autonomous from the state, and bound by a legal order or set of shared rules and it is an intermediary entity, standing between the private sphere and the state'. In this view, the distinction between state and civil society is emphasized and characterized in positive terms. Putnam (1995) is another contemporary proponent of Tocquevillian thought. He laments the decline of a spirit of association or what he terms 'social capital': 'networks, norms, and social trust that facilitate coordination and cooperation for mutual benefit' (Cox, 1999: 27). As a solution to this decline, Putnam recommends a notion of civil society which pays attention to 'community spirit, volunteerism and association' (Van Rooy, 1998: 13). In such ways, the Tocquevillian liberal approach, with its emphasis on civil society as an expression of society and a form of 'associational life' (Edwards, 2004: 10), is still very influential today.

This liberal idea of civil society has, however, been given new meaning in the neoliberal era. International organizations (such as the WB, the EU and the WTO) have adopted an understanding of civil society that is based on providing funding to CSOs or NGOs for building and promoting democracy. This neoliberal view reinforces the idea that the power of civil society should be increased vis-à-vis the state through the input of international donor agencies, in order to both create an independent space for citizens and generate a retreat of the state from some areas. It is neoliberal in character, as Kaldor (2003: 9) points out, because 'civil society consists of associational life – a non-profit, voluntary "third sector" – that not only restrains state power but also actually provides a substitute for many of the functions performed by the state'. The neoliberal policies prevalent around the world encourage the establishment of more NGOs with pressure from the international donor institutions, and this effectively conceals the goals of creating a minimal state while producing a profit-seeking donor sector for NGOs.

Critics of liberal and neoliberal views of civil society often draw on Hegelian and Marxist traditions. In contrast to the emphasis on pluralism and associationalism in the liberal tradition, Hegelian and Marxist traditions equate civil society with bourgeois society. The Hegelian approach conceptualizes civil society as an entity which requires the supervision and control of the state (Keane, 1988: 50). Hegel defines civil society as a 'specialized and highly complex network of rules, institutions, agencies, groups, practices and attitudes [which] evolved within the legal and political framework of the nation-state to satisfy individual needs and safeguard individual rights' (Pelczynski, 1984b: 263). In this approach, the state is conceptualized as a guardian of individual freedoms. Further, Hegel (1998: 373) argues that civil society recognizes individuals as self-sufficient persons, separating them from family ties. Crucially, for Hegel, civil society is an important component of 'the totality of rationally structured modern political community' (Pelczynski, 1984a: 1).

In the Marxist tradition, civil society has been conceptualized more negatively, as a site of class struggle, with the state seen as the instrument of the bourgeoisie, unlike Hegel's 'universal state' (see Cohen and Arato, 1992). Marx (1994: 153) traces the emergence of the term 'civil society' to eighteenth-century property relations, which had already evolved from antiquity and medieval times. He associates civil society with bourgeois society as the growth of civil society was dependent on the development of capitalism and so clearly encompasses market relations (White, 2004: 8). Although both Hegelian and Marxist traditions accept civil society as a bourgeois society, they diverge in terms of their approach to the role of the state in relation to civil society. Whereas for the former the state is a body for 'harmonizing competing interests in self-interested and egoistical society' (Van Rooy, 1998: 10), the latter sees the state as subordinate to the dominant class (Kaldor, 2003: 20).

The classic Marxist understanding of civil society, which puts economic institutions at the centre of society, has been transformed since the middle of the twentieth century with the influence of Gramsci, who shifted the focus from the economic dimensions of civil society to 'civic, cultural, educational, religious and other organizations not directly related to the system of production' (Kumar, 1993: 383–4). For Gramsci, 'it is not "economic structure" as such that governs political action but the "interpretation of it"' (Kaldor, 2003: 20). Gramsci reinvigorated the Marxist understanding of civil society with an eagerness to understand the reasons 'why Communists in the 1920s and 1930s in Italy failed to execute the revolution' (Ketola, 2013: 15).

He suggested the 'notion of superstructure' to explain the perpetuation of capitalism in spite of the existence of the objective circumstances for a Socialist revolution. For him, superstructure has two components: 'one that can be called "civil society", that is ensemble of organisms commonly called "private", and that of "political society" or the "state"' (Killingsworth, 2012: 13). In other words, it is not enough to concentrate on political society or the state to reveal power relations (Ketola, 2013: 15). Gramsci (1971: 263) argues that capitalist hegemony is constituted by a mix of political society and civil society – the capitalist state exercising its power consensually through civil society but also, ultimately, through coercive force. In this way, the meaning of the notion of civil society changed considerably. In the Gramscian approach, civil society is delineated 'not as a part of society, but as a sphere in which battles for and against capitalism are fought and that sphere is occupied by a struggle for material, ideological and cultural control over all of society, including the state' (Van Rooy, 1998: 10). This approach, however, also captures the transformative potential of civil society and the possibility of an emancipatory counter-hegemony (Cox, 1999: 3).

An alternative view is articulated in the works of Habermas, in which civil society is treated as a means to realize the 'values of active citizenship and political participation' (Onbaşı, 2008: 80). Habermas claims that the development of a robust civil society is only possible through active participation in a liberal political culture (Habermas cited in Schippers, 2005: 347). He asserts the existence of public-political society, explains its links with civil society (Habermas, 1989) and argues for recognition of the public sphere and the state as mutually constituted rather than distinct areas (Habermas, 1996). According to Habermas and other critical theorists, a 'healthy civil society is one "that is steered by its members through shared meanings" that are constructed democratically through the communications structures of the public sphere' (Edwards, 2004: 9). Much like Habermas, Cohen and Arato advocate a three-part model, which distinguishes between civil society, political-administrative processes and economic processes. In this model, they define civil society as 'a sphere of social interaction between economy and state, composed above all of the intimate sphere (especially the family), the sphere of associations (especially voluntary associations), social movements, and forms of public communication' (Cohen and Arato, 1992: ix).

To sum up, civil society has become a contested concept, with differing versions put forward by liberals and their critics. Although the neoliberal view has become dominant in recent times, in the West and beyond, many conflicting notions of civil society nonetheless remain in circulation.

The triumph of neoliberal civil society?

The concept of civil society was revived in the late twentieth century in both Eastern Europe and Latin America. In those contexts, civil society has been placed outside the state as part of anti-totalitarian struggles and viewed as a space in which citizens can exercise some control over the conditions in which they live, through both self-organization and political pressure (Kaldor, 2003: 8). Because of its capacity to empower at the level of the individual (Kuzmanovic, 2012: 23), it is lauded as a democratizing force.

Whereas in CEE countries the debate about civil society revolved around the excesses of communist statism and the revival of associative initiatives of non-state organizations, in Latin American context the debate was couched in terms of the development and promotion of democracy. When the term 'civil society' emerged in Eastern European contexts in the 1980s, it was seen to have three core components: self-organization, civic autonomy and the creation of independent spaces (Kaldor, 2003: 21). It gained importance during the late 1970s and early 1980s during the rise of social movements against communist states in Poland, Hungary, Czechoslovakia and Yugoslavia (White, 2004: 7). The United States supported CSOs in such countries, both financially and diplomatically, and when the Revolutions of 1989 happened, 'civil society ... suddenly gained cachet in Eastern Europe as the key to democratization' (Carothers and Ottoway, 2000: 7; see also Ishkanian, 2009). Civil society was thus positioned in opposition to state despotism, as a sphere in which social groups were able to exist and flourish (Hall, 1995: 1).

As Watson (1997: 24) highlights, under communism, 'the state abrogated all prerogative in the public sphere and society became a "private sector" and the monopoly achieved by "prerogative state" over the public sphere corresponded to the comprehensive curtailment of any real rights of political and civil citizenship'. Most of the time, it is explained as 'civil society was practically non-existent under communism because almost every activity was in the hands of the state' (Koldiska, 2009: 555). In this sense, civil society has been popularized by Central European intellectuals as an instrument for showing an opposition to socialist states (Hemment, 2007: 49). In other words, civil society became a main concern of 'the project of "anti-politics", which is a stance that opposes the socialist state' (Hemment, 2007: 49; see Killingsworth, 2012). Since 1990s, increasing or even establishing the role of civil society actors has been one of the most important tasks in Central and Eastern Europe (Nagle and Mahr in Koldiska, 2009: 555). Western donors put some effort to strengthen and promote civil society and tried to persuade the public about the inevitable and natural relationship between democracy and civil society. Contrary to this, when the eradication of radical democratic ideas emerged in the 1980s, more established and less revolutionary neoliberal ones came into prominence (Howell and Pearce, 2001: 51). Civil society organizations lost their political edge, membership in organizations diminished and collective action was limited (Börzel, 2010: 4). This new period began to be described by some scholars (Lang, 1997) as 'NGOization' or 'projectization of civil society'. Even though the number of advocacy NGOs in the former socialist countries went up in the 1990s, it has not brought about genuine participation or greater public debate (Celichowski 2004; Hann 2004).

The accession of CEE countries to the EU was also supported by the 'conviction that, once in the Union, their own states will become more robustly democratic and be protected against authoritarian or totalitarian temptations' (Sadurski, 2004: 371). However, EU's impact on the civil society in CEE was limited and ambivalent as against a general assumption that EU promoted democracy thereby supporting civil society organizations through its instruments of political conditionality, transfers of EU rules and modes of governance and capacity-building measures (Kutter and Trappmann, 2010: 42). Like Kutter and Trappmann (2010), Börzel (2010: 4) does not see EU's rights, money and networks sufficient to empower civil society. He also points out that civil society organizations did not always want to make use of opportunities offered by EU enlargement when cooperation with state actors was required, for example, to access EU funds or participate in the implementation of EU policies. This is related with the idea of emergence of civil society against the state authorities.

In Latin America, the main axis of the debate turned on the task of increasing development and enabling international agencies and lenders to bypass the central state and deliver direct assistance to what they identified as the constituents of civil society (Khilnani, 2001: 12). In this sense, the idea that the development of civil society is linked to democracy has been widespread in Latin American countries (cf. Brysk, 2000: 151). 'The 1980s saw the return to civilian rule in much of Latin America although transition mechanisms varied from country to country' (Waylen, 1994: 335). Due to the economic crises of the 1980s (high rate of inflation, severe economic imbalances, large public sector deficits), Structural Adjustment Programme (SAP) was implemented to improve economic performance of the countries. During the late 1990s, the World Bank suggested a strategy for poverty reduction in order to lessen the side effects of SAP although its agenda was not different from the SAP.

Since the 1980s, NGOs played a significant role in politics and public policy in Latin American countries as they expanded, and individual and international agencies sought to build a democratic counterweight to the military regimes that were dominating the region. The economic crisis of the 1980s also encouraged the growth of NGOs that sought solutions to worsening poverty (Ewig, 1999). 'The democratic transition period that followed the military governments witnessed the growth of social movements, which had contributed to the downfall of the military regimes and many of these social movements have also gradually institutionalized themselves in the form of NGOs' (75). However, what we see is that the role of the state was limited and NGOs were turned into 'technically capable and politically trustworthy organizations to assist in the task of "social adjustment"' (Alvarez, 2009: 176). In Latin America, the World Bank's strategy of using NGOs to substitute for state services fits well into neoliberal programmes of 'cutting back the state's involvement in favor of private sector provision of services' in the form of decentralization of social services from state to NGOs by providing social development funds (Ewig, 1999: 76).

In the light of this discussion, it can be argued that the activist-based approaches to civil society that emerged in Eastern Europe and Latin America were incorporated into the neoliberal approach, mainly through the influence of international institutions (such as the WB, the EU and the UN). These institutions perceive civil society as a way of developing democratic governance by increasing the role and participation of CSOs (Ketola, 2013). They employ the concept of civil society as a policy tool for promoting democracy and development through their own policies and funding. In diverse non-Western contexts, civil society has been associated with the transition to democracy, and the opportunity to obtain assistance or funding for this transition has been linked to each country's eagerness and efforts to develop civil society. In this way, the concept of civil society has been used in non-Western settings to refer almost exclusively to donor-NGO relationships, and civil society development has been limited by the policies of international organizations.[1] It could be said that the current attraction of the concept of civil society relates to the global dominance of neoliberalism (Konings, 2009: 2), by which NGOs have been co-opted (Klees, 2002: 49). In short, what clearly emerges from the practices of international institutions worldwide is that civil society is seen as inevitable and necessary for democratization.

However, Marxists and Gramscians have criticized the neoliberal notion of civil society on the grounds that it separates civil society from the state. This neoliberal project 'conceals its own massive use of state power, transnational and local, for the purpose of constructing a civil society according to its own image' (Beckman, 1993: 30). The neoliberal agenda represents NGOs as apolitical by virtue of being part of a voluntary and non-profit sector (Kaldor, 2003: 9). This enables the concealment of oppressive bourgeois characteristics of capitalist society and the fact that NGOs come to perform many of the functions formally assigned to the state (9). The idea that neoliberal civil society is an empowering and democratizing force has also been challenged by postcolonial scholars. For them, civil society is an ethnocentric term, which cannot mediate 'between self and society outside a Western context' (Chatterjee and Hann cited in Kuzmanovic, 2012: 23) and should therefore not be applied globally as a general model. Such scholars also accuse global donor institutions of neglecting the peculiarities of local context and of importing culturally specific (Western) normative ideals of civil society into non-Western contexts (Van Rooy, 1998: 15) such as the Middle East.[2]

Contesting neoliberal civil society in the Middle East

The concept of civil society spread to countries in the Middle East and Northern Africa (MENA) in the 1990s as a result of processes of economic and political liberalization (Moghadam, 2002: 14). It has been employed in the region with the aim of transforming authoritarian regimes into democratic ones. This, to a certain extent, reflects the idea applied in Eastern Europe, of strengthening civil society against the state (Ibrahim and Wedel, 1997: 12–13). However, although the main goal of democratization is similar, the cases of Eastern Europe and Latin America on the one hand, and the Middle East on the other, differ in an important sense. In the former, civil society developed from below to defeat authoritarian dictatorships and military regimes, while in the latter, political change has – until recently[3] – been primarily driven by moderate liberalization measures and external forces rather than pressure from civil society (Wiktorowicz, 2000: 46–7). The 'development of civil society' in the Middle East has been facilitated specifically by the global tendency of donor governments and multilateral funding agencies to treat NGOs as allies in development, the corresponding shift in the development agenda away from economic development and towards political and social development (Moghadam, 1997: 25), all oriented to the main goal of undermining the state's repressive control over society. In this light, international organizations have focused their attention 'on building democracy from below, through building-up of civil society, understood as a sphere of liberal and democratic leaning' (Cavatorta and Durac, 2011: 9). Concurrently, Arab states in the early- and mid-1990s conducted several projects that triggered expectations for the growth of democracy within civil society (Carapico, 2002: 380).

The literature on civil society in the Middle East can be grouped into three categories – supportive, rejectionist and critical – reflecting, to some extent, the rival liberal and critical views outlined earlier. Supporters of the civil society project across the Middle East subscribe to the liberal view that civil society should be a separate entity from both the state and 'primordial organizations' of kinship, village, tribe and religious groups (Zubaida, 1992: 4). Such organizations are regarded as sources of coercion and authority 'which can oppress the individual and trample over human rights; by contrast, voluntary associations are areas which foster individual autonomy and provide

experience in the exercise of social and political rights and responsibilities'
(Zubaida, 1992: 4). According to this view, NGOs, as the key actors in civil
society, serve as agents of change and liberalization, thus contributing to
democratization in the Middle East.[4] In this vein, Eddin Ibrahim (1995: 27,
30) identifies 'the articulation of civil society' as one of four variables that
impact upon the democratization of the Arab world, despite evidence of
problems and time lags in this process.

In the rejectionist camp, there are two lines of thought. According to the
first, the Western, liberal view of civil society should be rejected in favour of
more communalistic notions of civil society and the state (al-Masri cited in
Pratt, 2005: 124), and NGOs are seen as Western creations. This approach holds
that 'civil society, NGOs, the state and good governance [are] the latest means
by which the West undermines the strength of sovereign nation states in the
Third world; therefore, NGOs are a threat to the organic relationship between
the state and civil society' (Pratt, 2005: 124). The second line of thought
in the rejectionist approach suggests that civil society cannot be practised in
the Middle East as 'Islam' and 'traditionalism' are incompatible with civil
society. Gellner (1994: 29) adopts this view, arguing that 'Islam exemplifies
a social order which seems to lack much capacity to provide countervailing
institutions and associations' that are key to civil society. In the same vein,
for Sariolghalam (1997: 56, 60), the cultural preconditions necessary for the
development of civil society are missing in Middle Eastern societies because of
their particular social and state practices. Specifically, he asserts that 'the recent
return to traditionalism in the Middle East has made the possible emergence
of civil society principles even less likely' (Sariolghalam, 1997: 56).

There is a third category, which lies between the supportive and rejectionist
approaches, which is critical of the situation and role of CSOs in relation to
the state and informal relations in the Middle East. Scholars in this category
argue that the liberal view does not work in the Middle Eastern context, as
civil society is not a distinct entity from the state but rather repressed and
co-opted by it. This can be seen in the fact that most of the NGOs in the region
instrumentally act as a 'substitute for state involvement in social provisioning
for citizens', even though this should not be the case (Moghadam, 2002: 14).
Moreover, critical scholars claim that civil society is restricted, repressed and
co-opted by the state rather than being and acting as a distinct entity. In this

regard, Personal Status Law is given as an example for the considerable power of state institutions vis-à-vis CSOs in Middle Eastern countries (Zubaida, 1992: 5).[5] The Arab Women's Solidarity Association (AWSA), established in 1991 in Egypt by the feminist Nawal Al-Sadawi, was banned under the Personal Status Code, which gives the state a repressive power over voluntary groups, associations and organizations (Al-Ali, 2004: 78). Moreover, the state's control over NGOs can take the form of controlling the access to and management of international funding that is allocated to NGOs (Abdelrahman, 2004: 178, 183). Critics also argue that civil society is not distinct from informal relations in Middle Eastern societies. This is based on the idea that kin-based and communal relations are significant 'organizers of the social life' in the region (Joseph and Slyomovics, 2001: 12; also see White, 1996).

In actual fact there are two groups within the category of critical scholars: one which shows affinity to the liberal approach of civil society but is critical of the ways in which it is practised and applied, highlighting the need for further effort to achieve an autonomous civil society in the Middle East (e.g. Moghadam, 2002; Zaki, 1995), and one which is normatively closer to the Marxist, Gramscian and postcolonial views recounted previously, and which is critical of the main presumptions of the liberal view of civil society, such as the taken-for-granted attribution of the positive features of civil society.[6]

State and social relations in Turkey have been characterized in various ways that are reflective of the liberal, rejectionist and critical perspectives in the Middle East literature outlined above. Turkish scholars who take a liberal perspective on the characteristics of state-civil society relations until the 1980s emphasize that civil society struggled to develop freely in the Turkish case due to a strong and centralized state bureaucracy which was inherited from the Ottoman period (Heper, 1985: 16; see Toprak, 1996). From a liberal perspective, control of the state over civil society began to decrease in the 1980s as the top-down effort to build a Kemalist hegemony through civil society lessened (see Akboğa, 2013). The critical debates on civil society in Turkey reflect their counterparts elsewhere in the Middle East with their focus on the impossibility of maintaining distinctions between civil society and the state, and between civil society and informal relations (Dikici-Bilgin, 2009). Focusing on the former distinction, Gramscians and Marxists downplay the 'autonomy' of civil society. They – particularly the Gramscians – critique the liberal view on the grounds that it emphasizes autonomy and overlooks the way in which the Turkish state used civil society to generate 'consent' in order to manufacture hegemony. As Navaro-Yashin (2002: 119) neatly puts it, 'The state of the 1990s, a secular democracy, demanded a realm of civil society in favour of itself.'

In terms of the second distinction, critical scholars suggest that civil society in the Turkish context includes informal relations and networks. White indicates that civil society in the Turkish case challenges the classical Western approach to civil society by including 'personal, kin, and ethnic relations' (White, 2002: 179; also see Kuzmanovic, 2012). In terms of the circulation of neoliberal discourses of civil society, the Turkish case is not an exception to the regional experience. However, it differs from the rest of the Middle East in terms of the influence of the EU. It has been widely acknowledged that EU influence and, correspondingly, the AKP's commitment to democracy in Turkey have lessened since 2011 when the AKP entered its third term in office. Indeed, liberal and critical views converge in terms of their approach to the implications of the AKP authoritarianism on civil society as they emphasize the marginalization of some groups compared to others. As Özçetin and Özer (2015: 18) highlight, 'the ruling party's selective attitude towards CSOs is clear in the distinction it makes [between] "marginal", "problematic", "unacceptable" and "acceptable CSOs"'. In this way, secular CSOs are now navigating a more hostile environment. Indeed, it can even be argued that CSOs have organized themselves more collectively in recent years due to their dissatisfaction with government rule, as can be seen in the Gezi Park Protests of 2013.[7]

Despite the diversity in approaches to civil society in the region, there is a common problem in the conceptions of liberals, rejectionists and some critics, which has to do with their tendency to overgeneralize the concept. Whether they endorse civil society or assume it is a Western construct, commentators often fail to recognize the particularities of context and tend to homogenize the notion of civil society, overlooking its heterogeneity and diversity, and the contradictions within and between NGOs. In response to this problem, a group of critical scholars[8] have called for context-specific studies to analyse the position and role of civil society in relation to the state, and domestic and international institutions in the Middle East. It is this kind of approach I adopt in this book, with a country-specific focus on Turkey.

Civil society and the state in Turkey

What can we learn from the existing literature on civil society in Turkey? State and social relations in Turkey have been characterized in various ways that are reflective of the liberal, rejectionist and critical perspectives in the Middle East literature outlined earlier. Turkish scholars who take a liberal perspective on the characteristics of state-civil society relations until the 1980s emphasize that civil society struggled to develop freely in the Turkish case due to a strong and centralized state bureaucracy which was inherited from the Ottoman period (Heper, 1985: 16). The Ottoman Empire had a patrimonial structure in which the sultan acted as the supreme arbiter, and those working for him carried out the administration of the empire (Mardin, 1971: 200). Contrary to the feudal states in the West, the Ottoman state was autonomous and strong and was able to determine the structure of the whole social system without negotiating with society. People were asked to pay taxes and to partake in military service but were not seen as eligible to play key roles in state affairs (Sarıbay, 1998: 97). This top-down approach of the Turkish state has remained prevalent in the modernization process (see Keyman, 2005: 40). To illustrate, in the period of 1923–45, the bureaucracy and intelligentsia initiated a campaign for political socialization so as to integrate urban and some rural sections of the society into the 'political culture of modern national statehood' (Karpat, 1959: 48). In other words, the state has been conceptualized as a coercive force, perennially suspicious of civil society and reluctant to allow the development of social consensus (Toprak, 1996: 89). For scholars who take this approach, the dominance of the state over society engendered a 'conflict' rather than a 'compromise', and an autonomous civil society sphere free from the state could not be created (Çaylak cited in Çaylak, 2008: 117).

From the liberal perspective, the control of the state over civil society began to decrease in the 1980s as the top-down effort to build a Kemalist hegemony through civil society lessened. When political Islam and the Islamist movement emerged in the same period, it sought legitimacy using 'global [liberal] discourses on minority and human rights' in response to the Kemalist agenda of the nationalist secular Republic (Rumford, 2002: 272). The logic of the Islamist movement was in fact representative of a broader critique of the three pillars of the Kemalist regime: modernization,[9] secularism and nationalism. As Akboğa puts it, 'while many civil society organizations were founded with the goal of protecting the Kemalist principles, the 1980s witnessed the foundation of many civil society organizations that criticized the negative implications of these principles for some groups' (Akboğa, 2013: 7). What is notable, however, is that liberal advocates of 'autonomous civil society' viewed the process of Islamicization in Turkey as the emergence of civil society in opposition to the state after around seven decades of latency (Navaro-Yashin, 2002: 131). Kurdish CSOs were also formed to confront the nationalist and unitary discourses of the Turkish secular state. These organizations were defined as 'anti-establishment organizations, demanding the recognition of a separate Kurdish identity and collective cultural rights and denouncing the state's violations of human rights' (Kaliber and Tocci,[10] 2010: 192). Overall, in this liberal approach, whereas the state is considered as an area of power and increasingly a negotiating partner (Çaha 2005), civil society is thought to represent the people (*halk*) (Navaro-Yashin, 1998b: 57). This is the discourse many scholars used to interpret the development of civil society in Turkey during the 1980s.[11] These scholars also stress the value of civil society as a space for meaningful associational life, attaching civil society to democratic progress, demilitarization, pluralism and multiculturalism (Navaro-Yashin, 2002: 130). They see civil society as becoming more pluralistic and diversified with the growth of Islamist, environmentalist, Kurdish, feminist, Alevi and Kemalist movements since the 1990s (Şimşek, 2004: 48).

The critical debates on civil society in Turkey reflect their counterparts elsewhere in the Middle East with their focus on the impossibility of maintaining distinctions between civil society and the state, and between civil society and informal relations. Focusing on the former distinction, Gramscians and Marxists downplay the 'autonomy' of civil society. According to this view, the Republican period in Turkey saw civil society constituted as a domain of political society to establish hegemony (Dikici-Bilgin, 2009: 111). Underpinned by coercion, the establishment and reinforcement of the Turkish state consisted of 'forming a basis of consent in civil society and becoming hegemonic with a new world view acknowledged by the citizens' (Dikici-Bilgin, 2009: 112). Thus the state not only acquired the consent of society for Republican values and norms but also transformed society. For instance, the establishment of organizations such as Türk Kadınlar Birliği (Turkish Women's Union) in the

1940s was construed as a sign of the will of the state to win consent from civil society (Dikici-Bilgin, 2009: 112). In this way, the critical view echoes the liberal account. However, the proliferation of civil organizations in the 1980s is explained not as civil society becoming more autonomous but in terms of state delegation of responsibility, which occurred due to the implementation of a neoliberal agenda and a reduction in welfare provision. With the neoliberal turn in mind, critical approaches – particularly the Gramscians – critique the liberal view on the grounds that it emphasizes autonomy and overlooks the way in which the Turkish state used civil society to generate 'consent' in order to manufacture hegemony. As Navaro-Yashin (2002: 119) neatly puts it, 'the state of the 1990s, a secular democracy, demanded a realm of civil society in favour of itself'.

In terms of the second distinction, critical scholars suggest that civil society in the Turkish context includes informal relations and networks. Thus White's study shows us that there are hybrid groups in Turkey, which are neither kinship-based nor formed of 'contractually bound individuals' and which are 'concerned with addressing local conditions: lack of water and electricity, the need for health care, or the need for job training for girls' (White, 1996: 142). In this way, she indicates that civil society in the Turkish case challenges the classical Western approach to civil society by including 'personal, kin, and ethnic relations' (White, 2002: 179; also see Kuzmanovic, 2012). This resonates with the work of a small group of Islamist thinkers who reject the Western liberal view of civil society. Arguing that civil society cannot be independent of religion, they include foundations (*vakıflar*), religious associations (*dini cemaatler*), sects (*tarikatlar*), and religious Sufi lodges and orders (*tekke ve zaviyeler*) in the category of CSOs (Bulaç, 2014). Among such groupings, foundations played a particularly key role in conducting charity work in the Ottoman era; they 'have made a comeback over the last two decades as a major conduit for charity work' and are 'particularly important in the Islamist organizational network' (White, 2002: 200–2).

In terms of the circulation of neoliberal discourses of civil society, the Turkish case is not an exception to the regional experience. However, it differs from the rest of the Middle East in terms of the influence of the EU. Turkey's eagerness to become a member of the EU has important implications for how civil society is understood in the country, as scholars widely acknowledge.[12]

The EU accession process has paved the way for constitutional reforms to meet the Copenhagen Criteria and increased the flow of funding from the EU to Turkey. In this context, many reforms, namely the 'adaptation package', were made in the areas of minority rights, human rights and the civil-military relationship, with help from CSOs (Çaha, 2013: 65). In contrast to other Middle Eastern countries, Turkey's civil society has been promoted and developed via EU funding and policy reforms. Since 2006, there has been a programme of EU funding allocated for the furtherance of the EU-Civil Society Dialogue in Turkey, with the specific aim of encouraging civil society engagement. Being an EU member candidate country has brought about 'new legal and institutional frameworks supporting a role for civil society for socio-political development and democratization in Turkey' (Kuzmanovic, 2010: 431). Civil society actors, particularly business actors, were very active and effective in terms of putting pressure on the government to pursue Turkey's membership (Öniş, 2007: 247). When the AKP came to power in 2002, it saw EU accession as an important dimension of developing civil society in Turkey. The EU-induced democratic reform process has evidently influenced the AKP's emphasis on democratization via civil society promotion.

The EU accession process has had significant outcomes for the gender policy in Turkey. The Turkish state, the EU and the women's organizations, particularly the feminists, have all played a key role in policy changes namely for Civil Code, Penal Code and the Labour Law (Marshall, 2013: 4).[13] Civil Code was amended by the Turkish Grand National Assembly in 2001 with the aim of hindering the arrangements that put women in a secondary position in marriage (Arat, 2010: 235).[14] Afterwards, in 2004, a new Penal Code, 'which eliminated reference to patriarchal concepts such as tradition, custom, honour, chastity and morality in regulating sexual crimes', was accepted (Güneş-Ayata and Doğangün, 2017: 613). Turkey made changes in its social security system, particularly the Unemployment Insurance Law (Law 4447), with the aim of raising female labour force participation (Marshall, 2013: 67; Güneş-Ayata and Doğangün, 2017: 614). In this process, women's groups were very effective and employed various types of tools, namely press releases, protests, fax campaigns, establishing relationships with some politicians in parliament and developing connections with the EU via the European Women's Lobby to transform the traditional and family-oriented gender regime in Turkey (Marshall, 2013: 80).

Women's rights activists conducted transnational lobbying activities through the EU. The UN has also been a key international actor in their struggle for gender equality. In 2000s, women's rights activists had 'increased their advocacy and lobbying at the UN level through global women's coalitions in order to pressure the Turkish State to make legislative changes for the advancement of women's rights' (Marshall, 2013: 10, 78). Participation of women's rights activists to the 1995 UN World Conference in Beijing for the first time 'encouraged women's groups to organize better and women's organisations have started to put pressure on the Turkish state through the CEDAW committee' (78). Particularly, through shadow reports presented at these meetings in 2000s, women's organizations were able to produce alternative voices to the reports prepared by the state (81).

However, it has been widely acknowledged that EU influence and, correspondingly, the AKP's commitment to democracy in Turkey, have lessened since 2011 when the AKP entered its third term in office. Since then, the authoritarianism of the AKP has begun to increase and the party's religious-conservative vision of civil society has deepened (Tolunay, 2014). More specifically, the party, particularly Prime Minister Erdoğan, has taken an increasingly oppressive approach to visual and print media, increased control over the use of the internet, restricted abortion and caesarean rights, introduced limitations on the sale and use of alcohol, and antagonized mixed-sex student dorms (Yılmaz, 2015: 152). The contemporary situation of democracy in Turkey has been criticized by a group of scholars as 'post-modern authoritarianism' (Dağı, 2012), an 'electoral authoritarianism of a more markedly Islamic character' (Özbudun, 2014: 155) and 'a narrow vision of democracy based on an extreme understanding of majoritarianism' (Öniş, 2014: 5). Indeed, liberal and critical views converge in terms of their approach to the implications of the AKP authoritarianism on civil society as they emphasize the marginalization of some groups compared to others. As Özçetin and Özer (2015: 18) highlight, 'the ruling party's selective attitude towards CSOs is clear in the distinction it makes [between] "marginal", "problematic", "unacceptable" and "acceptable CSOs"'. In this way, secular CSOs are now navigating a more hostile environment. Indeed, it can even be argued that CSOs have organized themselves more collectively in recent years due to their dissatisfaction with government rule, as can be seen in the Gezi Park Protests of 2013.

In the post-2011 period, the AKP has also pursued authoritarianism in its gender policies by taking conservative and moral attitudes towards female body, promoting the idea of a 'strong family' and holding anti-feminist sentiments, and this has increased the significance of gender politics in challenging the state. A recent study conducted on the basis of the voices of activists from human rights and women's organizations highlights the problem of a high level of state control over civil society both in the form of repression and co-optation and underlines its impact as 'tempering the demand of CSOs and reducing their capacity to challenge the state power' (Doyle, 2017a: 1). Coşar and Yeğenoğlu (2011) call the outcomes of AKP's neoliberal, religious and nationalist politics as a 'new mode of patriarchy' that refers to gradual lessening of opportunities provided for women in spite of the legal advancements. Herein, the key concern of the women's organizations is 'the application of laws, promulgated by the EU pressure and transnational lobbying activities, on the ground and further the development of rights by continuing to pressure the state from and within the EU and the UN as well as protecting what has already been achieved' (Marshall, 2013: 81–2).

Engendering civil society and NGOs

Feminist critiques of civil society in the West

Feminists are concerned with how unequal gender relations structure civil society (Einhorn and Sever, 2003: 167) and with how this varies over time and in different contexts. In what follows, I will discuss the feminist literature on civil society, following Eto (2012), in terms of its critique of the public and private distinction, on the one hand, and the separation of civil society from the state, on the other. These two sets of criticisms are actually interrelated, although I distinguish them below.

First, the distinction between public and private has become an important 'organizing category' for feminist theorists in the West (Howell, 2005: 5). They argue that civil society[15] should be regarded as a gendered term; in Einhorn and

Sever's (2003: 167) words, 'the public/political sphere of civil society is neither politically, ideologically nor gender neutral'. The critique of the distinction between public sphere/civil society/state on the one hand, and private sphere/ family on the other, forms the basis of the feminist challenge to gender-based theories of civil society, since this dichotomy traditionally works to confine women to the private sphere while locating men in the public sphere (see Pateman, 1988, 1989; Fraser, 1992).

For feminists, the interaction between the public and private spheres is a key factor in shaping women's lives in contemporary Western societies (Benhabib and Cornell, 1987: 7). Feminist thinkers contend that this modern dichotomy should be rejected and the family be considered political insofar as it is structured by relations of power. As Kaldor puts it, feminists reject a 'public (state, market and civil society)/private (family) division since the family can be an oppressive and violent sphere' (Kaldor, 2003: 30). This critique dovetails with the broader feminist project of rejecting the confinement of politics to state affairs and calling for a reconsideration of 'the landscape of politics' (Hassim and Gouws, 1998: 57; see Gal, 1997; Seungsook, 2002).

The second focus of the feminist challenge to civil society in the West is in terms of its assumption of a universally applicable dichotomy between the state and civil society. To begin with, feminists question whether such a dichotomy is universally normatively desirable, particularly from the point of view of women. Liberals aspire to a civil society, which is an independent, autonomous, plural space, and claim that by separating the state from civil society – which means less interference from the state – citizens' rights and liberties are protected. However, one of the problems with this distinction from a feminist perspective is that it underestimates the importance of the state and overestimates the potential of civil society (Eto, 2012: 107). This may justify the state cutting back on its responsibilities, which can mean cutbacks to services disproportionately used by women, along with the transformation of women's organizations into apolitical service providers. As Phillips makes clear, advocacy of civil society as a substitute for the welfare state strikes feminist scholars as an ideological move which merely adds weight to the unequal burden already faced by primary carers, most of whom are women (Phillips, 1999: 4). Likewise, Young (2000: 156) rejects the approach to civil society 'as an alternative site for the public-spirited, caring and equalizing functions that have long been associated with governments' (180) and argues that strengthened relations between state institutions and civil society both improve democracy and diminish injustice (156–7).

In the light of the discussion above, it could be argued that there is a general agreement among feminist scholars that civil society in the West, and as diffused more widely, should be viewed through a gendered lens, and that the reliance on public-private, civil society-informal relations/networks, and state-civil society dichotomies is highly problematic. The strong consensus on this view is hard to rebut. However, there are important differences between feminist scholars in terms of their view of the possibilities that civil society may thereby offer to women. On the one hand, some feminists argue that civil society is so problematic that it is of no political use to women; on the other hand, some believe that it remains, to a certain extent, a useful concept. The former view can be found in the work of Pateman (1988, 1989), Phillips (1987, 1999, 2002) and Jaggar (2005), among others. These scholars see civil society as an intrinsically patriarchal concept, which cannot be used as an instrument to achieve an egalitarian society. Their approaches to civil society vary in their detail, but share this overall thrust. For instance, for Pateman (1988, 1989), the 'individual', 'civil society' and 'the public' are from the outset patriarchal categories, which gain meaning in contrast to womanly nature and the 'private' sphere (Pateman, 1989: 34). She asserts that civil society does not sufficiently include women or facilitate feminist struggles (Schippers, 2005: 349). Phillips 'attacks civil society itself for the danger it presents to women' (cited in Eto, 2012: 104), and wonders whether feminism even needs the concept of civil society (Phillips, 1999: 58). Phillips sees two main reasons for the incompatibility of feminism and the idea of civil society (1999, 2002). The first is that civil society marginalizes women as well as other subordinate groups; since there is no way to 'check that each citizen joins an equal number of groups or that each is equally active ... civil society is likely to reflect and confirm whatever is the distribution of sexual power' (1999: 3). The second is that as civil society is relatively unregulated, voluntary organizations may be coerced into adopting the agenda of dominant actors and those that discriminate against women (3). This argument dovetails with Jaggar's (2005: 10, 20) critique of civil society in the neoliberal state, where foreign funding to women's organizations limits 'women's empowerment as citizens' rather than enhancing it; for her, 'civil society as a terrain of democratic empowerment' should not be favoured over 'traditional state-centred politics'.

However, many feminists argue that it is still important to look at civil society from a feminist perspective. In other words, they highlight significant contribution of women to the site of civil society in the West. Women have taken part in the social movements as seen in the feminist movements of the nineteenth and twentieth centuries. Whereas the first wave of feminism, seized in Western Europe and North America, focused on the struggle for the civil and political rights of women, the second wave introduced the motto of 'personal is political' and turned to the issues of 'elimination of violence against women, the use of sexuality as a medium for male dominance, the misrepresentation of women in the media and the challenge against virginity tests' (Diner and Toktaş, 2010: 41). As well as feminist movements, women conducted several voluntary activities in NGOs, non-profit organizations (NPOs), and charitable associations, some of which target to improve 'women's status in society' by undertaking 'women's gendered roles as mothers and wives' rather than questioning male domination (Eto, 2012: 2–3).

Women in the West have been active agents of civil society and have sought to integrate the aspiration for gender equality into civil society debates, thereby helping to facilitate the creation of a more egalitarian and women-friendly civil society.[16] In my view, this approach is both more practical and more convincing. As an example, Young (2000: 156) underlines the crucial role of civil society in advancing inclusion, freedom of expression and critique for the achievement of 'deep democracy', even though she problematizes the idea that civil society is a desirable alternative to the state for the promotion of democracy and social justice. For Young, state institutions inevitably decrease oppression and domination, and promote justice and development, since 'many of the structural injustices that produce oppression have their source in economic processes' (155). Nonetheless, she ultimately argues that both civil society and state institutions should be strengthened because they have an essential role to play in promoting democracy and justice (see also Eto, 2012). Similarly, Howell (2005: 6) underscores the 'emancipatory potential' of civil society, which 'may provide a site for organizing around feminist issues, for articulating counter-hegemonic discourses ... for envisioning other less sexist and more just worlds'. This is despite the fact that she is wary, like Phillips

(2002), of the potential of civil society to become diffused with conservative ideologies which constrict women to the domain of the family and enhance their dependency (Howell, 2005: 6). As Hagemann (2008: 37) sums up, however compromised by neoliberalism and gendered inequality it may be, civil society 'is the most important space and form of action for articulating and enforcing feminist demands on the market and the state and for protecting women within the family'.

Feminist critiques of civil society in the Middle East

With regard to the Middle Eastern region, there have been diverse studies rethinking civil society by analysing women's position and the contribution of women's activism. Such studies shed light on the gendered dimensions of civil society and state, and the increasing significance of gender politics in challenging the state in the Middle East.[17] One critique of mainstream discussions that emerges from this literature is that it excludes women from civil society. In such a vein, Al-Ali (1997: 189) criticizes the work of Zaki (1995) on the grounds that it presents civil society in a 'male-centered' way and 'disregards women's roles in and contributions to civil society'. Additionally, Rabo (1996: 156) pays attention to how androcentric and ethnocentric assumptions dominate the debates about civil society, by drawing on examples from Syria and Jordan. Furthermore, feminist scholars of the Middle East highlight the disregard for secular women's associations in the mainstream literature. On this issue, Al-Ali criticizes studies on the emergence and performance of civil society (e.g. Zaki, 1995; Zubaida, 1992) for ignoring secular feminist associations and limiting consideration of women's status to discussion of religious and minority rights (Al-Ali, 1997: 189).

This last point is worth dwelling on at more length. Feminist scholars are critical of the dichotomy of East/West or traditional/modern, and of the way in which it influences the conceptualization of civil society and women's organizing in the Middle East. In this vein, Al-Ali argues against the dominant trend of positing strict divisions between a 'modern, secular and westernizing voice' and a 'conservative, anti-western, Islamic voice' because she considers that this conceals 'the overlapping, contradictions and complexities of discourses and activism' (175). In this dominant approach, whereas modernity is related with political development, authenticity is associated with the implementation of Shari'a (188).[18] Al-Ali emphasizes rather that secularism does not automatically designate 'an anti-religious or anti-Islamic positions' (Al-Ali, 2004: 4). Connectedly, Badran (2009) underlines the cooperation between Islamic women's organizations and secular feminists by arguing that they are not in conflict or opposition to each other; on the contrary, they intersect and in some cases support each other.

Scholars of this persuasion also highlight the fact that women in the Middle East are active agents who, despite constraints, establish groups or act collectively to advance their interests (Chatty and Rabo, 1997: 8). More nuanced analyses which take into account heterogeneity and particularity indicate that women's movements in the Middle East are not imported from foreign countries; rather, they 'have emerged from within' and their agendas have been formed in relation to 'the specific characteristics of the societies in which they have been active' (Arenfeldt and Golley, 2012). Likewise, in her study of women's rights activism, Stephan (2012) asserts that women activists in Lebanon have actively contributed to the advancement of women's rights by developing strategies rather than 'passively submitting to the religious and patriarchal political apparatus'. In the same vein, Lewis's (2012) work on Egyptian women's activism refutes the general hypothesis in the West that Muslim women 'are the passive observers on their own lives, oppressed in turn by fathers, husbands, social norms and legal institutions'. On the contrary, she argues, many outstanding Egyptian activists, who are agents of change in their own lives and society, have been religious – mostly Muslim or Coptic Christian. She touches upon an additional misunderstanding regarding the Egyptian women's movement: that Egyptian feminism is anti-religious and 'a negative and corrupting import from the west' (Lewis, 2012).

Feminist scholars underscore the democratizing role of women's NGOs in the Middle East, whether secular or Islamic. According to Al-Ali, whereas women's NGOs must be linked with the state and the constituencies of civil society in their struggle for women's civil rights, they may also challenge these spheres, which could contribute to democratization in Egypt (Al-Ali, 1997: 174). Her position gains support from Moghadam, who asserts that 'women's rights or feminist organizations are the most significant contributors to civil society and citizenship' (Moghadam, 2002: 16), as in many Arab countries, 'the struggle for civil, political and social rights is led by women's organizations, which are composed of highly educated women with employment experience and international connections' (15; see also 1997; 2003). In this way, these scholars support the view, articulated earlier, that it is possible to foster the creation of a more woman-friendly civil society rather than attempting to do away with the concept altogether. However, feminist literature on women's NGOs in the Middle East also highlights the difficulty for women's groups to transcend the internal hierarchies and leadership structures which emerge in civil society organizations. In this sense, the work of Joseph (1997: 57) on Lebanese women's groups is interesting in revealing the 'paradoxes and contradictions' of the ways in which women's groups can 'reproduce hierarchical patron/client patterns of leadership such as those found in men's organizations ... even though their work may contribute to the improvement of women's situations in some ways'.

Turning to the Turkish context, some feminist studies have considered the gendered structure and role of civil society in the country and the impacts of women's activism (Çaha, 2013; Leyla Kuzu, 2010; Arat, 1994). Such studies mainly argue that women's and/or feminist activism contributes to the democratization process (Arat, 1994: 106), and that a new plural public sphere has been constructed in Turkey within which feminist approaches and practices have played a significant role since the 1980s (Çaha, 2013). Indeed, Çaha (2013; 2010: 92) claims that the political discourses developed by feminism – such as equality, difference and autonomy – contribute to the improvement of the position of diverse social groups in civil society, and to the pluralization of public spaces, helping to create a more woman-friendly civil society. Like some women activists from Egypt, women activists from Turkey 'have rejected hierarchical leadership and tried to implement democratic decision-making processes' (Al-Ali cited in Al-Ali, 2003: 226), which could be considered to have made a contribution to democratization in Turkey.

Among the studies on women's NGOs in Turkey, those of Çaha (2013) and Leyla Kuzu (2010) are crucial in examining the role of women's movements and/or groups in civil society. Çaha's book conducts a discourse analysis of fifty magazines published by women's groups between the 1980s and 2010. On this basis, Çaha argues that a new plural public sphere has been constructed in Turkey since the 1980s within which feminist approaches and practices have played a significant part. He problematizes the compatibility of Kemalism with independent civil society (60) and indicates how feminists have challenged official state ideology, thereby underlining the constructive impact of the feminist movement on the promotion of civil society in Turkey (75–86). He also points to the distinctiveness of Kurdish women's discourses, which articulates opposition to male dominance in the Kurdish movement and to the essentialist approach of Turkish feminists (178). Leyla Kuzu's work focuses more specifically on women activists' articulation of civil society itself. Her study analyses the role of women's movements in expanding the public sphere on the basis of in-depth interviews with two women's CSOs, namely KA-DER and KAGİDER. She looks mainly at the relationship between CSOs and the state, emphasizing not only the authoritarian rule of the state but also that it can act as a partner of civil society organizations. In this regard, she shows how the women activists emphasize the need for autonomous organizing and reveals their mixed attitudes to professionalization. For her, women's CSOs challenge uniform perceptions of civil society by 'making the public sphere women-sensitive' (Leyla Kuzu, 2010: 218). Taken together, these studies by Çaha and Leyla Kuzu challenge uniform approaches to both civil society and women's organizations in Turkey and highlight the complexities and multiplicity of women's voices.

Feminist critique of NGOs in non-Western contexts

While there is now a widespread understanding that NGOs should play an active role in establishing civil society, the definitions and functions of NGOs remain contested (Silliman, 1999a: 134). Karns and Mingst (2010: 249) point out that the view of NGOs 'as promising agents of progressive social change' is beginning to change. Increasingly, they are seen as having 'lost their political edge,' and membership has correspondingly diminished (Börzel, 2010: 4). As a result, NGOs have morphed into 'self-interested entities engaged in advancing their own agendas and often non-democratic, hierarchical groups concerned with financial and publicly perceived longevity' (Karns and Mingst, 2010: 249). A process that has been described by scholars and commentators as 'NGOization' (Lang, 1997) began in the 1990s. Lang (2013: 62–3) defines NGOization of civil society as 'a shift from rather loosely organized, horizontally dispersed, and broadly mobilizing social movements to more professionalized, vertically structured NGOs'. Many NGOs have become transnational by connecting themselves with international donor agencies and professional networks, receiving their monetary resources and their neoliberal practices and agendas (Bernal and Grewal, 2014: 5–6). Indeed, Petras (1997: 12) claimed that NGOs, particularly women's NGOs, are the 'community face' of neoliberalism, 'intimately related to those at the top and complementing their destructive work with local projects'. As the potential for NGOs to affect policy has increased and their access to funds has expanded (Silliman, 1999b: 136), they have become more dependent on funding, which brings about the necessity for fixed organizational structures, professional staff and fiscal accountability (Hawkesworth, 2001: 230). In this context, a group of scholars caught our attention, specifically due to the drawbacks of professionalized NGOs. They underscore that professionalism is an '"anti-politics machine", diluting NGOs' alternative political practices', while some others view it as 'a technical improvement making NGOs more efficient and efficacious' (Murdock, 2003: 510).

Feminist scholars are particularly concerned that the priorities of women's NGOs may be determined according to 'the priorities of government or international organizations instead of supporting alternative changes' (Silliman, 1999a: 138). To illustrate, international directives and imperatives make more funding available to groups, with efforts to improve the situation of women by providing them with resources, access to healthcare, skills training and so forth rather than efforts to transform their situation (138). Calderia (cited in Hawkesworth, 2001: 230) has criticized the foundation of NGOs as 'the premier women's organizations' on the grounds that local women's NGOs have not achieved a state of empowerment and have been unable to determine their own agendas, due to their dependence on government and donor funding. It is argued that the NGOization process transformed political aims into technical project goals and militancy into 'activism', weakening the political content of the feminist movement (Bora and Günal, 2002: 8–9).

These critiques are indicative of a more general skepticism towards NGOs and their ties to the state and international organizations. Dominance of the state as well as international organizations' priorities in women's NGOs is so powerful that it weakens the consciousness-raising role of grass-roots women's groups aiming to challenge patriarchal relations. However, as Lang (2013: 9) argues, NGOization is not always and necessarily bad. What is more, assuming that women's activism is determined and shaped by the processes of NGOization may overlook the discourses and practices of women's agency within organizations. Unlike the argument that most of the NGOs/women's NGOs are the vehicles of state and international donor agencies, Bora and Günal (2002: 17, 178) regard this claim as a cliché, which shows distrust in women's power and regards women as passive agents of NGOs. There is a need for context-specific studies to identify 'which actors, discourses, practices and organizational forms prevail or are most politically visible at any given time in a given socio-political context' (Alvarez, 2009: 182), as well as close attention to the articulations of NGO members. Only through such research is it possible to examine under what circumstances and to what extent women's NGOs, in general, retain a capacity to challenge the power and scope of the state and international agencies (Tinker, 1999: 88) even though they are under their influence.

The term of NGOization aims to capture a picture of whole economic, social and cultural interactions between state, society and NGOs in different contexts, namely in Latin America, Russia, Central and Eastern Europe, Asia, South Africa and the Middle East (Lang, 2013: 63). To illustrate, in the Latin American context we see a focus on the autonomy of NGOs, which are put at risk as a result of the subcontraction of women's NGOs by the state for 'advising on or carrying out government women's programs' (Alvarez, 1999: 183). Murdock directs our attention to the different aspects of NGOization, which consists of the impact of 'professionalization' of women's NGOs in Medellin, Colombia. She suggests that NGO strategies may differ due to 'the interactions between diverse set(s) of social actors', thus it is crucial to look at the 'lived experiences of NGOs' since the women working in NGOs are 'complex social subjects who operate within a broader context that both constrains and produces their actions' (Murdock, 2003: 508, 524). Specifically, she highlights that we should be hesitant to offer that 'those NGOs "resisting" professionalization may "do good" while others not' (510). In the same vein, Hemment's (2007: 75) work on Russia challenges the donor assumption that when state socialism in Russia collapsed, social groups and interests would rise up, and women's groups would follow the same trajectory as civil society advocates. From a broader perspective, she argues that we should go beyond the polarized discussions that tend to regard NGOs as either 'good' or 'bad' since both are intertwined and interdependent on NGOs (Hemment, 2004: 218; see Fisher, 1997). In the Russian case, 'women have found a niche in the nascent non-governmental sphere and for many it is perceived as a counter model to the "dirty" realms of politics and business' (Hemment, 2004: 219).

The scene in Central and Eastern Europe is not very different.[19] Following the collapse of communism, it is widely argued that Western donors fund women's NGOs in the CEE in accordance with their economic and political interests, which are important to promote their own agenda of transition in the region. The key implications of the Western donor intervention have been denoted as turning women's NGOs professionalized and making them operate in accordance with institutional rules and bureaucracy (Sloat, 2005: 440). However, the criticisms regarding the donor intervention may not always apply to the CEE context. Helms gives an example of the NGO, Medica, in Bosnia and Herzegovina funded for aiding war victims and refugees which in time created its own strategies for engagement with both women and the state and greatly contributed to the democratization process of Bosnia-Herzegovina (Helms, 2014: 34–5, 44). Knitting, sewing and similar activities, which are criticized by Western feminists as 'reinforcing traditional gender roles' actually bonded women together and served as a therapy. Instead of being loud about an explicit political agenda, Medica achieved significant policy changes on domestic violence, marital rape and so on by working 'behind the scenes' (36).[20]

NGOization has also been viewed as a problem in the Middle Eastern context including Turkey, and some scholars have questioned the taken-for-granted attachment of positive and democratizing attributes of NGOs. They have analysed the impact of increasing number of NGOs and the broader process of NGOization. Jad (2007: 234) notes that where the growing number of women's NGOs in the Arab world is considered to be a means of promoting 'bottom-up' democracy, this could also be regarded as a form of increased dependency on the West. She argues that rather than automatically identifying NGOs with 'healthy socio-political development', the rise of Arab NGOs, particularly women's NGOs, should be examined using a historical and empirical approach, which would enable recognition of the limitations on NGOs in achieving the goals of 'social change and democratization' (Jad, 2004: 34).

Within the context of the NGOization debate, the decline of voluntarism in NGOs against the rise of professionalism is also discussed in the Middle Eastern context (see Krause, 2008). Al-Ali claims that one of the major impacts of both donor institutions and the international women's movement on the Egyptian women's movement has been the 'professionalization of the previously voluntary welfare sector'. She highlights the benefits and drawbacks of this issue when she states:

> Being a woman activist can be a 'career' in contemporary Egypt, where a new field for jobs has been created within the wider NGO movement. Unfortunately, professionalism and careerism often involve competition for job opportunities, funding possibilities and travel grants, which, in turn, may breed envy and rivalry. (Al-Ali, 2004: 81)

Particularly regarding the NGOs in Egypt, Abdelrahman (2004: 169–70) makes an interesting point on voluntarism by emphasizing the new meaning of it intertwined with professionalism:

> Voluntarism is believed by people working in the NGOs sector to be the 'backbone' of their work. However, one of the main complaints in Egypt is the shortage of volunteers and absence of volunteer spirit among the people ... In the contemporary development environment, voluntarism has developed a new meaning: it has become a profession; a paid job for which training is required and budgets are allocated.

The threat of being dependent on state/government is another issue that NGOs face in the Middle East.[21] A group of scholars emphasize that the liberal view supporting the belief that civil society should be a separate entity from both the state and 'primordial organizations' of kinship, village, tribe and religious group does not work in this context, as civil society is not a distinct entity from the state but rather repressed and co-opted by it (Zubaida, 1992: 4). This is evident in the fact that most of the NGOs in the region instrumentally act as a 'substitute for state involvement in social provisioning for citizens', even though this should not be the case (Moghadam, 2002: 14). Moreover, critical scholars claim that civil society is restricted, repressed and co-opted by the state rather than being and acting as a distinct entity (see Al-Ali, 2004; Wiktorowicz,

2000). State control over NGOs can take the form of controlling access to and management of international funding allocated to NGOs (Abdelrahman, 2004: 178, 183). However, as Al-Ali (2005) argues, women's organizations develop unique ways of organization and activity in order to gain autonomy from the state and to form a more democratic notion of citizenship.

In this regard, studies focusing on the voices of NGO activists are striking. Pratt's (2005: 131–2) study is on the discourses of NGO activists in Egypt, in that, it reveals being 'autonomous' from political society, including government and political parties, is a difficult task for NGOs in the Middle East as government control, in some cases, even harasses them. Thus, it is not an easy issue for NGO activists to work outside the state. Similarly, they show hostility to political parties since they are only interested in some specific issues that are in line with their interests. For those NGO activists it is significant to act as an independent NGO from both the interferences of the state and/or political parties. Similarly, in Kuzmanovic's (2012: 90–2) work on civil society organizations in Turkey, CSO activists attach a central role to 'autonomy' from the state, political parties and funding as 'the prime characteristics of a CSO', and they argue that keeping some distance from them makes them a sincere (*samimi*) CSO. In the same vein, Doyle's study, based on the voices of activists from human rights and women's organizations, analyses the situation of CSOs in relation to the state in Turkey and underlines the problem of a high level of state control over civil society both in the form of repression and co-optation. She underlines that its impact is that of 'tempering the demand of CSOs and reducing their capacity to challenge the state power' (Doyle, 2017a: 1).

Conclusion

This chapter focused on the literature on civil society, NGOs and women's activism in different contexts with a particular discussion on the Middle East. It underscored the ways in which civil society and NGOs were conceptualized by various actors such as international organizations and donors, governments and policymakers and paid attention to the feminist critique of the gendered exclusions of civil society and of the neoliberal limitations of women's organizing in the context of NGOization.

Four arguments in the course of the chapter should be drawn attention to here. First, and most obviously, it showed that civil society is a historically variable and politically contested concept. While its neoliberal formulation may be dominant today, as disseminated through international organizations, this should not be treated as fixing the meaning of civil society once and for all, particularly in the light of the many critical voices raised against the neoliberal view. Second, it argued in support of the view that overgeneralization and stereotyping of civil society and NGOs in the Middle East and beyond should be avoided, in favour of close contextual study. Third, this chapter underlined the need to reject both structural determinism, which emphasizes the overwhelming power relations within which civil society and NGOs are formed and which they reproduce, and uncritical celebrations of the agency of civil society and NGOs. Instead, it argued in support of attention to the ways in which NGOs are both produced by civil society and help to produce conceptualizations of it. Pratt, Abdelrahman and Kuzmanovic in different ways illuminate a path by which this can be achieved, through study of NGO and activist discourses in and about civil society, and the extent to which they reproduce or challenge power relations. Finally, this chapter gave credence to the feminist critique of the gendered exclusions of civil society and of the neoliberal limitations of women's organizing in the context of NGOization, but maintained, along with Howell, Hagemann, Al-Ali and others, that feminists ought to continue to engage with civil society as a site in which gender inequality may potentially be challenged. It also supported Alvarez's injunction to explore ways in which women's NGOs can contest as well as reproduce neoliberal and patriarchal relations of power.

These arguments inform my case study of the role and position of women's voices in the construction of civil society in the Turkish context. In this case study I will build upon the work of Çaha, Leyla Kuzu and Doyle who have studied the ways in which women's NGO activists participate in and articulate notions of civil society. But neither of these authors aims to analyse the connections between women activists' understandings of civil society and hegemonic official discourses circulating currently in Turkey, which may indicate women's articulation of feminist alternatives to hegemonic institutionalization. What is more, they do not focus on the responses of women activists to the institutionalization of civil society in Turkey by conducting a comprehensive study covering all types of women's groups from main political standpoints. Such an approach would offer the opportunity to compare groups by identifying commonalities and differences between them.

3

The sociopolitical context in Turkey: Official dominant civil society discourses

Introduction

The sociopolitical context of Turkey depicted in this chapter is a necessary precursor to the analysis of civil society discourses of women's organizations in the subsequent chapters, intended as it is to illuminate the context in which such organizations operate and its discursive constraints and possibilities. Drawing on secondary academic analysis to evaluate the political, social, cultural and economic circumstances of Turkey over time, this chapter discusses the dominant official civil society discourses circulating in Turkey by the state and political elites, CSOs, and the EU and addresses the development of women's organizations in distinct periods of Turkish political history. I found six official dominant civil society discourses, namely, 'repression', 'autonomy', 'democratization', 'dialogue-based', 'project-based' and 'authoritarian' (see Table 3.1).

This chapter aims to indicate the main features of each of them under four parts. First, I look to discourses circulating during the period from the establishment of the Turkish Republic in 1923 by giving reference to the Ottoman past to the beginning of the 1980s. Here I show the main features of the secular and nationalist Turkish state established after the dissolution of the Ottoman Empire, its relation to civil society and gender issues, and the hegemony of the 'repression' discourse. Second, I turn to the period after the 1980 military intervention, which brought about profound and sweeping changes in Turkish society, as well as sparked the rise of the women's and feminist movement. This is when an 'autonomy' discourse began to dominate understandings of civil society. The third part of the chapter turns to the period

Table 3.1 Typology of Official Dominant Civil Society Discourses in Turkey

	Until 1980s	1980–90	1990–2000	2000–10	2010s–today
Repression	X				
Autonomy		X	X		
Democratization			X	X	
Dialogue-based				X	
Project-based				X	
Authoritarian					X

during the 1990s when a 'politics of difference and intolerance' saturated Turkish society (Öktem, 2011). I highlight the implications of this politics for the emergence of new groups in civil society and within the women's movement. It was during this period that the autonomy discourse was supplemented by an emerging 'democratization' discourse. Finally, I elaborate on the 2000s until the present day. The period between 2002 and 2011 saw the victory of the Justice and Development Party (AKP) and Turkey's EU candidacy status, at which time the discourses of 'democratization', 'dialogue-building' and 'project-based civil society' became dominant. Since the AKP's third term in office (2011), however, a more 'authoritarian' discourse of civil society has prevailed.

The repression discourse: From the Republican period until the 1980s

The nature of the state and its relationship with the society is crucial to understand civil society discourses circulating in the Turkish context since the Ottoman Empire. The strong state tradition has been widely used to analyse the nature of the state in the Ottoman-Turkish polity. This tradition means that the Ottoman-Turkish state has been strong vis-à-vis the societal forces and has been autonomous from them, which brings about a weak civil society (Heper, 1985). As Mardin (1969: 264) highlights, 'the Ottoman Empire lacked those "intermediate" structures ... It lacked that basic structural component that Hegel termed "civil society", a part of society that could operate independently of central government and was based on property rights'. Unlike the feudal state in Western polities, the Ottoman state was strong and autonomous in order to be able to form the whole system without negotiating with the societal forces. This caused deprivation of confrontations between the state and the societal forces.[1] Thus, civil society was not a significant determinant of political process.

The Turkish Republic was established in 1923 with the goal of breaking away from the Ottoman heritage. Modernization, secularism and nationalism were the founding pillars of the new republic (Dikici-Bilgin, 2009: 115). In the early years of the Republican period, the Republican People's Party (Cumhuriyet Halk Partisi, CHP[2]) was in power under the single-party regime and the official political ideology was Kemalism, named after Kemal Atatürk, the founder of the Turkish Republic. The philosophy of Kemalism consisted of 'Republicanism, nationalism, populism, secularism, etatism and inkilâpçilik (revolutionism)', and these key ideas were to provide guidance for Turkish civilization (Kili, 1980: 387). The civilization project of the Kemalist elites was not solely about economic and political modernization; rather, the identification of 'modernity' with 'progress' was prevalent in the making of the modern Turkish nation through the insertion of Western rationality into the 'backward' and 'traditional' (Keyman, 1995). As well as 'the political commitments of the Kemalist project', the 'construction of a particular cultural identity' was deemed essential (Seçkinelgin, 2004: 175). This was because the Kemalist central state was 'more interested in the principles of secularism, in building a new nation-state based on rationalist, positivist values, rather than in democracy and individual freedoms' (Kardam, 2005: 38). Indeed, cementing a new 'self-conception of Turks' meant that the Kemalist project reached far beyond state reform because it was about transforming 'a multi-ethnic Ottoman empire into a secular republican nation state' (Göle, 1996: 21).

What these founding pillars of the Kemalist state indicate is that the Kemalist elites were not shy in confronting the tensions between secularism and Islamism. Indeed, in the founding years of the Turkish Republic, secularization was a key element of the project of *laicism* (revolution from above), and was equated with civilization and opposed to Islam (Kadıoğlu, 2005: 23). In spite of the goal of a modern democratic state, secularization in Turkey was not intended to pave the path towards a liberal democratic system and it was in fact often used to legitimate authoritarian politics (Göle, 2003).

In this regard, the disestablishment of Islam was important in the process of nation building and modernization in Turkey (Arat, 2009: 4). In order to realize this, legal and institutional reforms were put into practice. The caliphate was abolished, and the General Directorate of Religious Affairs and the General Directorate of Pious Foundations were instituted in the place of Şeyh-ül-İslam and the ministry of religious foundations respectively (4). Moreover, the New Civil Code, which 'prohibited polygamy, subjected marriage to secular law, outlawed unilateral divorce, recognized male-female equality in inheritance and guardianship of children' was adapted from the Swiss Civil Code in 1926 (Arat, 2009: 4). The founders of the Republic 'established secular systems of law and education; destroyed the influence and power of the ulema (learned men of religion) within the state administration; banned the unorthodox Sufi orders and outlawed the use of religious speech, propaganda or organization for political purposes' (Toprak, 2005: 170). Thus, Islam was taken out of the public sphere and confined to the private sphere, and, more importantly, the preservation of Islam in the private sphere was thought to be achieved by the regulation of religious affairs by the state (Tank, 2005: 6; Göle, 1997: 49). In brief, secularism, from its inception, was closely associated with state authority and used as an instrument to modernize and develop the country (Arat, 2009: 4–5). One of the consequences of Republican secularism was to divide the Turkish population into 'secularist' versus 'Islamist' camps, with the latter 'marginalized by the Republic and pushed out of the centres of political power, social status and intellectual prestige' (Toprak, 2005: 171). The exclusion of the Islamists from the political, social and intellectual arenas lasted until the Islamic revival in the 1980s.

Along with secularism, nationalism has been one of the most effective and powerful forces from 1923 onwards in the history of Turkish politics (Uslu, 2008: 73). Ziya Gökalp was the early ideologue of Turkish nationalism from the Ottoman era. He believed it was necessary for Turkey to implement a range of reforms in order to embed nationalistic features in Turkish culture and to decisively support secularism. In the early Republican years 'the state was not only justified by the Nation, it was also responsible for the development of the Nation's consciousness which was bound to excel by its non-religious character' (Seufert, 2000: 29). This really meant separating governmental affairs from Islamic influence and its oriental traits (Karpat, 1959: 25–6).

Yet, even though nationalism had 'a secular tone, it internalized Islam as a psychological glue to ensure that ethnically different populations within the boundaries of the new Turkey remained united' (Uslu, 2008: 84). This being the case, Turkishness was to be based on the acceptance of Turkish culture – 'Turkey's language, its customs, its historical traditions' – rather than on race or blood (74). While the official goal was to unite ethnic groups in the name of Turkish national identity, this resulted in a great degree of intolerance towards Kurdish and Armenian populations. Overall, the role of the state was to create a Turkish nation, and since nation and state were to share the same goals, there was little space to manoeuvre for different interests and for associations to resist the nation-state (Seufert, 2000: 29). In effect, the nationalization project legitimized the co-optation of civil society by the secular state (Ketola, 2011: 93), and the particular form of imbrication between the civil society and the state in Turkey was a result of their attachment to the nationalist project (Seçkinelgin, 2004: 176).

Secularism and nationalism were very much part of the broader project of modernization in Turkey. Among other things, modernization is based on the dichotomies between the East and the West, 'modern and traditional, secular and religious, civilized and barbarian, democratic and dogmatic' (Göle, 2003: 18). The modernization approach assumes that whereas the West is characterized by secular democracy, rationality, individual freedom and technological advancement, the East is shaped by Islamic norms and values such as relatedness, honour and social harmony (Kardam, 2005: 3). The modernization project in Muslim countries seeks to 'Westernize' not only 'the cultural code, modes of life and gender identities' (Göle, 1996: 21), but also political discourse and practices.

In light of this discussion, I would argue that repression emerges as the official dominant discourse of this period within which the state represses civil society, even though the state created a platform for civil society by establishing 'a secular legal system which recognized gender equality, secular education, and a conception of public service', which was not premised on ethnicity, class differences or kinship ties (Toprak, 1996: 87). Foundations, which played a key role in conducting charity work in the Ottoman era, became of secondary importance with the establishment of the Turkish Republic and thereby associations began to work towards disseminating Republican values and ideas

(White, 2002: 200). Under the rule of the CHP as a single-party, the Turkish Hearts (Türk Ocakları) and the Turkish Women's Union, formed respectively in 1932 and 1934, were abolished in spite of the fact that they endorsed a similar 'civilizing and nationalizing project' (Seufert, 2000: 29). In sum, the hegemonic civil society discourse circulating in Turkey from the early years of the Republic until the multiparty system period (1950) was strongly shaped by the Kemalist and etatist mindset, informed by two key goals: guaranteeing the state's responsibility for democracy and ensuring the development of society within the boundaries of the Kemalist project (Seçkinelgin, 2004: 175).

The organizing of Kemalist women was a crucial element in the top-down effort to build Kemalist hegemony through civil society. The dichotomy between Western and Islamist values, and the secular Kemalist state and its nationalistic features, have crucial implications for women's rights and feminism in Turkey (Kardam, 2005: 3). Kemalist women were an important part of secular civil society but their mobilization was encouraged and channelled by elites as a key part of the instrumentalist approach to civil society at the time. In essence, Kemalist women were mobilized to build social support for the three pillars of the Turkish Republic. In this context, the Turkish Women's Union, which was established in 1924, and the Association of Professional Women (Meslek Kadınları Derneği), (re)established in 1949, promoted Kemalist ideology and principles (Çaha, 2013: 58). In this sense, it could be said that the Kemalist activist women and their organizations were an important part of secular civil society (Seçkinelgin, 2004: 175). Still, secularism was key to state ideology and partly shaped the extent of reforms regarding gender relations and civil society.

The repression discourse held sway in the 1950s and 1960s although it somewhat changed after the transformation from a single-party regime to a multiparty regime in 1946. The victory of a centre-right party – the Democrat Party (Demokrat Parti, DP) – in 1950 seemed to prepare the ground for supporting popular control of the state, religious freedom, democracy and a liberal economy. Indeed, DP rule between 1950 and 1960 was characterized by 'the downgrading of the secularist tendencies of previous governments, rapid economic development, the political and military integration of Turkey into the Western alliance and the growing financial dependence on US' (Zürcher, 1997: 5). Religious groups, associations of businessmen, labour unions, peasant groups, media groups and various political groups were developed (Çaha, 2013: 31). For instance, the Confederation of Turkish Trade Unions (Türkiye İşçi Sendikaları Konfederasyonu, TÜRK-İŞ) was established in 1952 as the first labour confederation in Turkey (Zürcher, 1995: 330). Although the DP was in conflict with the prevalence of 'the bureaucratic intelligentsia' of the state, it did not challenge the sovereignty of the state itself (Heper, 1985: 100, 109). In 1957, the devaluation of the TL (Turkish lira) and rising inflation contributed to the decrease in electoral support for the DP, and Turkey very nearly experienced a repeat of the single-party regime of etatism and suppression of opposition (Kalaycıoğlu, 1998: 118–9). However, although the DP did bring about substantive change in many respects, the understanding of sovereignty of the state vis-à-vis the people and civil society did not really change under their governments in the 1950s. The discourse of repression continued its hegemony, and civil society remained under the sway of the state.

On 27 May 1960, military junta launched a coup d'état against the DP.[3] The next civil government formed in 1961 and was led by a coalition of the Republican People's Party and the Justice Party (Adalet Partisi, AP).[4] The military intervention 'opened a political space for parliamentary opposition' after ten years of rule by the DP (Toprak, 1996: 91). The 1961 Constitution prepared after the coup was regarded as a 'much more liberal constitution' (Zürcher, 1997: 5). For instance, modifications were made to the prevalent Westminster majoritarian electoral system, an independent judiciary was established along with a Constitutional Court, and autonomy was granted to university institutions and organizations operating radio and television. These reforms were intended to check governing institutions, and, in particular, to oversee the executive body (Kalaycıoğlu, 1998: 119).

Importantly, these reforms also prepared the ground for associationalism (*dernekçilik*) (Kalaycıoğlu, 1998: 119). Statistically, in this period, there was an increase in the number of civil society organizations, including business chambers, trade unions and associations together with political parties (Bikmen and Meydanoğlu, 2006: 36). Despite the rise in civil society organizations, the shift towards associationalism in Turkey was minor; civil society was not independent from the state (Yerasimos, 2000). In practice, the state only listened to those organizations with an outlook that was in line with the principles of the secular state (Ketola, 2011: 93). The military memorandum of early 1971 is typically seen as proof of the suppression of civil society by Turkish state elites.

Instability and extremism were rampant in Turkey before the 1971 coup, in large part due to the 1970 world economic crisis (Zürcher, 1997: 5). Ahmad reminds us of the situation in that period:

> By January 1971, the universities has ceased to function, students emulating Latin American urban guerrillas robbed banks and kidnapped US servicemen, and attacked American targets. The homes of university professors critical of the government were bombed by neo-fascist militants. Factories were on strike and more workdays were lost between 1 January and 12 March 1971 than during any prior year. The Islamist movement had become more aggressive and its party, the National Order Party, openly rejected Atatürk and Kemalism, infuriating the armed forces. (Ahmad, 1993: 147)

In this atmosphere, the 1971 coup d'état occurred with an aim to 'suppress opposition forces with alternative political projects' (Toprak, 1996: 91). In the name of reconstructing 'law and order' the left was repressed (Ahmad, 1993: 148) and Islam was manipulated. The main political changes that the military regime brought about were the dissolution of all political parties, amendment of the 1961 Constitution, establishment of special courts in charge of dissent resolution, control of universities to restrain radicalism and weakening of the trade unions by abolishing the Worker's Party on 20 July 1971 (Ahmad, 1993: 152, 156). The Islamic political movement National Outlook (Milli Görüş) emerged in Turkish politics with the establishment of the National Order Party (Milli Nizam Partisi, MNP), an Islamist party, in 1970. The party was closed down due to its threat to form an Islamic state in May 1971 (Atacan, 2006: 45) and was succeeded by the National Salvation Party (Milli Selamet Partisi, MSP). What is important here is that since the foundation of MNP, 'Turkish Islamism has been incorporated into the political system and legitimated by the parliamentary system' (Göle, 1997: 47).

In the 1970s more women's associations promoting the Kemalist ideology were established, such as the Turkish Mother's Association (Türk Anneler Derneği) and the Federation of Women's Associations (Kadın Dernekleri Konfederasyonu). However, around this time, women began to mobilize as part of leftist groups via associations (Çaha, 2013: 59). This represented a shift in organizing in the Turkish left, since prior to this time, women's issues were not regarded as worthy of attention (Berktay, 1990: 274). In this context, the Progressive Women's Association (İlerici Kadınlar Derneği) was formed by the Turkish Labour Party (Türkiye İşçi Partisi) in 1975 and the Ankara Women's Association (Ankaralı Kadınlar Derneği), named after the Federation of Revolutionary Women's Association (Devrimci Kadınlar Derneği Federasyonu), was also formed to organize campaigns and protests, particularly for working-class women (Çaha, 2013: 59).

I could argue that there is no significant discursive change in the decades after the early Republican period, despite some Westernization, and that it is with the military coup of 1960 that space was opened up for associationalism. Despite granting this space formally, in practice the state remained in control of civil society. The repression discourse was the official discourse and only a narrow range of groups emerged, with demands in line with the Kemalist agenda. When a wider range of radical movements emerged in the late 1960s to early 1970s, and there was social upheaval, the state responded by suppressing alternative visions, hence the 1971 coup d'état. In light of this, the state was very much reliant on military intervention to maintain support for the three pillars – modernization, secularism, nationalism – of the Kemalist project. In sum, the Kemalist secular nationalist state created its own civil society and Kemalist women became the 'carriers' of this system, or in Kadıoğlu's (2005: 26) terms, the 'images of modernity'.

The 'autonomy' discourse: Civil society and women in the 1980s

In September 1980, military elites decided to overturn the civil government again, this time using the rationale that Turkey was too politically, economically and socially unsteady to continue being governed under the present regime. After the 1980 military intervention, Turkey became a setting for deep and widespread social change. The military intervention brought about the dissolution of political parties and several civil society organizations, including those formed by students and academics. The 1982 Constitution, written after the intervention, limited civil rights and liberties, and prohibited ethnicity and class-based organizational activities (Mousseau, 2006: 306). Additionally, the military junta used Islam in their fight against the separatist and leftist movements which emerged during the 1970s and prepared a policy called 'Turkish-Islamic synthesis' in order to weaken the clashes between the left and right groups (Ketola, 2011: 93). Simply put, there was another cycle of repression of the left and a repeat in the manipulation of Islam for political purposes after the 1960s and 1970s. Indeed, Islam was construed as one of the founding components of Turkish society that had the power to unite the disparate groups within it (Akboğa, 2013: 7).

Three years after the military intervention, 'free' elections were held, authorized by the army. These elections were, symbolically at least, geared towards reconsolidating 'secular democracy' and sparking the emergence of a more autonomous civil society (Navaro-Yashin, 2002: 123). In the 1983 elections, the Motherland Party[5] (Anavatan Partisi, ANAP) formed the Özal government. This change in government marked the beginning of a new period of reform and change in Turkey, based, on one hand, around Özal's liberalization policy, and on the other, on the emergence of Islamism.

'Global market forces and logic of liberal market economics entered Turkey in 1980s, punching holes in insular and protective economic policies that had dominated until then' (Ketola, 2013: 67). Under the Özal government, the 24 January Decisions integrated Turkey into the global capitalist economy through economic liberalization, and economic policy was transformed from being based on import-substituting to export-promoting industrialization (Keyman, 2005: 43). With the Özal government, Turkey strengthened neoliberal economic and social policies which had already been realized to some extent by the military regime (Akça, 2014: 19). Through Özal's economic liberalization and anti-statist policies, Turkey aimed to integrate into the global capitalist economy (Keyman, 2005: 43). In this period, Turkey started to implement 'long-term structural neoliberal reforms under the auspices of the International Monetary Union (IMF)' and the World Bank had given to Turkey five structural adjustment loans successively until the mid-1980s (Ketola, 2013: 67). The main motivations of these market-based reforms were 'trade liberalization, privatization and a growth in exports' (Öniş and Şenses in Ketola, 2013: 67). Whereas the anti-statist discourse of the Özal government signalled the emergence of a liberal civil society discourse and the rise of NGOs, the introduction of neoliberal policies meant that civil society was reduced to the realm of market relations and the economy more broadly (Sarıbay, 1998: 103–4).

Although these neoliberal restructuring policies bolstered economic growth and triggered the creation of a new capitalist class, especially in Anatolian cities, they unfortunately led to poverty, increased social inequalities in terms of income and lifestyle (Kardam, 2005: 48), rising unemployment, inflation and mass migration from rural areas to urban centres (Delibaş, 2009: 96). The pro-Islamist Welfare Party (Refah Partisi, RP), successor to the MSP, was established in such an environment in order to create an 'alternative political voice appealing to the grievances of the urban poor' with an ever-increasing level of political support until the 1997 memorandum (Delibaş, 2009: 97). Although the integration of Islam into politics in Turkey has a history dating back to the transition to a multiparty system (1950s), in the 1980s, Islamist movements began to grow through the rise of RP in both local and national arenas (Özdalga, 1997: 75). One of the crucial strategies of the Islamist movements was to 'develop an educated counter-elite as a base of support' (Narlı, 1999: 40). To clarify, the migration of peripheral groups to the urban centres enabled new groups to attain secular education, which provided an 'opportunity of upward social mobility' and allowed them to 'come to terms with modernity in general and with secular elites in particular' (Göle, 1997: 52–3).

As noted, the Turkish state strictly controlled rights and freedoms through the 1982 Constitution, 'which, inter alias, prohibited education in languages other than Turkish (Article 42)' (Kaliber and Tocci, 2010: 195). Partly in response to such measures, in 1984, a guerrilla war against the Turkish Republic by the Kurdistan Worker's Party (PKK) began, in order to establish an independent Kurdistan, and 'the state has responded with heavy military' (Öktem, 2011: xiii). In this context, Kurdish[6] nationalism developed as a mass movement in Eastern and South-Eastern Anatolia for the Kurds to claim their cultural rights (Diner and Toktaş, 2010: 42).

What is more, the role of the EU membership process in the emergence of the autonomy discourse is undeniable, as it has triggered Turkey to make a stride to consolidate democracy and to assure rule of law particularly after the 1980 coup d'état. Although the relationship with the EU has accelerated after gaining candidacy status in the 1999 Helsinki Summit, the membership process dates back to 1959 when Turkey applied for the European Economic Community to be an associate member (Çakır, 2011a: 1). Four years after this application, the Ankara Agreement was signed with the EU, which 'recognizes Turkey's eligibility for membership and explicitly stated that full membership at a future date is possible if the obligations rising from the agreement were fulfilled by the parties' (Marshall, 2013: 84). Turkey, 'being the only country that has had a long relationship with the European Community', failed to get full EU membership due to not taking necessary steps to meet the economic and political criteria of the EU Treaty (84).[7] Although the EU was critical of Turkey after the 1980 coup d'état due to 'its lack of commitment to consolidating democracy and ensuring the rule of law', with the shift to civilian government in 1983, the new government showed its engagement with the EU membership through making amendments to the Constitution and economic policies (84). However, the EU did not accept the application of Turkey for full membership in 1989 because of economic and political reasons such as anti-democratic policies of the Turkish state and its human rights violations (Usul, 2011: 1). However, many circles have interpreted the refusal of Turkey's EU membership as a double standard given the fact that Turkey has shown eagerness to be part of the EU since the Second Enlargement (1981) (Çakır, 2011b: 39).

Within such a context, CSOs have proliferated with the goal of prospering civil society and contributing to democratization by weakening the power of the state and military in accordance with the EU conditionality of Turkey. In other words, the main role of civil society actors was to 'push the military authority for this end' and their influence on political change in Turkey (Seçkinelgin, 2004: 173). To illustrate, the ANAP's victory in 1983, after the three-year military junta, was interpreted as a response of civil society to the authority of military (Mert in Şimşek, 2004: 47). In this sense, the ANAP government replaced 'the discourse of existence of individual for state' with the 'discourse of existence of state for individual' by supporting the discourse of 'national will (*milli irade*)' (Sarıbay, 1998: 103). In this way, the 'democratization of the state' became a key manifesto pledge for right-wing parties (Bora, 1994: 14). At the same time, the rise of civil society helped to popularize policies which valued private enterprise (Sarıbay, 1998: 103). Importantly, the number of Islamic CSOs rose significantly, especially in the post-1983 period (Kadıoğlu, 2005: 28).

The increase in the number of NGOs created an idea of expansion of civil society vis-à-vis the state in Turkey. Thus, the autonomy discourse was the official hegemonic discourse of the 1980s. This discourse largely stems from a liberal approach to civil society where civil society is autonomous relative to the state, and the separation between state and civil society is valued. Whereas the state is considered as an area of power, civil society is conceptualized to represent the people (*halk*) (Navaro-Yashin, 1998b: 57). Democratization and demilitarization were particularly key, as the latter helped to define civil society as a 'non-military' space and an 'area of freedom' (Bora, 2005: 264). Despite the limitations and critiques of civil society practice in Turkey, it was perceived normatively with positive connotations, viewed as 'a realm of possibility for change' (Rumford, 2002: 273). What is notable is that advocates of 'autonomous civil society' viewed 'Islamicization in Turkey as the awakening of civil society against the state after seventy or more years slumber' (Navaro-Yashin, 2002: 131).

During the years of widespread politicization in Turkey – in the 1970s and 1980s – women's organizations were predominantly the appendage of leftist parties and groups and the Association of Progressive Women merely struggled against 'the difficult conditions of working-class women' (Tekeli, 2010: 120). Crucially, towards the end of the 1980s, women's groups started to be distinguished from each other with regard to their ideological persuasions (e.g. radical, liberal and socialist feminists), their choice of type of organization (i.e. establishing formal organizations or remaining informal, non-hierarchical networks) and their location (e.g. the groups in İstanbul and Ankara) (Kardam, 2005: 45). However, some women's groups hesitated to be referred to as civil society activists because of the historical tendency of civil society to be co-opted by the Turkish state. This issue became more important for women's organizations in Turkey in the 1990s and 2000s when the donor-CSO relations began to impact civil society, which will be elaborated in the next part of this chapter.

To conclude, in the political climate of the 1980s, according to the official discourse, civil society was recognized as an associational sphere and through demilitarization, began to become autonomous relative to the state. Pluralism was allowed and practised to a certain degree.

The 'democratization' and 'deepened autonomy' discourses: Civil society and women in the 1990s

The 1990s are crucial years in Turkish history because of the rise of the Islamist and Kurdish movements, the 1997 military intervention, the headscarf ban and the EU candidacy status with the Helsinki Summit (1999).

The 54th government of Turkey was formed by rightist political parties, namely RP, having an explicit Islamist origin, and True Path Party (Doğru Yol Partisi, DYP) on 28 June 1996. However, this government was short-lived due to the so-called reactionary (*irticacı*) politics of the RP government; trade unions and professional groups organized against the government, 'with words of encouragement by the army to join the "battle" between the MGK [National Security Council] and the government' (Seufert, 2000: 34). The 'Civil Initiative Five', composed of the employer and labour unions TOBB (The Union of Chambers and Commodity Exchanges of Turkey), TESK (Confederation of Turkish Tradesmen and Craftsmen), TİSK (Turkish Confederation of Employer Associations), DİSK (The Confederation of Progressive Trade Unions of Turkey) and TÜRK-İŞ (Confederation of Turkish Trade Unions), published a notice in February 1997 criticizing the reactionary politics of the RP government, and advocating a struggle for secularism and democracy. This initiative could be viewed as an example where the mainstream actors of Turkish civil society agreed with and supported the Kemalist military generals and officers of the 1997 coup d'état, aiming to highlight the possible threats posed by an Islamic government to the secularist Turkish state. With the pressures from the secularist camp, a modern coup-d'état occurred on 28 February 1997 and the RP government was abolished by the military junta.

In the aftermath of the 1997 coup, the conflict between Islamism and secularism was reignited when the government decided to ban the donning of the headscarf/turban[8] in public spaces such as universities and public institutions. Wearing a headscarf had been subject to state regulations rather than law because of the rising number of headscarved university students since the 1980s (Akboğa, 2013: 2). In this context, the headscarf became symbolic of the Islamization of Turkish society. Regarding its outright ban in public spaces, the dominant argument circulated by the Kemalist women was that wearing a headscarf is an obstacle for women to liberate themselves. Unsurprisingly, this engendered heated debate between Kemalist and Islamist groups. Importantly, the struggle of the Islamist groups against the headscarf ban was institutionalized (Akboğa, 2013: 1). CSOs such as AKDER, ÖZGÜR-DER (The Association for Free Thought and Educational Rights) and Mazlumder (Association for Human Rights and Solidarity for the Oppressed) were established in order to challenge the authority of the state and military, and fought against the headscarf ban (Kadıoğlu, 2005; also see Pusch, 2000).

Another divisive issue that caused unrest during the 1990s centred on Kurdish nationalism, which was salient internationally as well as domestically. Because of the aim of the PKK to form 'an independent Marxist state', the Turkish state and its allies such as the United States and the EU viewed the PKK as a 'terrorist movement' and responded militarily (Gunter, 2013: 88). In other words, 'at the beginning of the 1990s the military opted for a new strategy that totally militarized the Kurdish question and destroyed all hope of a political solution' (Akça, 2014: 24). Exceptionally, in 1993, Turkish President Turgut Özal seemed to accede to negotiate with the PKK but this plan was left unfinished after his unexpected death, and, thereafter, the military response became more severe (Gunter, 2013: 88). In such an environment, alongside the Islamist movement, the Kurdish movement began to be institutionalized. Political parties that gave priority to resolving the Kurdish problem were founded in the 1990s, and they found a support base from Kurdish people who were politicized through the Kurdish mass movement (Çağlayan, 2007: 126). People's Labour Party (HEP) was the first pro-Kurdish party established in 1990. Democracy Party (DEP, 1993), People's Democracy Party (HADEP, 1994) and Democratic People's Party (DEHAP, 1997) followed HEP after it was shut down due to allegations of aiming and acting to dissolve the state's indivisible integrity (NTV, 2009). Kurdish CSOs were formed as part of the institutionalization of the Kurdish movement, in order to confront the nationalist and unitary discourse of the Turkish secular state. Importantly, new Kemalist CSOs emerged in the early 1990s to challenge the rise of Islamist and Kurdish movements and reconsolidate 'the official Kemalist ideology';

that is, Kemalist civil activism was seen as inevitable for hegemony-building in the area of civil society (Erdoğan, 2000: 250). In this regard, Kemalist organizations mirrored the role of the authoritarian Kemalist state in seeking to protect 'national unity and laicism' (Erdoğan, 2000: 250).

In the 1990s, ethnic and religious minorities in Turkey began to raise their voices 'against policies that they felt were aimed at undermining their cultural and ethnic identities' (Özçetin and Özer, 2015: 18). With these events and developments in mind, the official-dominant civil society discourse was undoubtedly one of democratization. This discourse overlaps the autonomy discourse outlined in the previous section because of the way it constructs the independence of civil society as inevitable for the formation and promotion of democratic society. The democratization discourse developed in two particular ways in Turkey, specifically, through the juxtaposition of civil society (*sivil*) against the military, and through the pluralization of civil society, which reflected the fissures in Turkish society.

First, democratization was assumed to be occurring because CSOs were heavily contesting military authority. Political elites and analysts shared the view that the dominance of the military, displayed through its interventions in 1960, 1971, 1980 and 1997, was the main barrier to creating a free and associative space for the civils. In this light, trade unions (*sendikalar*), associations (*dernekler*), foundations (*vakıflar*), sectoral associations and chambers (*odalar*), bar associations (*barolar*) and fellow countrymen associations (*hemşehri dernekleri*) were viewed as promoting democracy when fighting against the authority of the military in the ruling of the country (Seçkinelgin, 2004: 173). What is notable about the democratization discourse is that the concept of civil society was employed together with the notions of democracy and democratization without any further analysis (Şimşek, 2004: 46).

Nonetheless, the democratization discourse also found some justification in the pluralization of civil society in this period. There was a sharp increase in the number and diversity of CSOs and civil society was construed by the state as an actor able to play an essential role in the processes of democratization and Turkey's EU accession (Keyman and İçduygu, 2003). During this period, the idea that the state had abandoned its policy of suppression and was actively seeking to encourage autonomous civil society intensified (Şimşek,

2004: 68). The transformative power of the EU on Turkish civil society since the Helsinki Summit (1999) has engendered the increased interaction between local (domestic civil society organizations) and European actors (EU) (Ergun, 2010: 513). This direct relationship between the CSOs and the EU has contributed to the idea of autonomous civil society as well.

However, dominant democratization and deepened autonomy discourses of the 1990s offered only partial accounts of civil society at this time. In particular, the idea of pluralism was not respected and never really materialized. Conflicts among different groups, especially between secularists and Islamists, still dominated politics by drawing a line between state and civil society, and relations within civil society (Ketola, 2009: 92). From the 1980s onwards, confrontations between Turks and Kurds, Alevis and Sunnis, Islamists and Kemalists have been dominant (Şimşek, 2004: 63). The exclusion from civil society of new groups which did not share the Kemalist line of thinking was particularly prominent, as this period was characterized by 'the emergence of rather vocal Islamic groups and of groups questioning the ongoing military involvement, its grounds and implications in the south-east throughout the 1990s' (Seçkinelgin, 2004: 177). What this makes clear is that the discourse of democratization was profoundly flawed; followers of this interpretation had 'confused a changing discourse or technique of state power with an autonomous rise of civil society and the idea of a separate realm of society was used by politicians seeking legitimacy, more in this particular historical period in Turkey than any before' (Navaro-Yashin, 2002: 132). They had, moreover, overlooked 'the tension-ridden struggles between diverse organs of the state on the one hand, and members of social movements on the other' (Navaro-Yashin, 2002: 132). Put differently, the deepening autonomy discourse hides the fact that civil society became an area to promote the legitimacy of the state.

The implications of these changes and tensions for women in the civil society arena were profound. The 1990s were the years when institutionalization both at the state and women's movement level was observed. In 1990, the General Directorate on the Status of Women (KSGM) affiliated to the prime ministry was founded with the aim of promoting gender equality in Turkey. Similarly, the 1990s were characterized by the institutionalization of the women's movement. Women's organizations increased in number, from around 10 between 1973 and 1982, to 64 between 1983 and 1992, and more than 350 in 2004 (Uçan Süpürge in Arat, 2008: 400), and they focused on various issues such as violence against women and women's human rights (Çubukçu, 2004: 99). Furthermore, these organizations started to develop strong political ties, lobbying activities and network structures (Uçar, 2009: 4). Despite their common concerns and ability to form coalitions, it was during this time 'the challenge of the Islamist, Kurdish, nationalist and lesbian-gay-bisexual-transsexual (LGBT) movements, each of which had diverse world views with respect to the causal roots and solutions to women's problems' (Diner and Toktaş, 2010: 42) created polarization and division within the women's movement. In the same vein, Coşar and Onbaşı (2008: 325) characterize the women's movement in Turkey during the 1990s as being divided along religious, ethnic and class lines on the basis of the divisive debates about the headscarf issue, the Kurdish issue and class issues. On the one hand, the 'headscarf issue cross-cut women's movement and call[ed] for a step beyond issue-based cooperation among different women's rights organizations' (Coşar and Onbaşı, 2008: 326). On the other hand, the Kurdish and Islamist women criticized mainstream feminists as 'being ethno-centric and exclusionary of other identities' (Diner and Toktaş, 2010: 47). 'Flagging of Kurdish and Islamic specificity has led to a clash with old-school republican feminists who fear that such women undermine nationalist, secularist ideals' and clashes with secular, 'liberal (–leftist)' activists who 'are suspicious, above all, of religious women as agents of an Islamist agenda' (Fisher Onar and Paker, 2012: 382).

Religious women who did not become part of any feminist movement in the 1980s developed feminist demands in relation to Islamist and Kurdish movements and organized in accordance with these demands (Bora and Günal, 2002: 8). They became more educated and got high-status professional jobs. In this context, religious women, who had already been an active part of Islamist movements, had another mission in the 1990s. They started to criticize traditional gender roles (Çayır, 2000: 52). As opposed to the religious women of 1980s, they began to interrogate the instrumental role given to women by their male counterparts in the Islamist movements. The 1990s witnessed the demands of religious Muslim women of 'participation' in place of 'representation' and they started to establish many organizations in order to participate in the public sphere, and thus this has transformed the woman-man relations within the Islamist movement (Çayır, 2000: 66–7). Especially with the revival of the women's movement after the Beijing International Women's Conference (1995) and the Habitat II Conference (1996), religious Muslim women founded various NGOs and formed platform coalitions, consisting of specific associations, enterprise groups and commissions (Özçetin, 2009: 111–12). With the main concern of headscarf ban, Gökkuşağı Kadın Platformu (The Women's Rainbow Coalition) in Istanbul, especially its member organizations AK-DER and Hazar Grubu (Peacetime Group), and HEKVA (The Foundation for Women's Education and Culture), Baskent Kadın Platformu in Ankara were founded (Pusch, 2002 in Özçetin, 2009: 112).

With the goal of protesting against the double burden of being exploited by the Turkish state and the patriarchal culture in the region, the Kurdish women's civil society organizations such as KAMER, SELİS, VAKAD (Van Women's Association) and DİKASUM (Diyarbakır Research and Implementation Center for Women's Affairs) were founded in Eastern and South-Eastern Anatolia, where there has been an ongoing conflict between the Turkish government and the Kurdish people since the 1980s. Women's issues have been integrated to the Kurdish nationalist agenda by the Kurdish women, and the Peace and Democracy Party (Barış ve Demokrasi Partisi, BDP) played an important role in this regard as 'being the most gender equitable of Turkey's political parties with quotas for women candidates during elections, and a separate women's assembly' (Fisher Onar and Paker, 2012: 390). However, BDP's women's branches prioritized to put an end to the oppression faced by the Kurdish people over solving women's problems (Fisher Onar and Paker, 2012: 390). Some Kurdish women's organizations including KAMER critiqued this understanding by 'objecting to patriarchal relations and multiple forms of violence against women' and giving precedence to the feminists concerns, but they were also blamed by the Kurdish nationalist for 'damaging the image of the Kurdish people' due to their focus on honour killings and incests (Fisher Onar and Peker, 2012: 390).

To sum up, democratization and deepened autonomy discourses were the official civil society discourses of the 1990s in Turkey. The next part of this chapter will ask whether or not this has changed during the terms of the four AKP governments.

From 'dialogue-based' to 'authoritarian' civil society discourses: Civil society and women in the years of the AKP

The victory of the Justice and Development Party (AKP) in the last four general elections (2002, 2007, 2011 and 2015), with increasing votes, has enabled the party to set the agenda for Turkish politics during the 2000s and beyond. Since 2002, the party has established single-party governments and the CHP has been the main oppositional party. The AKP is regarded as a continuation of the DP (1950) (Mert, 2007) and most of the party cadres were supporters of the National Outlook (Milli Görüş) tradition, which is represented in Turkish politics with the establishment of the Islamist party, namely MNP in 1970, and succeeded by MSP, RP, Virtue Party (Fazilet Partisi, FP) and Felicity Party (Saadet Partisi, SP) (Atacan, 2006: 45).[9] The AKP formed after the dissolution of the FP by the reformist faction of the party, and to distance themselves from hardliners in that party. The main aim of the AKP has been to challenge the Kemalist establishment across administrative, judicial, military, economic and social levels.

What makes the AKP's power unique in the Turkish case is its endeavour to integrate not only conservative and Islamic values but also a neoliberal programme into political discourse and practice. The 'AKP revitalized the neoliberal hegemony by "the absorption of Islamism into secular neoliberalism more or less successfully at the levels of the hegemonic formation"' (Tugal cited in Akca, 2014: 30). The period of the AKP's rule can be divided into two parts. The first period, of victory in the 2002 to 2011 elections, is identified by the discourses of 'democratization', 'dialogue-building' and 'projectism' shaped by the EU accession process and the associated democratization programme. The second period began after the 2011 elections, from which point we see the rise of an 'authoritarian' civil society discourse.

Dialogue, deepened democratization and project-based civil society: AKP power until 2011

Dialogue discourse

Despite portraying itself as a 'conservative democracy' (Yıldız, 2008: 43), the first AKP government gave priority to 'market rationality' and economic goals by implementing a far-reaching neoliberal programme rather than neoconservative policies (Acar and Altunok, 2013: 2). Connectedly, the AKP aimed for EU accession and showed commitment to the principles of Western democracy and liberal economics, particularly between 2002 and 2007 (Acar and Altunok, 2013: 2). The EU accession process played an important role in forming a dialogue discourse in Turkey.

Since the 2000s, the EU has suggested dialogue-based and bottom-up relationships, alongside the promotion of multiculturalism, as ways to enhance the civil society-democracy relationship in the Turkish context. The EU's policy on civil society in Turkey is also viewed as a way of transforming 'the state-centred nature of Turkish politics and policy-making' (Ketola, 2010: 105), which proposes to take into account different and diverse voices in the civil society area through dialogue and to let them participate in decision and policymaking processes. What is more, in Turkey's EU accession process, the latter granted a significant role to the cooperation and dialogue between Turkish and EU citizens. To serve this aim, in 2005, the EU suggested 'a strategy designed to strengthen civil society dialogue amongst candidate countries and EU non-governmental organizations and named this strategy as "Civil Society Dialogue (CSD)"' (Ministry of EU Affairs, 2017). The target group of these CSD programmes was voluntary organizations namely associations, foundations, platforms, citizen initiatives, professional organizations, commercial and industrial chambers, cooperatives and unions.

Dialogue-based civil society discourse in Turkey cannot be considered separately from the civil society discourse circulated by the EU, mainly in the candidate countries. In line with the EU motivation, the AKP sought to present 'itself as the representative of Turkish civil society' (Dikici-Bilgin, 2009: 117). It was seen as offering 'renewed opportunities for civil society development and was met with high expectations' (Özçetin and Özer, 2015: 18). The 'dialogue' discourse became dominant as successive AKP governments stressed how they prioritized civil society differently from the previous governments (AKP, 2012). They intentionally employed new rhetoric to emphasize that they welcomed the participation of CSOs in the decision- and policy-making processes. The dialogue-based conception of civil society is therefore about considering the voices of a diversified civil society sector. In this period, the number of civil society organizations increased and the interests pursued continued to be diversified: from various women's issues to environment, from gay and lesbian rights to homelessness, from language rights to ethnic groups and prison reform associations. Thus, we see a 'less formalized' and 'more diffused' CSO sector at this time compared with the period when it was comprised of more traditional organizations (Seçkinelgin, 2004: 174).[10]

Although the changes in the structure of CSOs were remarkable, civil society was still at a level where the hegemonic struggle between secular and Islamic circles remained predominant (Ketola, 2011: 92). The sociocultural reflex was 'contracting more frequently in the first years of the 21st century than it did in the last 30 years of the 20th and the emergence of politicized religious groups in particular motivated such a situation' (Seçkinelgin, 2004: 177). In the 2000s, the headscarf ban continued to be one of the decisive issues in Turkish politics. On 9 February 2008, the parliament's proposal for a constitutional amendment to lift the headscarf ban in higher education was accepted (BBC, 2008). However, on 5 June 2008, the Constitutional Court rejected the proposal on the basis that it was against the principle of laicism and the unchangeable provision of the Republic (Bianet, 2008). In 2013, the AKP government removed the ban, except on public prosecutors, police officers and judges, in the so-called Democratization Package (Radikal, 2013).

However, what we also see in this period is a sharp increase in the number of religiously motivated associations (RMAs) in Turkey, which played a key role as social assistance providers (Göçmen, 2014: 92; Kaya, 2015: 59). The AKP government(s) have sustained the idea introduced by the RP, using social provision as a way of 'bringing Islamic ideals and ethics into capitalist economy and creating a community around these ideals' rather than introducing state redistribution or broadening the range of welfare policies (98). Not only neoliberalization but also the rise of political Islam has been influential in this approach (93). 'While neoliberalism aggravated the socio-economic terrain of the poor and the needy, political Islam's moral obligation to alleviate poverty created a constituency, which sustained its growth and nurtured RMAs' (Göçmen, 2014: 96; see Kaya, 2015). Kaya (2015: 58) characterizes this 'neoliberal provisioning policies partly delegating welfare provision to faith-based voluntary associations' as a way of 'Islamization of society and politics' in Turkey. Herein, it is significant to highlight that the legal amendments done by the AKP government(s) have brought some advantages to RMAs (Göçmen, 2014: 98). More concretely, introduction of new regulations making the establishment of new associations and foundations easier under the new Associational Law in 2004 and Foundation Law in 2008, introduction of tax exemptions for companies which would enable them to be the possible donors for CSOs and the launch of the Awards of Association for Public Interest Status promoted RMAs both in terms of number and area of operation (98).

Islamic women's CSOs have increasingly worked as charity organizations and thus substituted welfare state functions in this period. The AKP favours these Islamic CSOs, which have grown in number and influence (Dikici-Bilgin, 2009: 117), and in some cases, employs them in achieving particular policy outcomes that are closely aligned with the government's objectives. As scholarly expressed, the state co-opts Islamic women's CSOs in Turkey and marginalizes the others (see Doyle, 2017a; Negron-Gonzales, 2016). Put differently, with the increase in the role of Islamic CSOs, including women's CSOs, in delivering welfare services, secular NGOs/women's NGOs have been gradually sidelined. This indicates the perpetuation of the hegemonic struggle between secular and Islamic circles within the civil society terrain.

Deepened democratization discourse

Dovetailing with the dialogue-based civil society discourse, the democratization discourse became much more prominent in the 2000s with respect to the EU accession process. Before turning to the Turkish case, I would like to discuss the EU's view on civil society[11] in general. The emphasis on civil society in the EU has gradually increased with the aim of promoting the policies of democracy (Raik, 2006: 1). The Draft Treaty establishing a Constitution for Europe (2003) emphasized the 'principle of participative democracy' and that 'institutions shall maintain an open, transparent and regular dialogue with representative associations and civil society'. Generally, civil society is thought as a way of overcoming the limitations of parliamentary democracy and 'building alternative mechanisms of legitimation into the system of governance' (Armstrong, 2002: 106). Moreover, the increase in the international visibility of civil society through international meetings is the other reason EU institutions engage with civil society (Salgado-Sanchez cited in Bayraktar, 2009). All EU institutions make the involvement of civil society in EU affairs a primary concern (Kohler-Koch, 2010a: 101).

The EU associates the consolidation of democracy with civil society development, as became obvious during the accession of CEE countries. One of the important motives of CEE countries to support accession to the EU was the 'conviction that, once in the Union, their own states will become more robustly democratic' (Sadurski, 2004: 371). In this context, civil society is construed as serving as a channel between citizens and the state to provide leverage for democratic change. Turkey has not been free from this kind of approach after experiencing several military interventions and the growing motivation for the EU membership. In 1999, after obtaining EU candidacy status in the Helsinki Summit, Turkey begun to receive financial grants.[12] Being such a large country, the economic and political impacts of possible Turkish accession on Union politics have generated much anxiety among Western European commentators (Hughes, 2004), as has the extent to which this Muslim-dominated country can embrace concepts of civil society and democracy that originate in the West (Kubicek, 2005: 362). Nonetheless, Turkey has been participating in EU Programmes.

After gaining candidacy status, in March 2001, the Accession Partnership was adopted by the European Council for Turkey and determined the conditions to open accession negotiations at the end of 2004 (Bayraktar, 2009: 48). With thirty-five chapters, accession negotiations commenced in 2005. EU interest in civil society and its actors, particularly CSOs, had risen in the wake of this process. Obtaining candidate status to the EU has been considered significant for the 'development of a pro-democratic civil society' in Turkey (Şimşek, 2004: 70). There were two main impacts of the EU accession process on civil society: (1) 'proper ground for changing the legal system', and (2) 'EU financial support' (Çaha, 2013: 67). In this regard, considerable political attention has been given in Turkey to the necessary reforms to meet the political demands of the Copenhagen Criteria, 'which is served as a basis for the further democratization of the state–society relations' (Keyman and İçduygu, 2003: 224). Several reforms were made within the areas of the civil-military relationship, and minority and human rights under the title of the 'adaptation package' (Çaha, 2013: 65). In the reform process, civil society actors, particularly business actors, were very active and effective in putting pressure on the government to fight for Turkey's membership (Öniş,

2007: 247). In 2002, 175 CSOs published a joint declaration to show their eagerness for the integration of Turkey into the EU, since they believed that accession could result in 'a more democratic, modern, open, and a secular system as well as a powerful and consistent economy and welfare society' (Çaha, 2013: 66). Among the EU reforms in Turkey, the new Association Law, executed in 2004 and Foundation Law in 2008, brought about important changes for associations and foundations. It eased regulations concerning the establishment of new associations and allowed them to conduct shared projects with international organizations (66–7). 'Although Constitutional regulations comply with the European Convention on Human Rights (ECHR), the legal framework still contains numerous incompatibilities with international standards and restricts CSOs activities' (ICNL, 2018).

As remarked earlier, the AKP government's close relationship with the EU, particularly in the first period, was remarkable and this led to a certain change in Turkey. EU membership is identified with Westernization and modernization, initiated by the foundation of the Turkish Republic in 1923 and by the Turkish political and military elites (Tocci, 2005: 75). The AKP is a political party that formed itself as a strong proponent of the EU-motivated reforms (Öniş, 2007: 247) and formulated its democratization agenda within the context of the EU harmonization process. The motivation of the AKP for EU membership is based on two points: 'its interests' and 'ideology-related explanations' (Tocci, 2005: 80). Whereas the former is about how the EU accession process helps the AKP become more legitimate through jettisoning 'its Islamist past vis-à-vis the international community and the secular establishment in Turkey', the latter is about how the EU helps to ensure democratic reforms that the AKP needs (80). In this light, 'Civil society has been both a subject and an object of the EU reform process' and the reform process has lent more credence to, and empowered, CSOs in Turkey (80–1).

The democratization discourse also encouraged negotiations with women's CSOs (Coşar and Onbaşı, 2008: 326). Indeed, it can be argued that the AKP's support of Turkey's accession to the EU offered women's organizations a crucial role 'in bargaining with government authorities' during this period (331). Although there was no shared 'frame of political reference' among such groups, they were able to apply significant pressure on the government (326), contributing to the implementation of CEDAW, the development of a new

Turkish Penal Code (2004), the amendment to the Law on Municipalities (2005), which obliges municipalities with more than 50,000 inhabitants to open women's shelters, and the formation of the Parliamentary Commission for the Equality of Opportunity for Women and Men (2009). These gender-sensitive reforms were all achieved under the AKP (Coşar and Yeğenoğlu, 2011: 562). Particularly in the penal code reform process, the AKP government showed eagerness to make civil society organizations participants of the decision-making process (Negron-Gonzales, 2016: 202). During this period, the AKP 'achieved remarkable legal regulations on protection against male violence and nullification of the statement "man is the family chief" from its civic code', even though it could hardly be described as a 'pro-women's rights political party' (Yılmaz, 2015: 157). What is more, cooperation among the women's groups was much more strong in this period. For instance, US organized the first and the largest women's NGO meeting in Turkey, namely the Civil Society Forum, in 2003 in which various women's groups gathered and discussed women's issues (Landig, 2011: 207).

The democratization discourse was also promoted for some time as the AKP sought to address the Kurdish question by peaceful means. This was especially clear with the reforms planned in many areas – including the Kurdish question – in order to meet the EU Copenhagen political criteria after Turkey's acceptance of EU candidacy and the PKK leader Öcalan's arrest (Çelik, 2014: 5). The coalition government (DSP, ANAP and MHP) enforced crucial EU harmonization reforms with respect to the Kurdish question such as 'a gradual ending of the emergency rule in the Southeast, allowing television and radio broadcasts in Kurdish, making Kurdish language training possible' (Pusane, 2014: 84). These EU harmonization reforms for the Kurdish question lasted in the first AKP government with a goal of 'eliminating the practice of torture and ill-treatment, [extending] the freedom of expression and association, [amending] the broadcasting law to allow for broadcasting in languages other than Turkish by public and private radio and television stations, and [permitting] the granting of Kurdish names to children' (85). After a period in which Erdoğan 'adopted a nationalistic and hard-line rhetoric during the 2007 elections campaigns' (85), a Kurdish Opening or Kurdish Initiative (also called the Democratic Opening) was launched in 2009 by the

AKP government (Gunter, 2013: 88), although 'government constituencies' and 'pro-secular' groups reacted strongly to the Opening (Somer and Liaras, 2010: 152). Through the Kurdish Initiative, the AKP government aimed to stop the war between PKK guerrillas and the Turkish military, to come up with a solution to the Kurdish question and to enhance the human rights of the Kurdish population living in Turkey. It was said to tackle democratic deficiencies of the regime by highlighting problems such as obstacles to education in the mother tongue, prosecution for 'demonstrating, writing, or speaking in support of Kurdish-nationalist ideas' and the 10 per cent threshold. It also seemed to cement the party's aim of 'reaching a peace agreement with the PKK' (Updegraff, 2012: 120–1).

However, such democratization goals did not last long. The Kurdish Opening process failed 'shortly thereafter following the increased number of deaths among the Turkish military and the PKK, which led to increasing social polarization between Turks and Kurds' (Çelik, 2014: 5). The pro-Kurdish DTP[13] (Democratic Society Party) was closed by the Constitutional Court on December 2009 due to its affinity with the PKK, and about 1,500 people, including politicians, human rights advocates, writers, artisans and leaders of CSOs, have been arrested because of membership of the KCK (Kurdish Communities Union) since April 2009 (Gunter, 2013: 89).[14]

Project-based civil society

Project-based civil society was yet another official discourse in Turkey in the 2000s. The increase in international funding, specifically from the EU, being channelled to CSOs in Turkey was tied in with the accession process, with funding regarded as an instrument to integrate EU principles into Turkish society. In this way, CSOs have been viewed as carriers of these principles (Erdoğan-Tosun, 2008: 137–8). With the funding provided by the EU as well as other international organizations, CSOs, including most of the women's organizations in Turkey, have been receiving funding from the EU to sustain themselves, while there are others which reject such funding or are not able to apply due to bureaucratic obstacles. The funding is used to pursue projects regarded by the EU as a way of promoting the democratization process in Turkey (Gazioğlu, 2010).

Although the EU also propounds a democratization discourse, in non-member countries that are regarded as in need of development, its dominant approach to civil society fits more closely with neoliberalism; it emphasizes the idea of encouraging the growth of civil society through strengthening the role of CSOs and thus promoting democracy and a free market economy. A prominent feature of EU civil society discourse in terms of its funding framework is the presumption of a causal and linear relationship between civil society and democratization. The EU has thus directed attention towards Turkish civil society as a partner 'to bring about social and political change, and to buttress the development of participatory democracy and NGOs in particular, [which] are seen as prime local agents of social change to implement the strategies of the international donor' (Kuzmanovic, 2010: 431). The EU civil society development projects, as well as EU strategies and policies, have had some impact on determining and framing the domestic agenda and ensuring the rise of the project-based version of civil society.

Turkey has received pre-accession funds from the EU since 2005, and state institutions or CSOs can obtain these funds according to the project title and scope (Delegation of the European Union to Turkey, n.d.). As well as MEDA and the Civil Society Development Programme of the EU, as highlighted under the 'dialogue' discourse, there has been a programme of EU support allocated for the furtherance of the EU-Civil Society Dialogue (CSD) in Turkey with the specific aim of encouraging civil society engagement with the accession process. The funding provided by this programme as CSD I (Promotion of the Civil Society Dialogue between the EU and Turkey Project) and CSD II (Turkey and EU Civil Society Dialogue Project) enabled nongovernmental actors to involve in the implementation of EU programmes promoting democracy and human rights. CSD I has promoted development of dialogue between municipalities, professional organizations, universities and youth in Turkey and the EU. This programme was completed on November 2009 and 119 projects have been awarded with a total amount of 19.5 million euro grants. CSD II, which is launched in 2011 as a continuation of the Promotion of the Civil Society Dialogue Project between EU and Turkey, has been included into the IPA (Instrument for Pre-Accession Assistance) 2007 programme. The overall objective of this project is to obtain better knowledge of the Republic of Turkey in European Union, including Turkish history and culture in order to create better awareness about the opportunities and challenges for future enlargements (Ministry of EU Affairs, 2007). This programme is carried out by the Ministry for EU Affairs with a grant fund of 5.3 million euro. Through all these grants, there have emerged several activities 'directed to particular civil society organizations in Turkey to promote democracy such as project-cycle and project-management seminars, technical training of staff and volunteers, and assistance with horizontal and vertical network-formation' (Kuzmanovic, 2010: 432). In this context, the Civil Society Development Centre (Sivil Toplum Geliştirme Merkezi) was established in 2005 and many project-writing and implementing companies were formed thereafter.

To conclude, dialogue and project-based civil society and deepened democratization were the official dominant civil society discourses of the 2000s in Turkey. Although dialogue and democratization were the official discourses of the AKP government until 2011, the AKP nonetheless took a 'majoritarian approach to politics', which 'equated democracy with winning elections' and 'representation rather than participation' (Özçetin and Özer, 2015: 8).

The authoritarian civil society discourse: The post-2011 AKP period

In the post-2011 period, the AKP reinforced 'patriarchal and moral notions and values, often framed by religion' in terms of organizing in and across social, cultural and political realms (Acar and Altunok, 2013: 2). The party, and particularly Erdoğan, has taken an increasingly oppressive approach to everyday aspects of life such as control over the media and internet use, bans or limits on abortion and caesarean rights, and prohibition of the sale and use of alcohol (Yılmaz, 2015: 152). This has had different implications for shifting civil society discourse in Turkey, mainly by bringing to the fore authoritarian conservative values and norms, and diminishing the impacts of the Kemalist/secular project. This has been done without undermining the neoliberal agenda. In this context, it is important to look at the ways in which AKP authoritarianism makes an impact on civil society in Turkey.

The Ergenekon (a clandestine organization) and the Balyoz (sledgehammer) trials, and KCK operations, can be seen as examples of the AKP government's attempts to 'dominate the key arms of the state' (Tolunay, 2014), and thereby signs of escalating AKP authoritarianism. In this regard, the AKP has used civil society as a legitimate ground for standing against the ideology of Kemalist elites and military dominance in state institutions in Turkey. CSOs have been instrumentalized to legitimize its policies. For instance, with the aim of strengthening civil society against the military, the Ergenekon and Balyoz trials were on the AKP's agenda to challenge the 'alleged clandestine network that, according to prosecutors, has been operating since AKP's first victory in 2002 in order to facilitate and eventually stage a military coup' (Milan, 2013). Hundreds of military officers, journalists, writers, as well as academics were imprisoned during these trials (NTV, n.d.). In the meantime, in 2012, under AKP rule, a parliamentary commission was formed to investigate military interventions and memorandums in Turkey, which was presented as an important step in practicing civil politics rather than military-backed politics. What is more, the KCK operations which started in 2009 – as indicated earlier – have continued during the third term of the AKP government, with 'a massive police operation against activists, advocates, academics, and publishers who are pro-Kurdish on the grounds of alleged links to the outlawed the KCK'; many individuals, including mayors, party affiliates, organizers and activists, were arrested and imprisoned (Abu-Rish, 2011).

The post-2011 period also witnessed the Gezi Park Protests which took place in late May and early June. What began on 27 May 2013 as an environmentalist protest, organized under the CSO umbrella Taksim Dayanışması (Taksim Solidarity) against the demolition of Gezi Park and construction of a shopping mall, soon turned into a massive protests against the AKP in Istanbul and other cities in Turkey. The rising authoritarianism of Prime Minister Erdoğan, the disproportionate force used by the police, and infringement of democratic rights and restriction of freedoms were seen as the main reasons why the protests emerged (Bilgiç and Kafkaslı, 2013: 8). Erdoğan 'sees the "ballot box" as the only legitimate instrument of accountability in a democracy and describes the anti-government demonstrations as an attempt by the minority to impose its will on the majority by unlawful means' (Özbudun, 2014: 157).[15] The Gezi protests were followed by contestations with the Gülen Movement (with which the AKP were previously in collaboration) and the trials of four AKP MPs for corruption, and this has resulted in deepening tensions around

AKP authoritarianism and the polarization of society between supporters and non-supporters of the AKP.

In the post-2011 period, the AKP has also pursued authoritarianism in its gender policies by taking conservative and moral attitudes towards the female body, promoting the idea of a 'strong family' and holding anti-feminist sentiments, and this has increased the significance of gender politics in challenging the state. As argued by Güneş-Ayata and Doğangün (2017: 2), 'the AKP has promoted a religio-conservative gender climate that simultaneously trivializes legal advances carried out since the 2000s and unleashes traditional forces in a strongly traditional society'. Coşar and Yeğenoğlu (2011) call the outcomes of AKP's neoliberal, religious and nationalist politics as a 'new mode of patriarchy' that refers to gradual lessening of opportunities provided for women in spite of the legal advancements. In terms of revealing the AKP's stance on the female body and sexuality, it is helpful to turn to the large-scale campaign organized by the various women's organizations in May 2012, in response to the draft law that would ban abortion. Before the discussion of the abortion ban, in October 2008, Prime Minister Erdoğan declared that 'each woman should have at least three children' (Hürriyet, 2008).[16] The Erdoğan government attempted to impose limitations on abortion and caesarean section in May 2012. It stated that it was working on a bill to change the period of lawful termination from up to the tenth week of pregnancy to up to the fourth week, apart from in emergency cases (Guardian, 2012). The legalization of abortion, obtained in 1983, was one of the most important outcomes of the women's movement in Turkey. Therefore, immediately after the AKP's declaration, women's organizations formed a platform called 'Abortion Is a Right and the Decision Belongs to the Woman' and organized a pro-choice rally in the city centres of Istanbul, Adana, Mersin, İzmir, Diyarbakır, Çanakkale, Sinop, Antalya, Eskişehir, Van, Ankara and Sakarya to protest the ban. After the protests, even though the AKP government took a step back, it continued working on the Bill of Reproductive Health (Radikal, 2012). What is more, it sought control of women's bodies in other ways. To illustrate, in July 2014 Turkey's Deputy Prime Minister Bülent Arınç declared that 'women should not laugh loudly in public' (Radikal, 2014), which was fiercely criticized by feminists.

In addition, it is obvious that the 'family' has been a central topic of the AKP's conservative social policy agenda. First, the Ministry of Women and Family was replaced by the Ministry of Family and Social Policy in 2011. In this way the emphasis on 'woman' was replaced with an emphasis on 'family', thus glorifying motherhood and equating it with womanhood (Çelik, 2014: 5). The AKP government, particularly Erdoğan, has also reinforced its hostility towards feminism, and denied the equality of women and men. President Erdoğan declared in November 2014, at the KADEM (The Women and Democracy Association) Women and Justice Summit, 'woman and men are not equal. This is against difference of nature or disposition (*fitrat*)' (Diken, 2014). He also stated during the same event, 'feminists do not accept motherhood' (2014). Erdoğan had made a similar statement in 2011: 'I do not believe in the equality of men and women. I believe in equal opportunities. Men and women are different and complementary' (quoted in Kandiyoti, 2011a: 10). As Kandiyoti aptly puts it, these interventions 'signalled that regardless of Turkey's signatory status to CEDAW, the prime minister had chosen to nod in the direction of *fitrat*, a tenet of Islam that attributes distinct and divinely ordained natures to men and women' (Kandiyoti, 2011b).

The authoritarian stance of the AKP governments, especially the last one, reflects the marginalizing attitude they have held towards some CSOs and particularly women's organizations. 'Though the AKP governments have repetitively declared their willingness to dialogue with civil societal actors', write Coşar and Yücesan-Özdemir (2012: 298), 'in practice they have acted selectively, excluding class-based and gender-based organizations deemed radical and/or marginal'. Thus since the 2007 elections, the AKP government has negotiated more selectively with women's organizations (Coşar and Onbaşı, 2008: 326). Women activists complained on being excluded from the policymaking and policy-implementation processes since the third term of AKP and they voiced this problem in the 2010 CEDAW report that 'dialogue between the State Ministry of Women's and Family Affairs, the national machinery and women's NGOs remains limited and constrained' (Negron-Gonzales, 2016: 206–7). Women activists are aware that the AKP government tries to find favour with some women's organizations by, for instance, inviting them to policymaking meetings, while marginalizing other groups, especially those with more radical views on the body and sexuality. To illustrate, Prime Minister Erdoğan met with the representatives from some women's CSOs on 18 July 2010 as part of the process of the above-mentioned Kurdish Opening (Bianet, 2010). In this meeting, 'Erdoğan interpellated the women present as mothers saying that "their voices would drown out the sounds of bullets" since no pain equals that of a woman whose son has fallen victim to war' (Kandiyoti, 2011a: 10). This is despite the fact that 'among the 80-odd attendees were members of NGOs with established feminist credentials such as KA-DER and the Foundation for Women's Solidarity, among others' (Kandiyoti, 2011b). Even if the invitation to attend meetings is accepted and participation occurs, women activists are aware that their demands are not fully taken into account in the law and policymaking process (KESK, 2012). For instance, in the preparation of the Law on Family Protection and Preventing Violence against Women (6284 sayılı Ailenin Korunması ve Kadına Karşı Şiddetin Önlenmesine Dair Kanun), women's groups were invited to the consultation process by state officials and bureaucrats. However, their recommendations were only partially taken into account and the law still does not fully meet their demands, as stated by the 237 women's organizations that gathered under the Platform to End Violence (Şiddete Son Platformu). Conversely, the AKP favours the Islamist and/or pro-government civil society women's organizations, which have grown in number and influence during this period (Dikici-Bilgin, 2009: 117). There is a growth in 'counter-[feminist] movement of pro-family civil society organisations' (Negron-Gonzales, 2016: 208). An example for this is the TÜRAP (Türkiye Aile Platformu/Turkish Family Platform), founded in 2012, which is a coalition including over ninety CSOs targeting to foster pro-family values and agendas (Negron-Gonzales, 2016: 208). In March 2013, KADEM was established by a group of educated, upper-class and conservative women The vice president of this association is Sümeyye Erdoğan, daughter of the president of Turkey. The headquarters of KADEM is in Istanbul but the association has branches in almost every city. This women's NGO, formed with the support of the AKP government, has the mission of prioritizing the concept of 'gender justice' by supporting the idea of complementarity of man and woman and recognition of natural differences between them by referring to Islam, over 'gender equality' (Yılmaz, 2015: 112). This approach has been critiqued by the other women's NGOs in Turkey in that it would maintain traditional gender roles and patriarchy and thereby deconstruct feminist consciousness and activism.

Authoritarianism of the AKP has escalated with two current developments. First, Kurdish issue in Turkey has transformed into a security-oriented, essentialist and unitary approach with the re-emergence of armed conflict after the general election of 7 June 2015 (Tekdemir, 2016). More specifically, AKP changed its approach to the Peoples' Democracy Party (HDP)[17] and blamed HDP for being supportive of the PKK after HDP passed the 10 per cent threshold for the first time (Hughes, 2015: 6). With the failure in establishing a coalition after the elections of June 2015, new elections were conducted on 1 November 2015. Before the November 2015 election, polarization within the society has been rising and violence in the south-eastern region has been increasing. On 20 July 2015, ISIS (also known as Daesh) bombed Suruç due to which '34 pro-Kurdish young socialists who had been en route to Kobane to provide humanitarian aid and solidarity' were killed. Afterwards, two Turkish police officers were killed by the PPK and subsequently Turkish military bombed 'ISIS targets not only across the Syrian border but also PKK bases in the Qandil Mountains of northern Iraq'. ISIS executed a terror attack in Ankara on 10 October 2015, which 'targeted a peace rally organized by trade unions and leftist groups to protest the intensifying conflict between the PKK and the military' and 102 people were killed and more than 400 wounded (Hughes, 2015: 6). After the November election, violence and secularization policies have continued. MPs from HDP, including the party leaders, were jailed for terrorism-related charges in 2016, which hindered the existence of different voices in the parliament.

Second, the 15 July 2016 military coup attempt[18] could be seen as a turning point in Turkish history since it has serious implications for the society as a whole and civil society in particular. The CSOs in line with the Gülen movement were closed and dissident voices were muted. By 18 October 2017, the Turkish government has promulgated thirty statutory decrees under State of Emergency and seven of them became law by the approval of the parliament (Hürriyet, 2018). Five of these statutory decrees have a direct impact on civil society organizations, by which 86 foundations, 1325 associations including women's organizations[19] and 19 trade unions were closed (T24, 2017).

In sum, from 2000s until the third term of the AKP, civil society continued to be seen as autonomous from the state even though it is clear that this is an ideological manoeuvre; the AKP government has gestured towards listening to the ideas and criticisms of CSOs by producing a dialogue discourse and deepening the democratization discourse. Moreover, in those years, the project-based civil society discourse emerged due to the EU funding in Turkey. The EU's dominant discourse of civil society echoes the neoliberal approach by drawing attention to the idea of developing civil society through strengthening the role of CSOs in promoting democracy and a free market economy. Importantly, this discourse is not in conflict with the AKP government's approach to civil society and CSOs. Overall, the dominant civil society discourses of the 2000s rests on the idea that CSOs are/should be autonomous, be able to form dialogue with the state institutions, and have a capacity to obtain international funding and thereby promote democracy. Since the third term of the AKP, however, authoritarianism has escalated, with important implications for the civil society arena in Turkey, generating a disjuncture from the democratization and dialogue discourses of the previous era, with negative outcomes for some sections of society and for women's organizations.

4

Mapping civil society as a voluntaristic, autonomous and mediatory agent

Introduction

This chapter and the subsequent one identify and analyse the civil society discourses of women activists in Turkey by offering a detailed analysis of data based on primary empirical research, including interviews with members of ten women's organizations in Turkey and the campaigning literature available to me at their offices or online. The organizations, selected using the sampling criteria discussed in the introduction, are TKB and TÜKD (Kemalist groups from Ankara), AKDER and BKP (Islamist organizations from Istanbul and Ankara respectively), KAMER and SELİS (Kurdish groups from Diyarbakır), Istanbul feminists KA-DER and their Ankara counterparts US, and finally the anti-capitalist SFK (Ankara) and AMARGİ (Istanbul).

What I find from my analysis is that the women activists from Turkey produce seven civil society discourses. Civil society is represented as: 'a space of voluntary activity', 'a sphere of autonomous organizing', 'an agent of mediation between state and society', 'an anti-systemic agent', 'an anti-hierarchical area', 'a space for democratization' and 'a co-opted and non-feminist force'. Moreover, women's discourses circulate in complex, overlapping ways and do not map neatly onto different group identities. In this regard, while political orientation plays a role in shaping civil society discourse, it is not determining of such discourse.

This chapter will focus on women's 'voluntarism', 'autonomy' and 'mediation' discourses and argue that they generally represent a mainstream idea of civil society by envisioning a voluntaristic, autonomous and intermediary civil society. However, what makes this chapter interesting is that it analyses differences between and within women's organizations in terms of how women activists construct and identify these discourses.

The voluntarism discourse

According to the voluntarism discourse, civil society is a space of voluntary activity, especially for women. Voluntarism is interpreted as an indispensable principle of civil society and identified with no personal gain. As the oldest interviewee from the Kemalist TKB states, 'everything you have done – all your labour and effort – is for an aim and there is no benefit from it ... No one forces us to do that; we do it on our own' (interview with Sevda,[1] 8 May 2012). This discourse is reproduced by almost all of the women from the feminist organization KA-DER, who posit voluntarism and self-determination as the main tenets of civil society and the guiding principles of the association itself. Rezan, the president of KA-DER, in her mid-fifties, described civil society in her interview (18 July 2012) as 'organized structures established by volunteers to intervene in politics for the sake of citizen's own rights'. In contrast, Islamist women made very few references in their interview to the voluntaristic dimensions of civil society. However, we still see an emphasis on voluntarism in their literature, such as in the book *From Yesterday to Today*. In this publication, BKP members highlight the principle of voluntarism with Özlem Gültekin stressing that 'every woman struggles for a work that yields no financial advantage and even has disadvantages, although they have so many responsibilities' (Gültekin, 2007: 9). Women from the second Islamist organization, AKDER, also circulate this discourse. Birsen, the youngest member of AKDER, puts it this way: 'Civil society comprises a group of people who act voluntarily, believe in the same cause and wish to be helpful for society. I mean, civil society organizations are non-profit organizations which aim to benefit society' (interview, 6 July 2012). An AKDER leaflet confirms this approach, stating 'AKDER is a civil society organization based on voluntariness continuing its fight for seeking right in all national and international platforms' (AKDER, n.d.).

Within this voluntarism discourse from Kemalist, Islamist and feminist groups, the identity of women activists is constructed in a particular way, as 'responsible volunteer women'. To illustrate, the Kemalists and some women from KA-DER linked 'being a volunteer woman' to the concepts of 'responsibility', 'duty' and 'commitment'. A gendered dimension to civil society discourse is introduced here in that the intersection of voluntarism discourse with responsibility centres on an image of women who do not anticipate or gain any benefit for carrying out their civil duties, and who are charged with the mission of civil society development as well as the promotion of women's rights. Moreover, voluntarism is explicitly not identified as a type of leisure pursuit or social activity, as made clear by the youngest woman from TKB, in her forties: 'I think any civil society work which is seen as a social activity will not go anywhere' (interview with Lale, 7 May 2012). Similarly, the president of KA-DER rejects voluntarism if it is informed by the following attitude: 'I can either work or not, depending on my mood' (interview with Rezan, 18 July 2012). To some interviewees from KA-DER, this kind of attitude demonstrates a lack of discipline in CSOs, acts as a hindrance to their institutionalization and certainly does not represent what they mean by 'voluntarism'. In this way, only the women's organizations have achieved the status of 'genuine' CSOs, as Tansu, an older woman activist from the TKB states:

> Only the women's organizations have civil society consciousness ... In other organizations, it is not as developed as in the women's organizations. They are called civil society organizations but there is no civil society in Turkey as conforming to our understanding in terms of context, aim, working format and the relationships with the state. (interview, 4 May 2012)

The responsibility aspect of the voluntarism discourse can also be seen in the emphasis on the educating and consciousness-raising roles of women's groups in civil society, with CSOs expected to reach out to people (*halka inmek*), inform them and raise them up, especially on the Kemalist view. This has functioned to reinforce a paternalistic, top-down positioning of Kemalist women as enlightened leaders in contrast to ordinary ignorant people, which is characteristic of the modernization discourse and which, as Kadıoğlu (1998: 94) points out, has been an element of the Kemalist education mission since the establishment of the Turkish Republic. As one woman from TÜKD puts it, 'the problem is how to reach to the people (*halk*) ... prepare more leaflets suitable for their level, you know, simplified motto, writings, spokesperson' (interview with Pınar, 30 June 2012). Or as the vice president of the same association, who is in her late fifties, elaborates, 'CSOs should inform people about ... topics – firstly recognize the problems; and secondly enlighten and educate the people' (interview with Sevim, 28 June 2012). The websites of both TKB and TÜKD place emphasis on this role. TKB's website states:

> We Turkish Women should get to the place we deserve in the social and political life. First of all, we need to raise awareness and educate the Turkish Women. We should explain to them that they should reach for more and explain to them how they would reach their goals. Our objective is to achieve the social, economic and politic equality of the women and men in Turkey. We should put forth effective work for advancing the education, togetherness and awareness levels to the level Atatürk envisaged for the modern Turkish women. (TKB, 2015)

Similarly, TÜKD's by-law states that one of the aims of the association is the 'enlightening of society, helping girls and women get education under modern conditions; contributing to spreading adult education and realizing projects regarding these issues' (TÜKD, 2010).

Connectedly, the voluntarism discourse is promoted through a critique of professional civil society organizations. Indeed, voluntarism and professionalization seem to be regarded as mutually exclusive processes, and it is through this distinction that the women activists from TKB maintain their self-understanding as a 'genuine' CSO. Whereas 'genuine' civil society is defined as voluntary-based and distant from political authority, the 'alleged' one is identified as male-dominant, professional, interest-oriented and close to political power/the state (political power and the state are used interchangeably). In this sense, some Kemalist women explain the lack of civil society consciousness in professional organizations by the non-existence of voluntarism and thus, as Buket in her late forties from TKB emphasizes, 'to a great extent voluntary organizations should be identified as civil society' (interview, 10 May 2012). To illustrate, Sevda from TKB criticizes the professional feature of some of the CSOs in order to bring the voluntary aspect of civil society to the fore: 'the TOBB [The Union of Chambers and Commodity Exchanges of Turkey] is a standard civil society organization. But, is it ever similar to us? All of the structures within the TOBB are professional' (interview, 8 May 2012).

There are other approaches to the relationship between voluntarism and professionalism, however. In stark contrast to the Kemalist women, some activists from the Islamist group AKDER partly view voluntarism in a negative light by identifying it with lack of professionalization. Perihan, who is the general secretary as well as an employee of AKDER, argues that voluntarism merely reveals the extent to which there is a 'lack of professionalization in civil society in Turkey' compared with European countries (interview, 5 July 2012). In addition, there is a group of women from TKB, TÜKD and KA-DER who do not support voluntarism exclusively; rather, for them, it should be accompanied by 'institutionalization' and 'professionalization'. For instance, the youngest interviewee from TKB argued that professionalization and voluntarism are complementary rather than in tension. As she puts it, 'civil society should be something professional ... I mean I have to work in order to survive but concurrently it is not very easy to be active in an association. Therefore, as well as the volunteers, there should be a professional team here' (interview with Lale, 7 May 2012). Similarly, an activist in her sixties from KA-DER underscores: 'The combination [of voluntarism and professionalism] must be made better ... In the West, it [civil society] is more institutional and professional and ours is more amateur; this must be more of a priority' (interview with Selda, 22 July 2012). Yet, this should not be equated to endorsement of a private sector form of professionalism. Indeed, the same interviewee also argues that projects managed by civil society are differentiated from the social responsibility projects of private companies, which are seen as marketing ploys to promote the image of a company. More generally, Selda points out what distinguishes civil society from professionalism of private sector:

Supposing that we are making a petition campaign and I view this from a professional standpoint. They say, for example, 'let's hire a person to conduct the petition campaign'. You can do that, you can hire a person for money but it is not the issue; if I, at my age, can set my table, collect signatures, explain my association to people, then the case is completely different. After all, if I hire a person, this person does not absorb what really matters for you [but] ... in the meantime, I may convey some messages, and they reach out to the right places. (interview, 22 July 2012)

Clearly, Selda wants to contest the meaning of professionalism to clarify that she does not endorse a kind of private sector professionalism in her effort to add to and improve voluntary practices.

The autonomy discourse

Moving on to the next discourse, women from all the groups in my sample, apart from anti-capitalist groups, underscore the autonomy of civil society in two main aspects. First, they articulate the view that civil society organizations are independent from and 'above' political parties, political organizations and ideologies. Women interviewees from Kemalist and Kurdish women's groups subscribe to this aspect of the autonomy discourse. Although the overwhelming majority of the women from both Kemalist organizations show sympathy with the main opposition party, the Republican People's Party, and take part in its activities,[2] they attach a pejorative meaning to 'politics' when practised by the CSOs. They are of the view that CSOs should be at a distance from any political party or ideological stance, as Nurdan, who is the president of TÜKD, indicates: 'We are independent. We are not following any political opinion; we are not a part of any political party/organization. We are autonomous and free' (interview, 29 June 2012). Similarly, it is stated in TKB's by-law that

> all activities of the organization are carried out with an awareness of being a civil society organization and with a sense of policy above political parties. People who are members of political parties may be accepted as members of the organization on condition that they act in accordance with the policy of the organization that is above all political parties and remain loyal. (TKB, 2015)

In the same vein, the Kurdish-feminist activists from KAMER argued for remaining 'above-state and political parties' (interview with Seda, 2 June 2012), 'not defending any type of politics or ideology carried by a political party/organization' (interview with Sevda, 20 May 2012) and 'surviving without anyone's support' (interview with Derya, 17 May 2012). However, the Kemalist women also clarify that to be distanced from political doctrine and party politics does not mean that their CSO is 'non-political'. A positive interpretation of 'politics' is attached to the activities of CSOs with regard to their involvement in policy- and decision-making. Among the women activists I interviewed, Pınar from TÜKD was clear about the value of CSO involvement in policy: 'Associations should engage in politics ... just as the business world oversees and directs the policy decisions, civil society needs to develop supportive and/or preventive policies especially for social issues' (interview, 30 June 2012).

The insistence that civil society organizations should be ideology-free also emerges on the subject of solidarity among politically active women. The women activists from the Kemalist groups that I interviewed frame 'womanhood (*kadınlık*)' as an identity that creates common ground for women's CSOs irrespective of ideological identification. Lale from TKB implies that as long as a CSO maintains autonomy from any ideological stance, creating a common ground among women's organizations is possible:

> Organizations share a common ground in that they are sensitive to women's issues and they detach themselves from any political thinking such as being headscarved or not [*açık/ kapalı*], believing in Islam or not ... In civil society it is necessary to prioritize women and women-sensitive policies, and to aim towards doing something both in law and practice in support of women. We can work together with an association for headscarved women. I don't care what she [headscarved woman] thinks but we have a common topic: woman. (interview, 7 May 2012)

Similarly, Tülin, in her forties and president of KAMER Batman branch, highlights the value of autonomy in terms of the freedom it gives KAMER to reach as many women as possible through autonomous organizing: 'I can reach all women, even if they are supporters of the CHP, or the BDP, headscarved or not ... You can be useful for them if you are independent. You cannot reach all women when you have a political party behind you' (interview, 18 May 2012).

However, after further probing on this issue, it became clear that the perceived solidarity of women has limits. Some interviewees from the Kemalist groups, in particular, find markers of Islamic identity and faith problematic. Buket's interview is striking because while the need for cooperation with headscarved women is acknowledged, it shows intolerance about the visibility of headscarved women in the public sphere: 'I get annoyed when I see headscarved women at the table in the Ministry of Environment ... It seems primitive in this decade' (interview, 10 May 2012). What the reproduction of the secularism-Islamism distinction here helps to reveal is the way in which the autonomy discourse is bound up for Kemalists with the ideal of Republican woman as 'educated, urban, non-headscarf wearing (Özçetin, 2009: 106). Kemalist women are quite explicit that women ought to simultaneously fulfil the roles of mother, wife and educated professional, roles which make up the Republican ideal. When the Republic model of womanhood is situated in the context of the autonomy discourse, it becomes clear that Kemalist women's organizations do in fact invoke ideology in their vision of civil society. This is because, in their view, civil society is an autonomous space that ought to be led by women who embody and represent the Republican ideal. Kemalist women simultaneously gloss over differences among women in an effort to be ideology-free and mask their ideological orientation in this very move by assuming that women's organizations in civil society ought to be occupied with the same mission.

Moving on to the second dimension of the autonomy discourse, activists from all organizations apart from anti-capitalist feminist groups put forward the idea of civil society as 'above government' and of 'non-partisanship (*tarafsızlık*)'. In this way, they assume that a free civil society is set apart from government and not controlled by it. The importance of a free civil society dovetails with, and can only be understood in light of, the distinction among activists between pro-government and anti-government organizations. For the Kemalist women, civil society contributes to the struggle for gender equality only if it keeps its independent and critical characteristics. This explains why they re-categorize CSOs in light of their dependence on their pro-government alignment, as Lale from TKB states:

> Our association is contemporary (*çağdaş*) and in line with democratic principles. Other associations consist of headscarved women, are pro-government. All their demands are met, for example, assembly hall and buses arranged to travel to the hall are free of charge ... But we organize by spending from our own personal pockets ... I mean the government always safeguards the civil society that is on its side and organizes activities to undermine the ones on the other side. (interview, 7 May 2012)

According to the Kemalists, pro-government organizations – in particular Islamist women's organizations – muddy the important distinction between civil society and government because they are not critical of the government. But, perhaps surprisingly, women from both Islamist groups in my sample agree that state control of civil society should be eliminated because it is contrary to the freedom of civil society, as Perihan, president of AKDER, indicates: 'If civil society activities are checked by the government, this is very problematic' (interview, 5 July 2012). Or as Hale from the same organization put it, 'CSOs are independent from the state and become an alternative to it by seeing what the state cannot see ... I mean do you think the cumbersome and giant form of the state enables it to keep up with societal changes?' (interview, 9 July 2012). Islamist women lament the lack of autonomy in civil society and criticize the power of the state to destroy its independent and critical dimensions. They argue that the state's distinction between the CSOs which are 'close to the state (*devlete yakın*)' and those which are 'opposed to the state (*devlete karşı*)' in effect subjugates the former to itself and imposes restrictions on the activities of the latter. Size matters here, as Birsen from the AKDER points out, 'the state may influence the big CSOs by being more committed to them, for example, by supporting their project, compared to the small ones' (interview, 6 July 2012). What is more, CSOs that do not share state ideology are at risk of being closed down, as one of the participants from AKDER recalls:

> Political power ultimately makes an impact on civil society ... For instance, during the 28 February [1997] process Anadolu Gençlik Derneği (the Anatolian Youth Association, AGD) was shut down. As you can see, the political power very easily closed down an organization which does not go along with it. (interview with Göknur, 11 July 2012)

Additionally, Islamist women argue that it is problematic when CSOs fail to interrogate state policy and act as a check on state power. Birsen from AKDER comments that 'civil society should be strong against the AKP partisanship ... it can cope with state power as long as it is strong' (interview, 6 July 2012). However, this is not the case in Turkey, as Ayşe who is vice president of BKP and in her late forties articulates: 'Unfortunately, a civil society which would foster politics is very weak in Turkey. A strong civil society is where people are aware of their rights autonomously from the state' (interview, 7 August 2012). In parallel, Perihan from AKDER states that 'there are some Islamic associations which turned into organizations anxious not to disrupt or pressure the government' (interview, 5 July 2012) and Nurten from BKP emphasizes that 'we are blamed by some people as being close to government, [but] this is not the case. We don't say yes to everything that the AKP does' (interview, 9 August 2012). It is clear that for these women activists, their organizations transgress government and political party norms and practices; they want to stress how they are not absolutely aligned with these groups and maintain their own autonomy.

Kurdish-feminist women also seek to maintain independence from the state. As stated in KAMER's book titled *We Can Stop It*, 'the principle of "independence" was the most important policy ... We created an independent space where we could be independent and think and debate to form ideas. Ever since, each and every one of us has had an idea to voice' (KAMER, 2011: 265). According to all KAMER members, state control of CSOs is unacceptable. In response, they argue for a 'non-partisanship' approach, which distinguishes their organization from CSOs, which are effectively interest-based and in a close relationship with the government (a view shared also by women from the feminist organizations US and KA-DER). Nuray, the president of KAMER and the oldest interviewee from this organization, expresses this point clearly: 'The most powerful CSO in a city is Ticaret Odası [Chamber of Commerce]. How can an organization that needs the approval of the government for a bid be independent?' (interview, 16 May 2012). This point can be better understood by recalling the fact that in Turkey, civil society consists of 'not only associations and foundations but also trade unions, political parties, chambers, universities and labour unions' (Göksel and Güneş, 2005: 57). Therefore, the prevailing CSO classification is questioned by the women from KAMER to such an extent that they reject the classification of interest-based organizations as part of civil society. As Seda from KAMER puts it, 'CSO is civic (*sivil*). These are the organizations that are above the political parties and the state. The others which behave for their own interests are chambers and trade unions which seek their own interests. None of them are a CSO ... they strive only for the rights of their own members' (interview, 2 June 2012).

Kurdish-feminist women from KAMER, differently from the other groups, relate ethnic identity with the autonomy of civil society. Just as interest-based organizations are regarded as working only for their members' rights and establishing close ties with the state, those CSOs which base their membership on ethnicity are viewed in a similar light. To reinforce that the women activists I interviewed from KAMER do not use ethnicity in this way, Nuray, the president of KAMER, states that women 'moderate (*hafifletme*)' their ethnic identity with respect to their organizing work so as to 'make room for other women to stand beside them and to become more independent' (interview, 16 May 2012). This point references other Kurdish women's organizations in the region, and the organizing work mentioned includes a proposal that in order to be more independent, the organizations need to have less identity-based relationships with other CSOs. In this sense, it could be argued that the autonomy discourse works to transcend ethnic differences in this case.

Though KAMER members recognize the benefits of independence, they are also attuned to the obstacles of maintaining independence, particularly in light of the ongoing conflict between the Turkish state and Kurdish people in South-Eastern and Eastern Anatolia. In this regard, two categories of CSOs appear in the women's spoken texts, namely, independent (*bağımsız*) and partisan (*yandaş*). Nuray states that, since its establishment, the KAMER foundation has been accused of 'being partisan toward the Kurdish political movement by the state officials or being dependent on the Kurdish movement due to striving for women's rights' (interview, 16 May 2012), but all the women that I interviewed from KAMER stress their difference from any partisan groups. This issue was also raised in their book *We Can Stop This*:

> During the time of our establishment, we experienced our greatest difficulties as a consequence of our principle of independence. This difficulty still continues – albeit somewhat lessened. Neither government agencies nor other organizations wanted to believe that we were independent ... They did not want to understand the fact that KAMER was on the side of women's human rights. (KAMER, 2011: 281–2)

Proving their independence to others and gaining trust are ongoing tasks. One strategy in this regard is to organize handcraft workshops to bring more women into the foundation in areas where partisan groups are especially dominant, as Nuray points out: 'Some people from the KCK came to us and said we can't do ... things without asking their permission ... women avoid talking to us because they are afraid ... We don't want to ask their [the KCK] permission, as such a thing will make us dependent on them. Thus, the only way for us is to ... open up a ceramics workshop' (interview, 16 May 2012).

The women from the second Kurdish group in my sample, SELİS, favour a confrontational (*çatışmacı*) rather than collaborative approach to the state. They are, therefore, sceptical of the view that civil society should be a negotiating partner and should function as an intermediary between the state and society. As Gökten, who is in her late thirties, puts it, 'civil society appears to me as being independent from the power (*erk*), from the governing body (*yöneten*) and where you stand comfortably for what you want' (interview, 24 May 2012). In this light, another woman, Ece, who is the youngest interviewee from SELİS and the president of the association, states that 'disclosing some issues, moulding public opinion, etc.' are key to the purpose of civil society. She voices the importance of having 'a civil pillar (*sivil ayak*)' in society functioning as a control mechanism on the state, trying to make the state act in new and better ways (interview, 15 May 2012). Overall, SELİS members 'expect the state to adopt an attitude that accepts the independence of CSOs ... otherwise, oppression from the power may come into existence in that area' (interview with Reşide, 22 May 2012).

Interestingly, activists across the Kemalist, Islamist and feminist groups in my sample stress the need to maintain financial independence from government. Indeed, they attach negative meanings to CSOs being supported by the state because of the way this potentially undermines CSO autonomy. Nurdan, the president of TÜKD, says that 'if the CSOs have an expectation from the state, they cannot keep their idiosyncratic features ... expecting any financial source from the state is inconsistent with my understanding of civil society' (interview, 29 June 2012). It seems, however, that rejection of financial support from the state is not a principle set in stone. Because of the financial difficulties experienced by many CSOs, some interviewees from the Kemalist groups are of the view that state support is welcome if it is used to support projects and consultation processes, and to buy essential resources. Lale, the youngest member of TKB, makes this quite clear: 'If the associations are for the public benefit, not for any personal gains, women, environment, health organizations etc. should be supported by the state' (interview, 7 May 2012). Similarly, among the Islamist women, public funding is endorsed if it is allocated to CSOs independently from the government; indeed, this is also viewed as one way of curbing the rise and dominance of government-supported CSOs in Turkey. Nurten from BKP addresses this more nuanced position: 'You can't always criticize someone or an institution you always take money from. There is such a risk ... [But] civil society should get project-based financial support from the state. This would enable a transformation to some extent' (interview, 9 August 2012). However, in the following excerpt from my interview with Rezan, member of the feminist group KA-DER, it is clear that full funding from the state remains compromising:

> I personally do not approve state's support for civil society ... it has been discussed a lot between women's organizations and there are so many women telling me that CSOs are engaged in very important activities and the state should support this but I do not agree. For example, I am saying that it [the state] should not help with anything except for rent allowance [for organizations] and insuring an employee ... in order not to establish dependency. (interview, 18 July 2012)[3]

The mediation discourse

The third discourse implies that civil society is an agent of mediation between society and the state, regardless of specific governments. Thus Sevda, the president of Kemalist group TKB, states that 'it does not matter which political party is in power, in general we request from them to have a close relationship with civil society ... because we are the eyes and ears of the public, we are the organized voice of the public' (interview, 8 May 2012). Further, TKB lists among its key objectives on its website the fostering of strong cooperation and solidarity with national and international CSOs, public institutions and local administrations, and creating joint projects with them (TKB, 2015). Similarly, for Begüm from the Islamist BKP, civil society is imagined as 'a channel between the people and political power'. Civil society is 'at the people's side' (interview, 1 August 2012). And the press statement issued by BKP regarding the 17 December 2013 corruption crisis in Turkey insists: 'Via civil society organizations the reflection of the national will on the decision-making processes is possible and necessary' (BKP, 2014). A final example comes from the Kurdish-feminist group KAMER, which stresses that it aims to increase collaborations with the public bodies:

> KAMER strives to take part in City Councils. It strove to collaborate with
> the KSGM (Directorate General on the Status of Women). It took part
> in meetings regarding preparations for the National Action Plan ... It is
> important for KAMER to be part of the Violence Monitoring Committee
> headed by the State Minister on Women, where there is a representative
> from each department and where it is possible to communicate about the
> difficulties encountered on the ground. (KAMER, 2011: 284)

There is a strong emphasis in this discourse on the active role of civil society
in shaping and pressurizing the government. As one interviewee from TKB
put it, 'the opinions of the civil society should be taken in every respect'
(interview with Buket, 10 May 2012). On the TÜKD website, 'working and
leading the way for a modern, secular Turkey with women pioneering for
change who can take active part in all decision making mechanisms as equal,
active and free citizens' is listed among principles (TÜKD, 2010), and TKB
similarly encourages women to take part in decision-making mechanisms
(TKB, 2007). Or, as a statement by Nurşen Orakçı on the website of BKP puts
it, 'As CSOs, we became well-aware that we have a very important mission
in the issuing and implementation of laws and we realised that we need to
work very hard' (Orakçı, 2007). The function of civil society as a pressure
group should be initially fulfilled before considering other strategies of civil
activism, as Lale from TKB explains: 'Civil society organizations function
as a pressure factor ... They should form relations with the government by
establishing communicative channels. If this is not managed, they should go
for demonstrations and protests, but not any violent activities' (interview, 7
May 2012). There is an accompanying emphasis in this discourse on dialogue
and negotiation: the state has a responsibility to 'listen' to what civil society
has to say, as Yasemin from AKDER explains: 'The state should listen and
invite the CSOs into the law-making process and should pay attention to
their suggestions and projects' (interview, 13 July 2012).[4] Seda from the
Kurdish-feminist group KAMER uses the example of when activist women
created a platform to push for change in the Civil Code to illustrate how
dialogue between civil society and the state can work productively: 'When
we detect some problems about women ... We say, you are the state, this is
your responsibility and you have to do it. As a CSO, we remind them of their
duties' (interview, 2 June 2012).

The women from feminist organizations US and KA-DER articulate a rather different approach to the mediating role of civil society, one which is more instrumental in character. They support this role only because they know that siding with the state brings access to resources, including valuable information, which they also acknowledge comes at a cost. Çiçek, who is one of the employees of KA-DER and has no political party membership, makes this point clear: 'If you say something contrary to the government today, you can't participate in a meeting organized by the government and you can't be informed of developments. Or for example ... if you have good relationships, you can learn the agenda of the parliament in advance' (interview, 21 July 2012). The by-law of KA-DER accordingly states that it strives to be 'in cooperation with all ministries, the Ministry of Family and Social Policies in particular, with the Committee on Equality of Opportunity for Women and Men of the Grand National Assembly of Turkey and with all other related commissions' (KA-DER, 2012). As well as fear about state repression, pragmatism and necessity of being in a relationship with the state inform this expression of the mediation discourse. As Emel, the youngest member of US, clarifies, 'It is obvious that it is not possible to do something [for CSOs] by positioning yourself totally independent from the state. So, civil society has to be a negotiating partner of the state' (interview, 26 June 2012). To illustrate, the US 'Route of Women in Democracy Project (Demokraside Kadın İzleri Projesi)' aimed to encourage participation in decision-making processes and to build a bridge between women's organizations and members of parliament, and a more continuous exchange of information (US, 2011: 1).

It should be noted that the women activists from Kemalist, Islamist and Kurdish-feminist KAMER also bring attention to a disjuncture between the ideal and the reality conveyed by the mediation discourse. Ideally, in their view civil society should act as an intermediary between the state and the people but this is very difficult to achieve in Turkey. Thus Kemalist women point to the ways in which the AKP governments have marginalized associations which advocate Kemal Atatürk's ideas and the idea of a Republican secular state, labelling them 'anti-government'. For women from TKB, this strategy has had quite concrete effects, because financial aid to the organization was cut under the AKP, and they have experienced a funding shortage. More broadly, Kemalist participation in policymaking has been restricted and this means, for the Kemalist women in my study, that their role in checking government power is undermined. For women activists from the Kurdish-feminist group KAMER, the disjuncture between the ideal and the reality in terms of the mediation discourse is due rather to the gender ideology of the AKP governments:

> We [KAMER] are trying to create a relationship [with the state] based on dialogue and empathy. Is it happening? Of course not. There are some political disparities (*politik farklılıklar*). For example, the government currently builds its politics around protecting the family ... we object due to various reasons, for example, the family is not strengthened unless you empower women, or emphasizing the family constantly can objectify women. We do try to criticize these policies. We have endless struggles and contradictions. (interview with Nuray, 16 May 2012)

Finally, despite their relative visibility under the AKP regimes, both Islamist women's organizations are also sceptical about their capacity to influence the government. As Göknur, a woman activist from AKDER in her thirties, explains, CSOs 'put forward something ... you create public opinion and this will be viewed as a step backward by the government' (interview, 11 July 2012). In general, and as discussed in the autonomy discourse earlier, Islamist women explain their relative marginalization from the AKP government by referring to their distance and deviation from what they regard as 'pro-government' organizations. However, some women activists from BKP echo the Kurdish-feminist women when they account for their organization's marginalization by making reference to gendered exclusions. Thus Nurten, for one, highlights 'a sardonic and trivializing viewpoint of the government or state officials towards the organizations working on women's issues ... this has a negative impact on the women's associations' (interview, 9 August 2012). She adds that what lies behind this attitude is 'the dominance of the male point of view and the man's fear of losing authority' in civil society (interview, 9 August 2012).

To sum up, women activists from all groups apart from anti-capitalist groups contribute to the idea of civil society as a volunteer-based site as well as autonomous and intermediary agent which generally represent a mainstream idea of civil society. However, what is striking here is that we also see tensions and ambiguities in the discourses of women activists, which will be analysed in Chapter 5 of this book.

5

Reconstructing the site of civil society: Alternative voices

Introduction

The discourses of women activists in Turkey are divided along the ones supporting the mainstream ideas of civil society and those challenging them. After dealing with how women activists produce a mainstream idea of civil society by envisioning a voluntaristic, autonomous and intermediary civil society in Chapter 4, this chapter turns to the challenging discourses of the women activists to the dominant view of the civil society by asking in what ways and to what extent women activists reconstruct the site of civil society. What is seen is that they build civil society as an oppositional, non-hierarchical arena and emphasize the democratic outcomes of the promotion of civil society differently from more liberal ideal of a voluntaristic, autonomous and intermediary civil society. This brings a critical approach to the concept and practices of civil society as opposed to the mainstream view discussed in the previous chapter. Interestingly, a group of women activists articulates a co-optation discourse, which identifies civil society as a depoliticizing and non-feminist force. I consider that this discourse has a particular importance since it seeks to resist civil society by foregrounding feminist agency and politics as the key vehicle for emancipation of women in civil society. This chapter also highlights the differences between and within women's organizations in terms of how women activists construct and identify these discourses.

The oppositional discourse

This discourse, produced by women activists from the Kemalist TKB, Islamist BKP and Kurdish SELİS, stakes out a more clearly oppositional position, insisting that civil society should be conceived as an anti-systemic agent. The women differ, however, in their perception of what the system is.

For a few Kemalist women from TKB, the 'established system' in Turkey is the AKP government regime. In this regard, repressive and anti-secularist elements of AKP rule such as the restrictions on the right to protest, the Ergenekon (a clandestine organization) and Balyoz (Sledgehammer) are highlighted as particularly disconcerting for the Kemalist women. On the basis of those concerns, Kemalist activists construct a binary opposition between pro-systemic, 'non-adversarial (*muhalif olmayan*)' and anti-systemic 'unorganized (*örgütlü olmayan*)' civil society, as Tansu from TKB elaborates:

> When you say civil society in Turkey, there are two groups: one taking a stand for the system and the other being out of the way or removed. For the one supporting the system, there are lots of opportunities ... Many people or organizations integrate to the system in order to stay on its good side. Well ... they are assimilated. (interview, 4 May 2012)

Using this categorization, these women position Islamist organizations as assimilated and their own associations under the category of 'anti-systemic' organizations, thus reproducing existing polarizations with the Turkish women's movement along secular/Islamic lines. The fate of anti-systemic women's CSOs is set to be one of marginalization and exclusion from opportunities. Tansu concludes that 'civil societies should not have a relationship with the power [political power] at all. Civil society means organizations; organizations exist to become oppositional ... They are not expected to be accepted by the government or political power' (interview, 4 May 2012).

For a small group of the Islamist women activists that I interviewed, 'the system' is identified with state tradition and ideology in general, and the authority of the Republican state in particular. In a reverse of the anti-systemic discourse of the Kemalist women activists, Islamist women's oppositional discourse centres on criticism of the laicist and Republican authoritarian ideology of the state. In addition, the legitimacy of the state is called into question, as BKP member Nurten explained: 'In Turkey, the state is very powerful. It tells me what kind of Muslim I should be ... The main dilemma of Turkey is being a laicist Republic, at the same time 99 per cent of the population of Turkey is Muslim' (interview, 9 August 2012). In this regard, civil society is produced as an alternative space to the established system; it is discursively referred to as a platform where people voice their criticism of the state. One woman from BKP spoke passionately of the value of an oppositional civil society:

> Civil society should be different from normal public institutions, I mean, different from the present or current 'system' ... It means to be able to produce an alternative to the system ... the present situation without accepting it as it is . . For instance, civil society organizations say that social norms such as 'man is the head of the family', should be altered and they run campaigns in order to fulfil this intent. This may necessitate long-term work and struggle. Those people who go against the system pay a price; in some cases, they may be killed. (interview with Nurten, 9 August 2012)

With this last point, Nurten illustrates just what can be at stake for those pursuing an oppositional vision of civil society.

Kurdish interviewees from SELİS uniformly articulated an oppositional anti-systemic discourse, but in this context, 'anti-systemic' refers to 'anti-state and anti-power'. They describe the state as a 'masculine state' and as a set of institutions that categorize some people as 'the other (*ötekileştiren*)'. This critique of the state is clearly more abstract and absolute compared with the views expressed by the Islamist and Kemalist women activists discussed so far. The target of critique here is not a specific state structure controlled by governments but the idea of the state itself. As one member of SELİS puts it, 'we are against the state approach. When there is a state, we see power and oppression' (interview with Reşide, 22 May 2012). In addition, activists from SELİS are very critical of the intertwining of state and capitalism, which results in the marketization of civil society. This is reflected in their critique of the now-established links between CSOs and funding, discussed earlier. Funded projects are considered to lead to the formation of power areas in civil society and obliterate its adversarial drive. It is in this light that we should understand the distinction between conformist and oppositional versions of civil society drawn here. In contrast to the ways in which Kemalist and Islamic groups map this division onto the secular/religious divide, Kurdish groups distinguish between the 'subservient (*itaat eden*)', 'non-oppositional (*muhalif olamama*)' groups that are male-dominated and take funding, and non-funded women's groups. Gökten from SELİS illustrates this in the excerpt below:

> Actually I don't think that the CSOs in Turkey have their own agenda any more. They operate within the framework of the power, but now they don't have an oppositional dimension … [But] I definitely believe that women's organizations have a special place in Turkey. Hierarchy is less, maybe due to woman's nature (*kadının yapısı*); they do not like hierarchical structure very much[1] … [and because] they are an oppressed class (*ezilen bir kesim*). I think that women's organizations are more dynamic although I said that governments have pressured civil societies but women's groups can go beyond the system much more [than the other CSOs]. (interview, 24 May 2012)

Overall, then, there are significant differences in how the system and opposition to it is theorized among these different women's groups. Yet there is also a shared, overwhelmingly normative vision of civil society, one which acknowledges that civil society may be drawn into the sphere of influence of the system, but which also clings to the possibility of a positive and supportive organizing space with the responsibility of scrutinizing and resisting the state.

The anti-hierarchical discourse

This discourse frames civil society as a potentially anti-hierarchical space. Echoing the structure of the anti-systemic discourse, this is a view critical of many civil society organizations, including women's organizations, which are dominated by hierarchical and unequal structures and problematic leadership practices. It simultaneously invokes an aspiration to create a civil society which pursues equality and an end to hierarchical social relations, whether such relations arise from within civil society or between CSOs and the state.

Challenging hierarchical and centralized forms of organization in civil society is a predominant concern of activists from groups across my sample, and is usually discussed in conjunction with the autonomy discourse, as shown when 'dependence' and 'hierarchy' are articulated together and framed as decisive problems in civil society. For example, the feminist organization KA-DER takes a stand against hierarchical formations, stating in its by-law that it has done so by removing the word 'educate' from its name and instead adopting a relationship based on sharing, not hierarchy (KA-DER, 2012). Importantly, the anti-hierarchy discourse is mainly discussed with regard to relationships *within* CSOs, and specifically the issue of representation and leadership, as a woman from KA-DER explains:

> I think that hierarchy is not viewed as a very big problem in women's organizations, but in fact, the thing is that CSOs ... are also hierarchical in themselves, and women's organizations are not excluded from this ... Women's organizations are represented by presidents as well as by an EC [executive committee], the members themselves are not part of these decision-making procedures and these discussions. (interview with Çiçek, 21 July 2012)

Or as Sevda from the Kurdish-feminist KAMER declares, 'we had meetings with the other CSOs. In some of them, the president has a separate room. Other people are working next to the president's office in such a small room with adjacent desks. I was shocked. This is nothing but hierarchy' (interview, 20 May 2012). In the same vein, for the Kurdish women activists in my study, the prevalence of hierarchical structures within and between CSOs is one of the most significant problems plaguing civil society, and their critique of it underscores how they try to create a non-hierarchical organizational structure in their own groups.

We see a subtle difference between activists in my sample in terms of their approach to hierarchy. On the one hand, the interviewees from the Kurdish-feminist group KAMER, and also from the feminist groups, argue that it is impossible to completely dismantle hierarchy, even within their own organizations. As Nuray puts it, 'it is a lie to say that there is no hierarchy in KAMER' (interview, 16 May 2012). The feminist groups suggest that, in order to work with the state or government, a hierarchical organizational structure may be necessary; furthermore, some KAMER members suggest that hierarchies based on differential knowledge and experience might be desirable. To illustrate, some interviewees from that group argue that anti-hierarchical structures can result in the 'devaluation of knowledge and experience' (interview with Nuray, 16 May 2012) and 'disharmony in an organization' (interview with Tülin, 18 May 2012). In line with this approach, KAMER documentation makes clear that its commitment to 'taking a position against hierarchy' is tempered by the need to have 'equality without devaluing knowledge and experience' (KAMER, 2011: 283). On the other hand, the women from the Kurdish group SELİS and the anti-capitalist AMARGİ strive to establish and maintain non-hierarchical structures in and between organizations. As Gökten from SELİS articulates, 'I believe there is less hierarchy in women's organizations. In SELİS, it is even less … we are doing our best not to develop such a hierarchy' (interview, 24 May 2012). AMARGİ emphasizes in its introductory leaflet: 'We do not want to resemble the system that we are so critical of, so we have no leader, but hold everyone responsible. That means no one decides for anyone. We implement our mission through working groups. We make decisions through consensus' (AMARGİ, n.d.1). Nonetheless, irrespective of whether they think hierarchy can be entirely abolished, all groups in my sample agree that an overemphasis on leadership positions in a CSO, specifically in a women's organization, is unacceptable.

For the women in the anti-capitalist organization AMARGİ, capitalism is one of the key sources of inequality within and between CSOs. This can be seen in the interview with Eda from AMARGİ, who declares that 'there are not enough alternative CSOs. We should have more CSOs that have problems with the system that have issues with capitalism, concern about the working class, and at the same time, sexism. We lack this type of CSO, we have to increase' (interview, 3 July 2012). For her, far too many CSOs are 'ends' in themselves rather than 'instruments' that bring about benefits for society as a whole. Other members of the same group lament the way CSOs function like a company, with the workers within it relatively detached and alienated from the group's goals. As Duygu from AMARGİ puts it, 'the CSOs are turning into places where you do your own task without attaching yourself to that space' (interview, 2 June 2012), and where one's marketable abilities, such as proficiency in English, override attachment and commitment to an organization.

More broadly, the critique of hierarchy dovetails for many of my interviewees with their critique of patriarchy. The women activists from the Kurdish groups SELİS and KAMER certainly identified male dominance as one of the roots of hierarchy. As Reşide, one of the youngest activists from SELİS, comments, 'We grow up with this hierarchical structure in which mother is always in the kitchen, is responsible for the child care and the father works outside. It is all these little things we grow up with' (interview, 22 May 2012). KAMER's documentation puts it this way:

> We realized that hierarchy was one of the pillars of the system, which was practiced with diligent care ... This system gave women the opportunity to exist only in men's shadow. Many of us believed that there were no forms of existence other than that as someone's daughter, wife, or mother. We were suffocating each other even while expressing our love. We stopped doing this. (KAMER, 2011: 268)

The fact that dominance in the family translates into dominance of men in mixed group decision-making processes in civil society annoys these women, and is contrary to their equality-based understanding of civil society. In line with this approach, the CSOs dominated by men and attributing traditional gender roles to women are called into question, as Reşide from SELİS articulates in the following extract:

> There are also some civil society organizations which ascribe gender roles to women, well, from how it should be at home to their point of view of the state ... For example, in one of the meetings I participated in, there were some women who said that 'if a woman does cleaning at home, gets along well with her husband, she is not exposed to violence' ... there are also civil society organizations [that support this kind of idea]. (interview, 22 May 2012)

As can be seen in this quote, for Kurdish women, the patriarchal system is not limited in scope to men's power over women, but is reproduced by women themselves. Tülin from KAMER underscores the point: 'It's a male-dominated system, I suppose ... women are affected by this. They may say "If men show off their power, I'll do the same to them" ... Women can also resort to violence in some cases, for example, when they become a manager' (interview, 18 May 2012).

It is in connection to this argument that the normative aspect of the anti-hierarchy discourse emerges, as it is suggested by some interviewees that the transformation of civil society can only be realized by feminism. While integrating a feminist approach into civil society is acknowledged as being 'difficult due to the dominance of hierarchies within and between the civil society organizations' by Çiçek from KA-DER (interview, 21 July 2012), Duygu, one of the oldest members of AMARGİ that I interviewed, argues that feminism has already had a significant impact on civil society. She says that 'it is feminism that will bring horizontal organization into the society ... and should develop relationships with civil society' (interview, 2 June 2012). Eda from the same organization agrees:

> I am sure that leftist CSOs and human rights associations fight against the problems of the civil society, but they don't fight for destroying the power domain. In those organizations, men are in power, so they don't want to give up their power easily, so they don't address these topics ... this is a problem of sexism ... they should learn from the feminist women's organizations ... it is not easy, it is still on-going. (interview, 3 July 2012)

In line with this view, women's organizations are framed by some interviewees *as model organizations for civil society* as a whole, exemplifying best practices for CSOs to follow due to their efforts at building bridges between organizations, notwithstanding any internal struggles they may have with hierarchy. An activist from US puts it this way: 'The primary duty of civil society [is] to come side by side. We can work on different subjects but we can get together for the issues. The women's organizations can do this and it sets an example for others in civil society' (interview with Didem, 19 June 2012).

The democratization discourse

The democratization discourse posits that civil society is an arena for non-discriminatory and active citizenship. Two distinct approaches to the connection between democracy and civil society can be discerned. While Kurdish women underscore the non-discrimination aspect of the democratization discourse, women from feminist US emphasize the development of democratic culture and active citizenship practices via CSOs. I will outline each of these approaches in turn.

The interviewees from both Kurdish organizations in my sample focus their attention on the need for civil society to combat discrimination. They frame discrimination between and within CSOs as a 'democratic failure', and their emphasis upon it is linked to the regional and ethnic problems they encounter as Kurdish women and as individuals working within Kurdish women's organizations. In the first place, they argue that they face discrimination on the basis of ethnic difference coded in geographical terms. Thus Nuray from KAMER mentions that she is bothered by some people from other organizations referring to her as 'coming from the *Eastern* part of Turkey' (interview, 16 May 2012), that is, the Kurdish regions of Eastern and South-Eastern Anatolia. As noted by Derya from KAMER:

> One of the problematic areas in the civil society is discrimination ... We can see it when we go to the West from the East [of Turkey] for project work. When I say I am from Diyarbakır [a city in Eastern Anatolia], you can see eyebrows are raised, because they have some type of profile in their minds, and they get surprised if the person they met doesn't fit into this profile ... when people or other organizations come to this side of the country [the eastern part of Turkey], they position themselves as the knowledgeable person; the person comes to give us knowledge or the person comes to save us. Ultimately, here we have also produced knowledge, experiences, data ... but when they come from the West there is a perception that they come here to teach or save us. (interview, 17 May 2012)

For Derya, this discrimination can even result in violence: she goes on to describe a Women's Shelter Congress held in 2012 in which 'Our women friends coming from the East and South-East were almost lynched, they had to be guarded and sent away after they felt their lives were in danger ... This is ridiculous ... This is where we are in civil society' (interview, 17 May 2012). In addition, discriminatory attitudes are explained as responses to the articulation of a particular identity, that is, '*being a woman from Diyarbakır*' rather than the more general identity of '*being a woman*'. In this vein, Reşide from SELİS discusses the same Women's Shelter Congress: 'We are accused of not dealing with women's issues, but dealing with regional issues'. She cites an example of a colleague reading a letter from a woman in prison and continues, 'We got a serious reaction; banging the tables, shouting "get out of here, you can't do it like that in Turkey, go to Northern Iraq, here is Turkey!" ... they never want to see SELİS in the decision-making process' (interview, 22 May 2012).

Unlike the women from KAMER, my interviewees from SELİS focus on the discrimination produced by the state and its policies in Turkey. They refer to 'divisions (*ayrışma*)' in society, whether taking the form of gender divisions between men and women, ethnic divisions between Turkish and Kurdish people, or religions divisions between Christians and Muslims, as resulting in 'othering (*ötekileştirme*)' by the state. As Gökten puts it:

> There is a serious separation in the society, the trouble or distress of one group is not felt by other groups. Men don't feel women's, Turks don't feel Kurds, and Muslims don't feel Christians. There is such a separation. Thus, civil society cannot unite and build more power as a bloc and obviously this doesn't help the democratization of the country. However, this separation is generated by the state's politics. Eventually, [for the state] it is easier to control and rule when you are separated. (interview, 24 May 2012)

In this way, the state is portrayed as a source of illegitimate power and oppression. Furthermore, in this context, the state is viewed as a masculine entity, which goes some way in explaining its abuse of power. Ece, an activist from SELİS, underscores that the masculine mindset of the state in Turkey effectively means it ignores women's problems and, at the same time, it has an interest in propagating an acceptable image of womanhood; those deviating from the state's image of femininity are subject to the process of othering (interview, 15 May 2012). The women from SELİS accuse the Turkish state for making organizations such as theirs or "the other (*öteki*)" through refusing to support them financially and indirectly forcing them to become dependent on EU and other sources of funding. As Ece remarks, 'if you don't mind the masculine state, you don't have those kinds of problems; your projects are approved by the state very easily' (interview, 15 May 2012).

Feminist groups also appeal to the democratization discourse, but differently from the Kurdish women activists, emphasizing how the development of democratic culture depends, among other things, on the idea and practices of active citizenship. For feminists, active citizenship is promoted and accommodated within CSOs since these organizations are ideally suited to representing 'the people'. This is particularly evident in the interviews with women from US. Civil society encompasses all citizens, and a broad definition of 'civil' is defended, as when Fulya from US refers to 'the people's sense of morality, their ways of working and their language ... which is defined in opposition to the "military (*apoletli olmak/olamamak*)" or "official (*resmi*)" definitions' (interview, 21 June 2012). Civil society is conceptualized as a space for organizing around, and providing representations of, citizens' voices, and in this way it contributes to the development of democratic culture. The projects conducted by US, such as Gölge Meclis Projesi (Watch Your Shadow) and Demokraside Kadın İzleri Projesi Broşürü (The Route of Women in Democracy), also confirm this standpoint. 'Through the Gölge Meclis Project', notes one leaflet, 'instead of having to go along with the services that are considered appropriate for themselves, women will be encouraged to set the agenda and to be active in achieving the result they want' (US, n.d.). Similarly KA-DER has projects such as Kadın Yurttaşların ve Aktivistlerin Seçmenler ve Aktif Yurttaşlar Olarak Güçlendirilmesi Projesi (Empowerment of the Women Citizens and Activists as Electorates and Active Citizens Project) which are 'supporting active and participatory citizenship by empowering women ... and in the long term encouraging the active participation of the women in politics' (KA-DER, n.d.). The aim is for women who are the targets of these projects themselves to become active in civil society. As Didem from US concludes, becoming part of a CSO both facilitates and enhances the impact of active citizenship:

> If there is a matter in the area you live in, to say that 'I feel uncomfortable about this situation' is the first step to being organized about it. Because those who are organized get annoyed about the pavement issue today, the day after the people should say, 'you don't build the right pavement for the suburbs', and this turns it into a class struggle ... An active citizen should be an activist. This kind of activism can happen on the streets, it happens by attending the council ... this voice of disturbance works when it is organized. That's why I believe in CSOs. (interview, 19 June 2012)

Overall, then, the feminist groups suggest that the power of civil society as a realm of active citizenship lies in the way it can shape the political agenda to include previously marginalized yet vital issues people feel strongly about.

The co-optation discourse

The final discourse is much less positive, hinging on the idea that civil society is an agent of co-optation. This view is articulated by the anti-capitalist feminists – all the women I interviewed from SFK and some from AMARGİ – along with some women from US. For these women, civil society in Turkey has been subject to co-optation by the state. Specifically, they pose a challenge to CSOs by framing civil society as a depoliticizing and non-feminist force. Their main line of criticism is based on unveiling the contradictions within the understanding and practices of civil society. In this context, civil society as it actually exists in Turkey is described as (1) depoliticizing in terms of the activity it promotes (2) status- and interest-seeking and (3) a buffer zone between the state and the market. I will deal with each of these points in turn.

The first dimension of the co-optation discourse constructs a dichotomy between civil society and feminist politics and highlights the de-politicization of civil society. That is to say, feminist organizations are positioned in contrast to other CSOs, and CSO politics more generally is viewed as reproducing capitalist structures and substantially concealing systemic inequalities by adopting a narrow, issue-based mindset where problems are viewed in isolation from each other. In this sense, these women activists use pejorative phrases like 'professionalism' and 'maintenance of the system' in order to describe civil society, and do not view it as an arena for transformative political struggle, as Burçak from AMARGİ makes clear:

> I don't respect civil society from my point of view, you can't respect it in a way. It is a nice thing, but not radical, it doesn't produce something different. It obscures the existing problem, does not say anything to transform it. It helps the continuance of it in a way and actually it makes the problems look nicer. (interview, 2 July 2012)

Whereas CSOs are described as 'conciliatory (*uzlaşmacı*)', feminist organizations are called 'critical', as stated by Betül from the same group: 'To me, feminism can't choose to conciliate, this is why I say a feminist organization is not a CSO, or it shouldn't be. Feminist politics should always be critical' (interview, 15 June 2012). In the same vein, some women from US construct a dichotomous relationship between civil societism (*sivil toplumculuk*) and revolutionism (*devrimcilik*). In the context of broader political struggle, 'civil society activism' is regarded as the lesser of the two practices, partly because of the way such activism shows signs of and enables co-optation by the state and the political power.

According to this view, the relationship of civil society to the state is one of conformity rather than an adversarial relationship. As Burçak from AMARGİ signifies, 'I believe it is built on the principle of avoiding any conflict' (interview, 2 July 2012). In this context, developments in civil society, such as NGOization and the rise of the funded project, are singled out as important instruments for creating a depoliticized space; as Betül from AMARGİ puts it, 'They [civil society organizations] are not able to transform the society due to lack of political attributes' (interview, 15 June 2012). More than this, civil society is limited by direct repression. For Emel from US:

> [Political] power has started to rule civil society. It used to be like, 'you have a field … play here' [but] … it is beyond that idea now … [Take] the example of Canan Arın. Well, she is a lawyer from the Purple Roof Women's Shelter Foundation (Mor Çatı) and she was taken into custody because she was talking about early marriages. A lot of people from KESK (The Confederation of Public Labourers' Union) were taken into custody. Therefore, it is beyond 'go on, you can play in the garden'. It doesn't even allow you to play. You will play in the garden in the way it [political power] wants. (interview , 26 June 2012)

State repression thus severely limits the actions and impact of civil society activists. The same activist employs a wall metaphor to show that activists are trapped within the boundaries of civil society: 'There is a wall but I am not very sure if hitting this wall wears it down (*aşınmak*). Does this wall erode? … What is wearing down, you or the wall?' (interview, 26 June 2012)

In this context, many activists from feminist and anti-capitalist groups refuse to refer to their organization as CSOs. This is not to suggest they seek the total abolition of CSOs and civil society. Zeynep from SFK, for one, acknowledges the importance of CSOs but insists that the role of the civil society should go beyond them:

> CSOs have many projects. Let's consider what is sought in single-purpose projects for women like advisory hotlines for domestic violence, etc. All

of these affect women's lives directly. But ... an organization like SFK ... takes women and turns them into political subjects (*politik özneler*). [CSOs and feminist organizations are] separate areas but mutually supporting areas. Political subjects themselves can take heart from the CSOs' research and projects, etc... . but I think politics cannot be restricted to CSOs only. (interview, 26 June 2012)

In this extract, there is a reference to a wider definition of politics than the world of CSOs allows for. In the light of all this, 'civil society' and 'CSO' are not seen as acceptable terms to use to identify the feminist political struggle and organizations associated with it. Within this context, the SFK manifesto starts with an approach that 'being independent from the state, capital and men' is an essential feature of feminist organizations. The organization does not suggest that CSOs should be autonomous from authorities in order to work properly in the site of civil society; rather, it challenges the idea and practices of civil society (SFK, 2008). Indeed, feminism can gain its meaning precisely from the contrast with civil society, as when Betül, one of the younger members of AMARGİ, explains: 'For me, civil society looks like a concept in which the meaning is emptied out, because it is very abstract ... because of that, there is still a reason to call myself a feminist. Because it [feminism] is not neutralized (*hiç etmek*) by power, as is the case for civil society' (interview, 15 June 2012).

More concretely, the incompatibility of feminism with civil society/ CSOs is emphasized by referring to the 'non-CSO' characteristics of feminist organizations. Thus some interviewees from AMARGİ prefer to see themselves as part of a 'women's organization' than a CSO, seeing this term as challenging the dominant perceptions of civil society as being 'above-politics' and specialized. As Esra articulates:

One cannot call AMARGİ a civil society organization. Because AMARGİ has a side, it produces political discourse (*söz*). Indeed, its side is very clear. Therefore it does not say that 'I am talking above politics' or 'I am creating a non-political discourse', rather, it states 'I am doing politics'. (interview, 16 June 2012)

In line with this approach, women from SFK prefer to employ the term 'democratic mass organization (DMO)' rather than 'civil society organization'. For all of the anti-capitalist feminists from this group, the site of civil society in

Turkey is divided into two groups: CSOs supported by international funding and DMOs. These two distinct groups are also defined respectively as the 'state-approved and non-state approved'. As Bilge from SFK puts it, 'there are government policies and opposing groups. The democratic mass organizations are the oppositional groups for me ... we don't use the CSO term' (interview, 15 June 2012). Similarly, Zeynep from the same organization describes SFK as a political movement rather than a CSO. In this way, SFK for her retains its political potential for transformative change:

> In a professional organization, you do advocacy, but feminism is not only advocacy, it is beyond that. Of course, you can do that as well, but it shouldn't be limited to that because feminism is more threatening, fights against the system by definition, fights against the patriarchal system. This is a total struggle that should include many areas. For example, a study against men's violence can make a crack in the system, but if you define that only from that perspective, if you don't make an overall system analysis and build an entire struggle, you can crack but cannot overturn the system. (interview, 26 June 2012)

The second dimension of the co-optation discourse is that civil society is considered an instrument for status and interest-seeking. When presidency, delegation and representation start to play a key role in a civil society organization, according to the anti-capitalist women that I interviewed, a CSO turns into an instrument for gaining capital and status and is easily manipulated by the state/governments. In other words, the internal organizational hierarchies of CSOs means that those leading the organization become detached from the membership profile, as Esra argues: 'Civil society has serious hierarchies within itself ... CSOs are becoming power domains as being a president or something else there is a prestigious thing' (interview, 16 June 2012). The solution to combat these problems is located in 'bottom-up politics' and direct political participation in decision-making procedures, rather than more representational procedures. For example, participation was emphasized and redefined in 'Beyoğlu'na Feminist Sözümüz Var (We Have a Feminist Word to Beyoğlu)' campaign brochures: 'If you do not see the obstacles in front of the participation of the women and the other disadvantaged groups and try to eliminate them with conscious interventions, the word participatory has no meaning' (SFK, 2013). At this point, feminist organizations are suggested as an alternative to representation-based organizations since they put an emphasis on horizontal and non-professional structures, rotational systems and collective and non-hierarchical decision-making processes. This perspective on feminist organizing prompts women to participate in the politics of organizing as well as in the politics of everyday life. It refers implicitly to the broader debate on 'bureaucracy versus collectivism' (see Martin, 1990) in the literature on feminist organizations, and aligns feminism with internal democracy, broad participation and minimal hierarchy.

The third dimension of the co-optation discourse is that civil society functions to serve as a buffer zone between the state and capitalism. Anti-capitalist women activists believe that when civil society plays this role, it permanently blocks the possibility of solving the problems of the capitalist system caused by both the state and market relations, as Elçin from SFK highlights:

> I think the civil society is an intermediate agent that would tolerate the inequalities faced by individuals, on their behalf, as a result of powerful attacks of capital and the state. I mean, it's like a welfare state. Like when capitalism became cruel and produced a deadlock, the welfare state project was developed. Nowadays, capitalism is more of a deadlock [than before] but the state does not want to take responsibility for the damage [directly]. They do this through civil society, sometimes through support provided by the state and by causing [people] to forget the reality that they are the state's main responsibility. (interview, 23 July 2012)

In order to illustrate this point, Burçak from AMARGİ discusses how a CSO may form a relationship with capital, giving the example of the alliance between TEMA (the Turkish Foundation for Combatting Soil Erosion) and Koç, the second largest company group in Turkey. When the latter 'occupied some forest area in Istanbul and built a university campus there [Koç University] ... not a single civil society organization gave a reaction about how valuable that land is and how that is an occupation' (interview, 2 July 2012). In this regard, the state is understood to be in need of civil society in order to manufacture consent; it is seen to gain legitimacy through civil society. As Esra from AMARGİ highlights, 'The state needs civil society to be able to promote politics, to create this hegemony' (interview, 16 June 2012). Because of this understanding of state-civil society relations, most of the anti-capitalist women activists characterize the dominant perception of civil society projects creating 'a free and equal world' as a 'delusion' as Betül from AMARGİ argues (interview, 15 June 2012).

Conclusion

The aim of Chapters 4 and 5 was to analyse the main features of the civil society discourses articulated by the women activists from Kemalist, Islamist, Kurdish, feminist and anti-capitalist women's organizations. I found that women's groups did not produce a unified narrative but rather many different discourses of civil society. I identified seven main ones, under the headings of voluntarism, autonomy, mediation, opposition, democratization, anti-hierarchy and co-optation, as set out in Table 5.1.

The autonomy discourse is the most prevalent, in which the Kemalist, Islamist, Kurdish and feminist women activists position civil society 'above politics and ideology' and independent from the state or government despite some divergences within it. The mediation discourse is the second most common discourse produced by the women from Kemalist, Islamist and feminist organizations, and the Kurdish-feminist organization, KAMER. This discourse implies that civil society plays a key intermediatory role between the state and society. Often closely aligned with the mediation discourse is the voluntarism discourse, which creates the idea of civil society as a space that is and/or should be reliant on voluntary activity performed by responsible persons who do not expect any personal benefit. A rather different meaning of civil society emerges with the opposition discourse that is produced by the Kemalist, Islamist and Kurdish women activists. This discourse assumes that civil society should be an anti-systemic agent, and criticizes 'non-adversarial or unorganized' civil society and the suppression of civil society by the system; yet the emphasis of the women from the Kurdish groups is distinct from the other groups.

The emphasis on the democratic outcomes of the promotion of civil society activism lies at the heart of the democratization discourse, which is circulated by the women from the Kurdish organizations and the feminist organization,

Table 5.1 Discourses of Women's Organizations

Discourses	Women's Organizations									
	Kemalist		Islamist		Kurdish		Feminist		Anti-capitalist	
	TKB	TÜKD	BKP	AKDER	KAMER	SELİS	US	KA-DER	SFK	AMARGİ
Voluntarism	X	X	X	X				X		
Autonomy	X	X	X	X	X	X	X	X		
Mediation	X	X	X	X	X		X	X		
Opposition	X		X	X		X				
Democratization					X	X	X	X		
Co-optation							X		X	X
Anti-hierarchy					X	X	X	X		X

US. Overlapping somewhat with the democratization discourse is the anti-hierarchy discourse, which is produced by the women from the Kurdish and feminist organizations as well as AMARGİ, the anti-capitalist organization. This discourse envisages civil society as a site in which CSOs should have a non-hierarchical and horizontal organizational structure, and suggests that the integration of feminist organizational principles and practices into civil society is one way of rebuilding civil society along non-hierarchical lines. In stark contrast to the connotations of the democratization discourse, the discourse of co-optation identifies civil society as a depoliticizing and non-feminist force, and challenges particular features of civil society in Turkey. Starting with the assumption that civil society has already been co-opted in Turkey, it rejects the idea of civil society from the outset.

In terms of the key factors shaping the women's articulation of discourses, political orientation of course plays an important role. In line with their political standpoint, almost all of the interviewees in my sampling – apart from the anti-capitalist women – make a distinction between pro-government and anti-government/state CSOs. This is important for considering how ideology works to shape the contestations and fragmentations between the women's organizations in Turkey. For instance, confrontation is apparent in the Kemalist and Islamist women's interviews, as they directly refer to each other as pro-government or pro-system. Kemalist women understand civil society as an area for performing and reinforcing the secular or Kemalist characteristics of the Turkish Republic, and the position and mission of Kemalist women's organizations are thus differentiated from those of the Islamist women, who are seen as too close to the government. In the mirror image of this perspective, the Islamist women accuse the Kemalist women's organizations of being overly partisan and compromised by close ties to the Republican system. Furthermore, political standpoint explains why different meanings and roles are attached to civil society in the same discourse. Thus women activists from the Kemalist, Islamist, Kurdish and feminist organizations all articulate opposition, democratization, and voluntarism discourses but divergent understandings of civil society emerge in each of these accounts because of the different political leanings of those who articulate them.

However, political standpoint is not the only factor shaping the articulation of civil society discourse. Each organization's approach to funding plays a crucial role – see, for example, how it shapes the Kemalist women's civil society discourses in terms of the relationship between voluntarism and professionalism. Generally speaking, the women activists from TÜKD, who are pro-funding, are positive about the integration of voluntarism with professionalism, while almost all women activists from TKB that I interviewed, who are sceptical of funding, repudiate this approach in the name of promoting a perception of 'responsible voluntarism'. Another example can be given from the anti-capitalist organizations. While SFK is an anti-funding organization and produces the co-optation discourse, anti-capitalist women from AMARGİ are open to funding and do not reject the idea of civil society, envisaging it as a non-hierarchical site for women and compatible with feminist goals.

Organizational structure is also influential in shaping the articulation of certain discourses. For instance, although I identified a good degree of convergence in the Islamist women's civil society discourses, the different organizational structures of AKDER and BKP partly influence their views on the relationship between voluntarism and professionalism. AKDER is semi-professional and supports the inclusion of professionalism in civil society while BKP depends on volunteers and tends to see civil society as a voluntaristic activity. This might be a decisive factor for their different approaches to the relationship between voluntarism and professionalism.

In addition, geographical location is a factor that explains why the Kurdish women's civil society discourses diverge from the women's organizations with different ideological leanings. As noted, the Kurdish women's organizations are located in Diyarbakır, in South-Eastern Anatolia, where the Kurdish population is concentrated and where there has been an ongoing war between the Turkish state and Kurdish militants led by the Kurdish Workers Party. Quite clearly, these organizations are affected by this regional politics, specifically the issue of ethnic identity and the ongoing war. I would argue that this is why women activists from both Kurdish organizations find common ground in the articulation of the democratization discourse, which envisages a non-discriminatory civil society.

Finally, the framing of women's rights and feminism is another factor that influences the articulation of women's civil society discourses. In particular, this impacts on their understanding of the gendered dimensions of civil society. The issue of women's rights and feminism can be framed according to the following categories: equality, justice-based equality, empowerment, emancipation and liberation for all groups. I would argue that whereas the women's groups using the first three categories to conceptualize women's rights – equality, justice-based equality and empowerment – mainly refer to the importance of women's activism in the site of civil society, those using the last two categories – emancipation and liberation for all groups – are more likely to address the hierarchical relationships and patriarchal features of civil society, and to emphasize feminist agency to tackle those problems.

6

Encounter with official civil society discourses: Reflection, negotiation, critique or resistance?

Introduction

This chapter presents the second stage of the textual analysis. It examines the interdiscursive dialogue between the official discourses circulating in Turkey and civil society discourses of the women's groups, identified in Chapters 4 and 5. It aims to analyse the discursive continuities and disjunctions between the two sets of discourses by identifying whether and how dominant discourses are reproduced by the women's organizations, how the interdependencies of the competing discourses are constructed and the extent to which women are '"transforming" text through encouraging a rethinking of their meanings' (Sunderland, 2004: 30). If there is such a transformation, this analysis will enable me to show the power of women's discourses to move beyond dominant discourses and create new meanings and visions of civil society. In light of the focus of this chapter, it is helpful to recall the two sets of discourses under analysis. I will refer to the current dominant civil society discourses in Turkey, which are autonomy, democratization, project-based civil society, dialogue and authoritarian-based, and the civil society discourses produced by the women's groups, namely, voluntarism, autonomy, mediation, opposition, democratization, anti-hierarchy and co-optation.

In what follows, I group the encounters between dominant and women activists' discourses around three categories which are also prevalent in the literature on civil society in the Middle East: (1) reflection and negotiation of liberal democratic discourse (2) critical engagements and (3) rejection. The first discusses the ways in which the women activists are endorsing the liberal view, at least to some extent, through both *reflecting* the dominant discourses and *negotiating* with these dominant discourses. The second examines the critical engagements of the women in my sample with the liberal approach to civil society by discussing their *critique of civil society* as well as their *resistance through challenges*; in other words, how the women activists contest civil society but continue to speak within the language of civil society. Last, I will discuss the rejectionist approach, which refers to '*resistance through alternatives*'. This means that the women activists strive to combine dissent with the production of an alternative framework for their activism and political visions. I will discuss in each case the gendered dimensions and implications for the women's struggle. Overall, this chapter could be regarded as an analysis of the ways in which power and gender relations are reconstructed in the interaction between women's civil society discourses and dominant discourses in Turkey.

Reflection and negotiation of liberal democratic discourse of civil society

Reflecting dominant civil society discourses

Women activists' civil society discourses show continuities with the dominant civil society discourses of autonomy, democratization and dialogue. I begin by showing the continuities with the autonomy discourse and arguing that this discourse is reflected in the women's interviews in two ways. First, they draw on similar linguistic terms to those found in the dominant discourse, such as free, autonomous, independent, voluntary civil society and CSO. Second, the intersections between the women's discourses bring about complex relationships with the dominant discourses. This is noted in the reproduction of the autonomy and voluntarism discourses by the women activists from Kemalist, Islamist, Kurdish and feminist women's groups.

By way of a reminder, the dominant autonomy discourse posits that since the 1980s, the state has been retreating from the area of society, and civil society is constituted as a realm for people's voices and demands. In other words, the issues that were previously not voiced by the people have begun to find an expression in the realm of civil society (Navaro-Yashin, 1998a: 57). It is also argued by scholars and activists that after the 1980 coup d'état 'various social groups such as religious groups, ethnic movements, women's movements, human rights activists and environmentalists, started to attempt to narrow down the scope of the state's economic, political, social and even cultural hegemony in favour of a civil society' (Çaha, 2013: xiv). In this sense, the autonomy of civil society from the state is promoted in academic circles as well as through international donor agencies, and sustained by the official discourse of the Turkish state elites. It is regarded as a means for forming a liberal and pluralistic civil society independent of the state's authority; in this view, the state is not a determinant or controller of civil society (Navaro-Yashin, 1998b: 57–8).

The women's CSOs reflect the autonomy discourse in two ways, by emphasizing autonomy from the state/government and autonomy from politics and ideology. Whereas the first dimension refers to the state or government, the second is a broader term which refers to ideas and social forces that subsume the state. In this sense, the autonomy of civil society from both is regarded by the women activists that I interviewed as a prerequisite for more freedom and the promotion of diversity in civil society.

Among the women's organizations, the interviewees from the Kemalist groups, the Kurdish group KAMER, and the Islamist and feminist groups emphasize autonomy, albeit in various ways. They invoke autonomy by envisioning a space of civil society functioning autonomously from the state/government and positioned above politics and ideology. It is interesting that the Kemalist women draw on an autonomy discourse that originated in opposition to the orthodoxies of Kemalism and secularism. In this sense, members from both Kemalist organizations conceptualize the area of civil society as supra-political and supra-ideological. Similarly, control of CSOs by the state is not accepted by the Kurdish women, particularly those from KAMER, since CSOs should retain their autonomous and critical features by staying 'above state and political parties' (interview with Seda, KAMER, 2 June 2012) and 'not defending the view of a political party' (interview with Sevda, KAMER, 20 May 2012). The women activists from KAMER aim to transcend a politically shaped civil society by distancing themselves from any ideology, as they also highlight in their documentation. According to the Islamist women, the area of civil society is constructed as an alternative to the state and market and is viewed as a distinctive space free from any conflict. Civil society is also located with the people and their demands, as opposed to the state and its rules and institutions. Thus, civil society is imagined as a reserved independent and critical site in which state scrutiny should be eliminated for the sake of the promotion of democracy in the country. Similarly, feminist women from KA-DER and US employ the term 'autonomy' in relation to full financial state support for the CSOs, and frame such support as a threat to 'being civil' or independent. They also argue that CSOs should respond to and solve problems and issues emerging 'from below', and should be considered distinct from organizations constituted 'from above', that is, political parties.

However, we see divergence in the women's autonomy discourse. This divergence is much more obvious in the Kemalist and Kurdish women's interviews in the sense that they stress their independence from different institutions in line with their distinct experiences as women's CSOs in the Turkish context. Most of the Kemalist women, mainly from TKB, emphasize their autonomy specifically from the AKP government rather than from the state per se. In contrast, the women activists from KAMER wish to be free from the supervision of not only the state but also any political organization located in the eastern and south-eastern region. This view is also articulated in their idea of civil society as 'above ethnicity'. KAMER is the only organization in my study to introduce a link between autonomy and ethnic identity. In this regard, moderating the Kurdish identity of an organization is suggested as a way of reinforcing the autonomy of a CSO. This is because some women activists from KAMER consider it essential to create independent and free CSOs that are inclusive and do not discriminate based on ethnic identity. This approach has to be understood in light of the aim of KAMER to change its image in the eastern and south-eastern regions because it is perceived by others to be too close either to the state or to the Kurdish Workers' Party.

Overall, I have two criticisms of the reproduction of the autonomy discourse by women's CSOs. First, the autonomy discourse tends to depoliticize civil society by reinforcing the state-civil society dichotomy established in the dominant discourse and drawing a clear boundary between the two spheres. It attributes distinctive characteristics to civil society, as if state and civil society were easily and entirely separable entities. What is more, the attachment of supra-political traits to civil society is an effort to differentiate the civil society sphere from not only the state/government but also from any kind of political and ideological force. When members of the women's organizations attach a pejorative meaning to politics and/or ideology, aligning with broader dominant discourses, they place civil society outside 'the political'. Second, the positive traits and functions ascribed to the concept of civil society through the normative definition of 'autonomy' in civil society threaten to essentialize the notion of civil society and to disregard the different and diverging interpretations of civil society that have emerged in the Turkish context. Notably, the autonomy discourse is not always reproduced as a stand-alone discourse, rather, it dovetails with the voluntarism discourse for several of the women's organizations (except for the Kurdish and anti-capitalist organizations, and the feminist US). By constructing a positive correlative relationship, voluntarism is presented as a necessity for ensuring the autonomy of an organization, and is addressed as a guarantee for autonomous associational life and the freedom of CSOs. In this way, voluntarism is pitted against professionalism, which is articulated as a threat to the independence of an organization.

The women's organizations also reproduce the dominant 'democratization' discourse, which is circulated currently in the Turkish context, mainly by the international funding agencies, and rests on the idea that a developed civil society will bring about democratic change and improvement, thereby creating a more liberal democratic society. This discourse regards the increase in the number and diversity of CSOs as a good indicator for realizing that aim; therefore, there is strong support for the inclusion of different groups and organizations in the civil society arena. This normative democratic model of civil society is reproduced in the women's interviews. Some of the Kurdish, Islamist and feminist women underscore a positive correlation between a strong, developed civil society and promotion of democratic culture.

Finally, the women's civil society discourses reproduce the emphasis on dialogue discourse used commonly in civil society discussions in Turkey. This dominant dialogue discourse prescribes the high participation of civil society organizations in decision-making and policymaking processes as a way of paying attention to, and taking into account, the voices of civil society actors. In this sense, the idea of a consensus-based relationship with the state prevails over any conflicting relations. Through their dialogue discourse, women activists from the Kemalist and Islamist organizations, KAMER and KA-DER similarly portray civil society as one of the channels between the state and society. Civil society is viewed as a space for policy-production and development and is deemed responsible for ensuring the problems of society are part of the public political agenda. For instance, the Islamist women suggest that a dialogue-based relationship with the state can be established if the state consults with CSOs during the decision-making process and if CSOs oversee state actions. Similarly, for members of KAMER, CSOs should be positive, problem-determinant and solution-oriented and thus should be in a constructive dialogue with the state institutions. Importantly, most of the women define the main function of CSOs as participating in the process of decision-making and policymaking, and influencing the implementation process.

A potential pitfall with women's reproduction of the dialogue discourse is that it glosses over more insidious power relations which not only impact on policymaking but operate throughout society. Although CSOs can play an important role in influencing laws and government policies, I would argue that 'getting access to power is not only a matter of participation in decision-making processes' (Townsend et al., 1999: 27) since power is not always identifiable or visible. The dialogue discourse can, in other words, function to mask power relations operating out of sight and behind closed doors, especially at state and policy levels. However, as I will discuss later, the depiction of women's participation in the decision and policymaking process is not uncritical. Almost all of the women I interviewed are aware of the power dynamics operating in those processes and pay particular attention to the ways state authorities marginalize women's organizations.

Negotiating dominant civil society discourses

The continuities and disjunctions between the women's civil society discourses and dominant discourses are often nuanced. To capture these nuances I use the term 'negotiation' to describe the ways in which the women activists that I interviewed reproduce dominant discourses but are somewhat critical of them at the same time. There is, therefore, a degree of compromise evident in the women's perspectives because the dominant discourses are both criticized and reclaimed. Negotiation occurs with voluntarism, dialogue- and project-based civil society discourses.

The meaning of voluntarism is negotiated in two ways in women's civil society discourses, specifically in those articulated by the Kemalist organizations, the Islamist organization AKDER and the feminist organization KA-DER. First, negotiation occurs by way of opening up the voluntarism discourse and bringing in the concept of responsibility, which effectively extends the boundaries of the discourse. In the women's interviews, voluntarism is presented as a responsibility rather than a free-time activity. Indeed, what is unique in these interviews is the image of women as committed and responsible volunteers acting in an autonomous site of civil society. For instance, for the women from KA-DER, the main responsibility of a CSO volunteer is to actively participate in the political arena. If an organization is comprised of self-disciplined and committed activists, they believe it is more likely to become institutionalized. The Kemalist women reproduce the voluntarism discourse but instead stress their responsibility to promote civil society as well as women's rights for the overall benefit of the society. Although the priorities of the Kemalist women and feminists from KA-DER differ, almost all of the women from these organizations extend the boundaries of voluntarism by integrating the idea of responsibility. What is also clear in the Kemalist women's discourses is that negotiation with the voluntarism discourse occurs by invoking the ideological commitments of Republicanism. As Tekeli (1981) aptly argues, women's rights function as a way of denying the Ottoman past and forming a 'democratized' Republic in light of Western ideas and practices. That is to say, women who were educated, enlightened, responsible and protectors of the nation were conceived as the bearers of modernization in the Republican period. By demanding commitment and duty-based voluntarism rather than being satisfied with civil society participation as a leisure-time activity, the Kemalist women reproduce a specific Republican gender identity for women. This identity is premised on feeling responsible for the development of civil society, and thereby enlightening other people and benefiting society. In this sense, there is a hint of elitism in the way Kemalist organizations negotiate and extend the voluntarism discourse.

Second, there is also an effort to negotiate the voluntarism discourse by opening up civil society to the promises of professionalism. Even though the women from some organizations associate 'genuine' civil society with voluntary-based organizations, the idea of civil society being a predominantly voluntary-only space is negotiated by some members of AKDER and KA-DER. They believe in the compatibility of voluntarism and professionalism within a CSO, and suggest that the two combined can increase the sustainability and efficiency of an organization. Indeed, this combination aids in the process of CSOs becoming institutionalized. For these organizations, such a negotiation of the voluntarism discourse is justified since combining voluntarism and professionalization is thought to be better for the future of the CSOs.

However, although there is a general view that voluntarism in an NGO helps women to gain skills through social networks and thus empowers them (Donoghue, 2001), a group of women activists in my sample, featuring voluntarist aspect of civil society, miss the point of many feminists who do criticize volunteering itself. They do not consider volunteering as being free use of women's labour, like household duties and childcare, thus perpetuating the patriarchal structure. Women as volunteers in civil society begin with the point where women no longer want to be limited to private spheres but want to be part of public sphere. For instance, women in Britain in 1970s felt like they could trust self-regulatory civil society based on voluntary actions more than a state which aimed to subordinate them (Phillips, 2002: 78). However, feminists noted that voluntary work in civil society organizations was usually preferred by married women as a substitute to paid work (Tiehen, 2000). This strengthens the role of women as caregiver rather than making them stronger. Many of the NGOs and organizations encouraged voluntarism as free labour and care work rather than fight against male dominance and do activism (Eto, 2012: 103; see Taniguchi, 2006). Feminists see this as a way of carrying the role of mothering to a public level. They also see voluntarism as a form of women's exploitation due to the fact that they do not get monetary benefit or insurance to secure themselves. This maintains women's poverty as well as their dependency on their husbands and fathers (Smith, 1975).

The groups in my sample also negotiate with the dominant project-based civil society discourse, which is constructed by the increase in international funding to CSOs in Turkey. Members of Islamist and feminist organizations, the Kemalist organization TÜKD, the Kurdish-feminist KAMER and the anti-capitalist AMARGİ do not oppose the idea of projects and funding. Except

AMARGİ, the main source of funding is the EU such as the Delegation of EU to Turkey and the European Instrument for Democracy and Human Rights (EIDHR). However, we also come across different sources for some organizations as well as EU sources. For instance, Islamist BKP receives funding from Islamic Development Fund, which is a multilateral development financing institution located in Saudi Arabia and they give prominence to female empowerment. The Kurdish-feminist KAMER gets funding from Open Society Foundation and Swedish International Development Cooperation Agency, both of which have a reference to promotion of human rights and strengthening of democracy in Turkey. Indeed, most of the members of these organizations believe in the power and capacity of funded projects to enhance civil society and the women's movement more broadly. However, this discourse contracts when the women activists from these groups acknowledge the limitations of projects and funding, especially those provided by state authorities and international donor agencies. This is where the interdiscursivity between project-based civil society and the autonomy discourses emerges. Women activists using the project-based discourse indicate that receiving international funding does not threaten their autonomy as long as funding bodies do not try to regulate CSO spending in accordance with their own goals, priorities and activities. Those CSOs which exist to solely seek funding or to bend to the will of donor agencies and the state are described as 'fake' CSOs in contrast to the 'real' CSOs, which are seen as standing strong against donor and state pressure. While accepting the reality of donor funding, the women's discourses recognize the possible threat of the power of capital to shape civil society and to encourage funded CSOs to abandon any critical stance. At this point, AMARGİ has a different sensitivity from the other women's groups, who accept to be funded by international institutions as they show feminist concerns when they choose their funder. They accept to get funding from Global Dialogue, Mama Cash and Henrich Boll and they emphasize that these funding bodies are attentive to promotion of human rights and feminist activism. In this regard, women's project-based discourses extend beyond the dominant form of this discourse to include a reflexive critique of the marketization of CSOs.

Finally, the meaning of 'dialogue' is negotiated in the women's interviews. A few women from the feminist organization US do not accept the dominant discourse of dialogue because of its restricted content. A feminist woman from US whom I interviewed states that civil society should 'deliberate and, if required, argue with and against the state rather than only establishing a dialogue with it' (interview with Didem, 19 June 2012). On the basis of their experiences with the decision-makers in Turkey, Didem suggests that activists should deliberate with the state on specific matters so as to establish accountability between the state and CSOs. In this way, the boundaries of the dialogue discourse are extended. In such ways, my interviewees extend the scope of voluntarism, project- and dialogue-based civil society discourses, and effectively carve out a wider, more critical space for the voices and actions of CSOs.

Critical approaches to liberal civil society

Critiquing dominant civil society discourses

This section takes me to the critical engagement of the women's groups with dominant civil society discourses. Almost all participants in my study identify a range of problems with civil society in Turkey which threatens the understanding of an autonomous, voluntary, democratic and dialogue-based civil society, and they particularly criticize the authoritarian civil society discourse of the current AKP government. When women adopt a more thoroughly critical approach to the current state of civil society, they move beyond the compromise with dominant civil society discourses, characteristic of practices of negotiation, to stress the hollow nature of dominant discourses and the inability of CSOs to conform to the standards of good practices implied in these discourses. Specifically, women's groups emphasize the unwelcome divergence from autonomy and voluntarism; the lack of democratization in civil society; and the problems with dialogue, project-based relationships and the authoritarian civil society discourse of the post-2011 AKP period. I will deal with each of these points in turn.

First, the interviewees refer to the problems of civil society in the Turkish context as an undesired deviation from the autonomy and voluntarism discourses. They assert their immanent critique of the gap between the ideals of civil society contained within dominant discourses and the lack of commitment to these ideals in practice. Connectedly, they position women's organizations as more committed to these ideals than other CSOs and in this way they remove themselves from being implicated in their own critique. This manoeuvre is clear in their production of binary categorizations. Women's organizations are often situated within the realm of a genuine, voluntary civil society while interest-orientated organizations like trade unions are situated outside this category. Similarly, the authenticity of CSOs which are 'pro-government' or 'partisan' is scrutinized while those which are 'anti-government' or 'non-partisan' are deemed to be better able to fulfil the demands of a CSO. What is more, the self-positioning of the women's CSOs becomes more obvious when gender enters the discursive equation. Members of some women's groups suggest that women and women's organizations are crucial agents in the development of an autonomous civil society. With the exception of the anti-capitalist organizations, the women activists from all organizations foreground this idea about women's role in civil society and their ability to resist the male-dominated and interest-seeking characteristics of other CSOs. For instance, the Kemalist women envision women's organizations as taking on a special mission in civil society in terms of their particular organizational consciousness and role of enlightening society. This mindset is also used to uphold the voluntarism discourse by pointing out its gendered dimensions. Male-dominated, non-voluntary CSOs are viewed as suspect and framed as less genuine than women's organizations.

Thus while the women activists' immanent critique of the autonomy and voluntarism discourses is laudable, it does contain some inconsistencies and tensions of its own. It establishes divisions between women's groups. Within the realm of women's organizations, some are viewed as more genuine than others; those women's organizations founded by a small group for social purposes are contrasted with organizations struggling to protect women's rights and to enhance women's social status. Thus only some politically orientated women's organizations become 'the most genuine and proper' civil society actors. The creation of the binary categorizations also undermines the promotion of democracy which the women's organizations intend to support. To illustrate, the confrontational relationship between the Kemalist and Islamist women does not conform to the normative demands of the dominant democratization discourse. The Kemalist women portray the Islamist women's organizations as pro-government CSOs and are intolerant towards women wearing headscarves in the public sphere. Indeed, the Republican ideal of 'womanhood' is used as a barometer to evaluate the aims and activities of other women's organizations in civil society. Likewise, the Islamist women's organizations emphasize the juxtaposition of Kemalist women's organizations with the secularist political party, the CHP. What is problematic here is that through constructing binary categories which are then mapped onto other CSOs, the women activists in my study situate themselves and their CSOs as worthy of operating in a democratic civil society, while excluding others from this realm. This may bolster their own sense of power but impact on their relationships with other organizations, and signifies their ambition to create a 'pure' civil society inclusive of 'good' CSOs only.

The second manifestation of the critical engagement with dominant civil society discourse is in the women's insistence on the limits of 'democratization' on the dominant view. The democratization discourse is found to be particularly hollow by the women activists from the Kurdish organizations because, in their experience, democratic principles are not adhered to *within* civil society. This critique is informed by their first-hand experience of ethnic discrimination from other CSOs. For instance, the women activists from KAMER recalled how people from other organizations would refer to them as 'coming from the Eastern part of Turkey' (interview with Nuray, 16 May 2012) in meetings. More generally, the Kurdish women activists recalled how treatment of their ethnicity frequently made them feel like 'the other' and exposed the hierarchies within civil society. The critique here is that CSOs themselves may not endorse democratic values such as equality and non-discrimination, and this is a key factor undermining the democratization function of civil society. Indeed, this goes some way in explaining why the Kurdish women activists offer an inclusionary and non-discriminatory approach to civil society.

The third point of critique focuses on the dialogue-based relationship between civil society and the state in Turkey and how this manifests in an authoritarian tone particularly in the post-2011 AKP period. The interviewees assert that rather than establishing a 'dialogue-based' relationship with CSOs, the AKP government shows authoritarian attitudes to the CSOs in line with its authoritarian policies in other areas. Although the Islamist women have less problematic relations with the government, activists from all of the women's groups criticize the AKP government's exclusionary stance toward some CSOs and women's CSOs in the decision-making and policymaking processes. The extent of state acceptance of CSOs as proper negotiating partners is debated by most interviewees. For example, the Kemalist women criticize the dominant authoritarian civil society discourse of the AKP by calling attention to the marginalization strategies of successive AKP governments from the policy- and decision-making process, and the lack of state support for their facilities and projects. Marginalization is construed as blocking the Kemalist women's CSOs more generally from checking and shaping government policies. Similarly, as a feminist from KA-DER underlined, women's organizations which did not conform to government ideology were effectively excluded from the process. Likewise, despite more visibility in current times, the Islamist women show a common concern about the extent to which they are perceived as genuine negotiating partners by the government and the extent of their impact on policy. Even though they are aware that the AKP has been partisan towards some civil society groups, they continue to expect the state to accommodate real dialogue to support women-friendly policies only if sufficient pressure is applied to the state by CSOs. In this sense, the Islamist women in my study believe that CSOs have to become stronger to pressure the state into forming dialogue-based relationships.

Several activists that I interviewed explain that the AKP government's strategies of exclusion and marginalization are gender-based. Although some women's organizations support the dialogue discourse, what really stands in their way is the government's disrespect for women's CSOs in line with its authoritarian civil society discourse. In this regard, a group of women from the feminist organizations criticizes the exclusionary attitudes of the state towards particular women's organizations that do not think or work in line with the government's ideology. In the same vein, the women activists from the Islamist organizations refer to the different experiences of women and men in civil society and their participation in the policy and decision-making process. They highlight men's easier and wider access to funding networks than women's, as well as the unequal distribution of resources to organizations based on gender. Because of 'the dominance of the male point of view and the man's fear of losing the authority' (interview with Nurten, BKP, 9 August 2012), women in the CSOs can have some problems with the state institutions when conducting their projects. What is striking here is that the Islamist women explain the reason for the government's exclusionary attitude in terms of their identity as a woman or a women's organization rather than their Islamist/religious identity.

What I would like to highlight here is that despite several differences between the Kemalist and Islamist women, I see a significant commonality regarding their approach to the gendered dimensions of civil society. Although a few Kemalist and Islamist women put forth a gender critique, most do not, and overall, they tend to endorse gender norms. In other words, both pay little attention to the gendered features of civil society. These women are not sufficiently focused on the gender norms and hierarchies prevalent in civil society and they do not pose a discursive challenge to them; gender takes a secondary and relatively insignificant place in their civil society discourses. I would argue that established feminine and masculine roles in CSOs in Turkey, and more generally in the area of civil society, are not contested by the Kemalist and the Islamist women's organizations, and they ultimately fail to challenge patriarchy and women's subordination.

Resistance through challenging dominant civil society discourses

This section shows how women's civil society discourses oppose dominant autonomy, dialogue- and project-based civil society discourses. I argue that the women activists from almost all of the different political standpoints produce forms of opposition to the dominant discourses, question dominant views of civil society in Turkey, and call for the rethinking of the borders and meaning of civil society from women's point of view.

First, the very notion of 'autonomy' embedded in the dominant autonomy discourse is challenged by activists from the feminist KA-DER, Kurdish SELİS, anti-capitalist feminist SFK and Islamist BKP. To illustrate, for the women from SELİS, CSOs should have *absolute* independence from the state, as expressed in the quote from Gökten, member of SELİS, 'civil appears to me to be independent from power, from the governing forces' (interview, 24 May 2012). Bearing in mind the historical abuses of state power in Turkey, absolute independence implies being situated beyond the reach of state oppression and includes the demand that the state should respect CSO autonomy. Opposition to the dominant autonomy discourse takes a distinct form in the Islamist women's discourses, as they seek independence from Republican state ideology. In turn, they want to see the creation of alternative spaces in which the people can voice their issues and problems entirely unregulated by state ideology. Perhaps most radically, the women activists from anti-capitalist SFK resist the dominant autonomy discourse by reframing and redefining the understanding of autonomy as independence from the state, capital and men. Besides, civil society itself is regarded as one of the actors in the power terrain rather than merely functioning as a controlling and restraining agent on the state. Likewise, a feminist woman from KA-DER questions the dominant meaning of autonomy in terms of being above politics, and criticizes the voluntarism discourse as a key source of labour exploitation in CSOs (interview with Çiçek, 21 July 2012).

Second, the dominant dialogue-based civil society discourse is challenged by my interviewees. Kemalist women from TKB challenge the dialogue discourse by suggesting that civil society should adopt an anti-systemic character. As indicated previously, this was expressed by Tansu, a member of TKB, through her criticism of discourse which implies the 'inevitability of a close relationship between state and civil society', and her support for the view that 'civil societies should not have a relationship with the [political] power at all' (interview, 4 May 2012). In the same vein, Kurdish women activists from SELİS advocate building confrontational rather than dialogue-based relationships with the state. Both confrontational and anti-systemic arguments align with a sceptical attitude towards the notion that civil society is always a channel between the state and society and should behave as a negotiating partner with the state. SELİS members do articulate the importance of 'a civil pillar (*sivil ayak*)' – by referring to CSOs – functioning as a control mechanism on the state (interview with Ece, 15 May 2012). However, they highlight that this does not mean that relationships with the state are always dialogue-based and congruent; on the contrary, civil society should make no compromises to reflect its oppositional and critical character.

Moreover, some women from the feminist organizations, particularly US, oppose dominant dialogue-based discourse because of the way it masks the unequal power relationships between civil society and the state. In this sense, they argue that fear of being deprived of knowledge and resources only accessible through the state turns CSOs into negotiable partners. As touched upon previously, a woman participant from US, Didem, states that 'you cannot transform the things you want unless you integrate into the system; otherwise, the system reckons you as "the other"' (interview, 19 June 2012). This point is also referred to as one of the handicaps of civil society, which leads to a condition of 'not being able to reject power' (interview, 19 June 2012); that is, not being able to show an oppositional character to the system. However, those feminist women still suggest the possibility of transformation of the existing system from 'within', through being a part of civil society. A member of KA-DER similarly suggests that this transformation can be brought about by CSOs playing a radical rather than balancing role relative to the state. For the feminist women, dialogue-based discourse fails to admit the problematic outcomes of a desire to establish relations with the state; in particular, it masks the fact that partisan and non-partisan organizations are distinguished according to the unequal economic opportunities provided to each group by the state. This is presented as evidence for the fragmented and unequal civil society prevalent in Turkey.

Finally, the interviewees resist the dominant discourse of project-based civil society. They argue that civil society ought to be a non-marketized sphere, free of values which seek to instrumentalize relationships and promote a profit motive. In some ways, this resistance intersects with the women's autonomy discourse. For instance, some women activists from the Kemalist group TKB and feminist organization KA-DER voice opposition to projectism and funding because recipient organizations risk being regulated by donors and becoming dependent on donor funding. Çiçek, a member of the feminist organization KA-DER also highlights the necessity of not being funded by donors in order to maintain independence from the burdens of capital; in this sense, she thinks beyond the options of full or partial international funding articulated by other women's organizations (interview, 21 July 2012). Similarly, the activists from the anti-capitalist organization AMARGİ resist projectism. They argue that accepting funding forces recipient organizations to adopt the same language and framework as the funding organization, and effectively eliminates any discretion CSOs have when delivering their projects.

Interestingly, the Kurdish interviewees from SELİS do not link the project-based civil society discourse to the autonomy discourse, but instead critique funding and projectism as a part of power dynamics. The prevalence of funded projects is considered by these women to lead to the concentration of power in civil society, which consequently undermines its adversarial position. Furthermore, they argue that establishing relations of exchange as a priority of CSOs leads to members becoming alienated from their own labour and falling into the trap of pursuing a profit motive. In this context, resistance to project-based discourse stems from an unwavering anti-capitalist perspective.

The resistance of the interviewees in my study to particular dominant civil society discourses is complemented and deepened by their opposition to patriarchal relations in civil society. The Kurdish and feminist groups, along with the anti-capitalist AMARGİ, reveal the gendered nature and structure of civil society. To illustrate, Nuray, a member of KAMER, points to the dominance of masculine approaches in Turkish state institutions and CSOs, and suggests 'gender mainstreaming as a solution to this problems of civil society' (interview, 16 May 2012). Male dominance is recognized as part of a broader patriarchal social system. For the Kurdish women activists, the dominance of men's voices in decision-making processes in mixed groups is exasperating, and they stress that their aspirations for change stem from an equality-based approach. What is more, those CSOs which attribute traditional gender roles to women are called into question.

This critique of patriarchal relations, in particular, dovetails with a broader critique of hierarchy. The Kurdish activists, for example, point out that hierarchies are a source of domination which can be reproduced by men and women. They recognize that just as men exercise personal and structural power, women may have a capacity to dominate when they come to managerial positions. This is why the Kurdish women in my sample are critical of the constructed hierarchies in women's organizations which have significant leadership positions. In the same vein, the feminist organizations in my study frame hierarchical structures within women's organizations and CSOs as a significant and decisive problem of civil society, originating in the issue of representation in the CSOs. They argue that representation becomes problematic when it is illegitimately delegated to someone or a group of people to oversee work and deliver projects. In this sense, CSOs are contrasted with feminist organizations based on their hierarchical structure.

Furthermore, the issue of hierarchy also comes up when the possibility of feminist civil society is debated. Çiçek from KA-DER describes the task of integrating a feminist approach into civil society as 'difficult due to the dominance of hierarchies within and between the civil society organizations' (interview, 21 July 2012). However, there is, in my view, a positive and transformative role attached to the feminist movement itself, which is very active and independent in Turkey in terms of reinforcing women's organizations and differentiating them from the other CSOs. What is more, feminists that I interviewed suggest that women's organizations are model organizations for civil society because of their attempts to organize in non-hierarchical ways. Indeed, the women activists from AMARGİ do envision a non-hierarchical civil society if feminist goals are integrated, and, at the same time, patriarchal power structures and domination are challenged in CSOs. This discourse challenges the typical normative language used to frame civil society as an autonomous space which operates through voluntarism, and which functions as a channel between society and the state.

The rejectionist approach: Resistance through alternatives to civil society

Women's civil society discourses not only oppose dominant discourses but often seek to change them through rejecting civil society, and in this process alternative and transformative discourse emerges. I call this discursive move 'resistance through alternatives'. This form of resistance effectively advocates democratic mass organization or women's organization to replace civil society. Most obviously, anti-capitalist feminist organizations make this move since their resistance to civil society is accompanied by suggestions about ways of rethinking the concept of civil society and its relationship to feminist activism and politics. More specifically, they articulate two ways of thinking differently about civil society: advocacy of 'feminism' and advocacy of 'revolutionism'. According to this form of resistance, social transformation and emancipation cannot occur from within the realm of civil society and so it is essential to transcend the boundaries of civil society to achieve these aims.

For the first way of thinking, advocacy of feminism, the discourse of 'moving beyond civil society' attaches a positive and transformative meaning to the concept of politics and locates feminist politics beyond the space of civil society activism. Here, resistance is adopted against dominant liberal-democratic civil society discourses which, when taken together, are depoliticizing and non-feminist. A woman activist from AMARGİ claims that, the state, in the case of the AKP, 'needs civil society to be able to promote politics, to create hegemony ... I think the AKP is the one which uses it the best' (interview with Esra, 16 June 2012). Further, existing civil society is deemed to be non-political and cluttered with interest-based organizations which make demands on behalf of their own members to the neglect of broader social concerns. Likewise, project-based civil society discourse is resisted by anti-capitalist feminist women, particularly SFK, through emphasizing the position of civil society as a buffer zone between the state and market. They strongly support the independence of organizations from capital; they reject funding which leads to projectism and highlight the advantages of raising funds independently of the state, any organizations and/or any person.

By suggesting revolutionism as a term to identify their struggle, some feminist women from US and some anti-capitalist feminist women make a general challenge to the normative idea of civil society. To illustrate, these women pay attention to the instrumentalization of civil society due to it having become an agent of co-optation. In this context, they construct a dichotomous relationship between civil society and revolution. While the latter aims for political struggle, civil society is framed as a space that is depoliticized yet determined by enduring power relationships and oppressive institutional structures. This implies that a struggle to change the existing system 'from within' cannot be successful. Indeed, these women activists underscore the incapacity of civil society to form an oppositional bloc to dismantle existing power relationships and structures. By replacing the concept of civil society with revolutionism, some feminist women from US produce an alternative language to replace dominant civil society discourses.

These alternative approaches assume incompatibility of feminism with civil society. The women's organizations who advocate them do not go by the name of 'CSO' and, in fact, their 'non-CSO' features are emphasized. Instead, the women activists from SFK employ the term 'democratic mass organizations' and the women from AMARGİ use the term 'women's organization'. This subtle discursive strategy can be viewed as a way of resisting dominant images of CSOs as being above politics, and as offering expertise on a topic and representation of certain groups in society. These women do not see civil society as a space or an agent that should or could be reformed as it has already been co-opted by the state and political power. Currently, they support the language of 'feminist politics and women's organization' over 'civil society and CSOs'. For them, the concept of civil society is too closely associated with 'civil activism' and fails to offer any meaningful transformative politics.

Conclusion

This chapter set out to analyse the interdiscursive encounters between women's civil society discourses and dominant civil society discourses circulating in the Turkish context. I showed that the women's discourses engage with the dominant discourses in three ways, namely through (1) reflection and negotiation, (2) critique and (3) rejection.

Overall, I want to make three general arguments regarding interdiscursivity of the women's discourses and the dominant discourses. First, I argue that the women's groups are actively engaging with and contesting the dominant civil society discourses currently circulating in Turkey. That is to say, there are varying and sometimes contradictory continuities with and deviations from the dominant discourses, sometimes articulated within the same group. All (except women from the anti-capitalist feminist organizations), to varying degrees, mirror liberal pluralist, Western ideals of democracy and the role of civil society, specifically reproducing and/or negotiating with most of the current dominant discourses of autonomy, democratization, project-based civil society and dialogue in Turkey. In reflecting these discourses they universalize the Western, liberal model of civil society. In so doing, the activists demonstrate that they value and seek to promote the idea of liberal democracy and a strong and vibrant civil society. However, at the same time, all, to varying degrees and in different ways, they contest some components of the liberal-democratic, Western ideal and its institutionalization in Turkey. It is thus evident that, although the women are influenced by the structural factors such as donor policies through funding arrangements, they exercise significant agency in challenging the power and scope of state institutions (Tinker, 1999: 88), and in contesting mainstream notions of civil society. In Alvarez's (2009) terms, we should not overlook the agency of women's NGOs.

Second, women's articulations on civil society, to some extent, reinforce ideologically polarized and fragmented characteristics of Turkish civil society. For instance, women's differing approaches to voluntarism in civil society, identification of each other as pro-government/system, serve this purpose. Yet, these ideological divisions in the civil society sphere lessen when the issue of autonomy from the state and government enters the discussion. That is to say, they unite against the AKP governments' exclusionary attitudes to women's groups who are critical of them, despite ideological differences between them. Women from all groups except anti-capitalist groups highlight that state control of civil society should be eliminated because it is contrary to the freedom of civil society. Their assertion is that they benefit from sources and opportunities in a limited way, if they are not a pro-government CSO. The results underscore the problem of a state threat to the autonomy of civil society in the Middle East and how women activists are striving to preserve their independent stance when state conservatism increases, highlighted by Abdelrahman (2004), Dohle (2017), Moghadam (2003) and Pratt (2005). With an awareness of the critique of NGOization, I would suggest that women's NGOs are still important in Turkey as being a site of struggle against government control and the subordination of women. They still have a potential to be an arena for getting women's voices heard, particularly under anti-democratic and authoritarian conditions. As women activists emphasized, CSOs should be autonomous spheres for political struggle. Yet regarding this issue, due to the ideological divisions between them, the situation becomes much more difficult for them to listen to their concerns in a progressive manner. I consider that their common view around autonomy may provide the ground whereby they can surpass ideological divisions and jointly act for an autonomous civil society, which may contribute to mainstreaming women's rights in Turkey, albeit for the short term.

What is more, I would argue the critiques voiced by women activists, in general, and the rejectionist view, in particular, are important and merit further attention. Women activists from almost all of the groups (except the anti-capitalist SFK) indicate the ways in which relations and practices within civil society continually undermine the realization of normative ideals. They also challenge the gendered hierarchies and unequal power relationships that dominate the civil society by advocating women's and/or feminist politics. And the rejectionist approach, articulated by women from the anti-capitalist organization in my study, goes further by arguing for the replacement of civil society activism with feminist politics, as part of an alternative vision of a democratic Turkey, one that is less about adding women into civil society and more about foregrounding feminist agency. Despite the fact that it is articulated by a minority voice, this approach is important due to its explicitly feminist character and transformatory potential. It deserves to be more widely discussed within the women's movement in Turkey and among feminist scholars of civil society, as it points to the potential emergence of counter-hegemonic voices within civil society. In sum, in line with Pratt (2005), Abdelrahman (2004) and Kuzmanovic (2012), I would argue that the critical and rejectionist approaches of women activists are important for challenging the power relations that dominate civil society, and for creating new terms and language about civil society in the Turkish context.

7

Women's voices in civil society: Transformatory potential?

With the aim of contributing to theoretical discussions on civil society and its feminist critique, this book set out to explore how women's organizations in Turkey are affected by and responding to the site of civil society in the country, which was exposed to EU-driven reforms in 2000s but since 2011, to anti-democratic and authoritarian measures. More specifically, it asked two empirical questions: what are the main features of civil society discourses articulated by the women activists and what are the key factors shaping their articulation? Furthermore, in what ways and to what extent do these discourses reproduce and/or contest the dominant civil society discourses circulating in Turkey. To respond to these two questions, this book has focused on the Kemalist (TKB, TÜKD), Islamist (BKP, AKDER), Kurdish (KAMER, SELİS), feminist (KA-DER, US) and anti-capitalist (SFK, AMARGİ) women's organizations in Turkey.

This book has four main arguments. First, I have shown that women do not speak with one voice on civil society, rather, there is a multiplicity of women's discourses ranging from autonomy, voluntarism, mediation, democratization to (and, used to a lesser extent) opposition, anti-hierarchy and co-optation discourses. Second, ideology or the political standpoint of groups is important in shaping which discourses of civil society are articulated, and in what ways, but not determining. Women's organizations which diverge ideologically and politically in fact converge in their use of the same civil society discourses, and women who support the same political standpoint sometimes produce conflicting discourses. This means that civil society discourses circulate in complex ways in that they do not map neatly onto ideological group identities; several discourses may be used simultaneously by one organization, and some discourses cut across several organizations. In that light, I have suggested that factors such as funding, geographical location, organizational structure and the framing of women's rights and feminism also play a role in determining which discourse comes to the fore. Also, these factors are useful for explaining why discursive divergences occur within each political categorization. To illustrate, approach to funding shapes the women's civil society discourses in terms of the relationship between voluntarism and professionalism or how they approach to and define the site of civil society, while geographical location is a factor that explains why both Kurdish women's groups find common ground in the articulation of a democratization discourse which envisages a non-discriminatory civil society.

Third, I argue that the women's NGOs do not passively reproduce dominant discourses. True, they often mirror key tropes, with all except the women from the anti-capitalist feminist organizations, to varying degrees reflecting liberal pluralist, Western ideals of democracy and civil society, specifically reproducing the current dominant discourses of autonomy, democratization, project-based civil society and dialogue. In this, they still retain a normative commitment to the liberal ideal of civil society, with civil society represented as an active intermediary between society and state and envisioned as an independent space free from state regulation and ideological influence. These normative visions, however, are also used to critically evaluate the reality of contemporary civil society in Turkey, based on women's experiences of working within it. To illustrate, activists are critical of the interferences of government and/or funding agencies that undermine their organizational autonomy, and claim that it is increasingly difficult for them to act as an intermediary between the state and people in Turkey in the context of AKP marginalization of many women's groups. In this light, the activists I interviewed have had to negotiate with key elements of the dominant view, compromising on the meaning of voluntarism, dialogue and project-based civil society. And all the interviewees, to varying degrees and in different ways, contest some components of the liberal pluralist view of civil society and its institutionalization in Turkey. They do so by developing systematic critiques of the problems with mainstream theory and practice and attempting to resist these, pointing to, for example, the lack of meaningful autonomy, the harmfulness of projectism and insidious patriarchal hierarchies in civil society. I consider that particularly the women activists', apart from anti-capitalists, conceptualization of CSOs as autonomous spheres may surpass ideological divisions between them and jointly act for an autonomous civil society may contribute to mainstreaming women's rights in Turkey, albeit for a short term.

Fourth and finally, I suggest that both the critical and rejectionist approaches of women activists are significant for challenging power relations dominating civil society and for creating new terms for and language about civil society in the Turkish context. I want here to highlight particularly the rejectionist view adopted by the activists from anti-capitalist women's groups, and their articulation of an alternative vision of a democratic Turkey, one that is more about foregrounding feminist agency. I have claimed that this approach, despite the fact that this it is very much a minority voice, is important due to its explicitly feminist character and transformatory potential. It is thus worthy of further debate within the wider women's movement and of more attention from feminist scholars of civil society and others.

Wider implications on civil society, feminism and politics

What do the arguments above contribute to wider debates about civil society and among feminists? My book augments and sharpens the claims made in recent work paying attention to NGO activists' articulation of civil society in the Middle East region and in Turkey, as well as speaking to the literature on the women's movement in Turkey and to feminist theorizations of civil society.

To begin with, this book contributes to civil society literature by adding new insights to recent work on the construction of civil society by the women's NGOs, particularly in the Middle Eastern context. First of all, it specifically addresses that diversity and counter-hegemonic possibilities in the site of civil society are not unique to Egyptian context, as seen in the works of Pratt (2005) and Abdelraman (2004), but also found in Turkey. Abdelrahman (2004: 185) problematizes the dichotomy between Islam and secularism, by showing the differing approaches to civil society within both Islamic and secular NGOs (Abdelrahman, 2004: 185–90). This book shows that this phenomenon, to some extent, manifests also in the Turkish context, in that similarly diverse discourses of civil society can be found in both Kemalist and Islamist women's groups. In addition, I argue that the discourses of civil society that I identify often cut across women's groups, irrespective of their political standpoints. Turning to Pratt's study, she argues that Egyptian advocacy NGOs produce counter-hegemonic discourses in the form of arguments for autonomy and post-nationalism and in their critiques of patriarchy and neoliberal globalization (Pratt, 2005). This book emphasizes that some echoes of these arguments can be found in Turkey among women activists there, albeit the overall picture is more mixed. I find in some quarters a similar insistence on autonomy from the state and a hostility to Turkish nationalism, to patriarchy and to neoliberalism, but the context for and the content of these claims are very different from the Egyptian case. For example, a critique of Turkish nationalism is put forward particularly by Kurdish SELİS women, but not in a post-nationalist way given their simultaneous advocacy of Kurdish self-determination. Also, these counter-hegemonic dimensions of the discourses of women's organizations in Turkey are tempered by some mirroring of dominant liberal views of civil society. So even if there are some counter-hegemonic possibilities here meriting further attention, as argued earlier, I would not conclude about Turkey, as Pratt does about Egypt, that there is evidence of the emergence of a nascent, unified counter-hegemonic project.

This book also contributes to the recent works on the construction of civil society in Turkey by women's groups. On the one hand, my research adds breadth to these studies because it casts a wider net empirically by collecting both interview and documentary data from forty-one women activists from ten different women's organizations in Turkey, representing a wide range of political orientations. Most obviously, it enables me to show that women's groups in Turkey are more diverse in their discourses than previously acknowledged. Leyla Kuzu's focus on liberal and feminist contributions to civil society, for example, misses the distinctive articulations of Kemalist, Kurdish and Islamist women's groups. While these political perspectives are acknowledged in Çaha's research, he gives only cursory attention to anti-capitalist perspectives absorbing them under the wider category of feminism and thus missing the ways in which, as I have shown, anti-capitalist and feminist groups differ in their approaches to civil society. In addition, this book reveals the ways in which women's discourses of civil society cut across these ideological categories and also that women within such categories may articulate multiple and sometimes contradictory views. This is a corrective to, for example, Çaha's conclusion that Kemalist views are entirely incompatible with a plural and open civil society and Kemalist women have 'ceased to be a component of civil society' (2013, 60–1). Rather, my work shows that there is some variety of views among Kemalist women and that they are actively seeking to construct civil society. Moreover, I argued that there is a convergence between the approaches of Kemalist and Islamist women.

On the other hand, I cast a more critical light on the relationship between women and civil society than the current research because of my focus on encounters between women's civil society discourses and dominant narratives circulating in Turkey. For most of the women activists in my study, civil society is not unproblematically good and beyond critique. Some also argue for the transformative power of the discourses, demands and needs of women's CSOs. However, a few of them (the anti-capitalists) do not endorse the normative value of civil society, while others (Kemalist, Islamist) adopt an approach to civil society that is not transformative, and thus reproducing gender inequality rather than challenging it. These women's concepts of civil society neglect or reify gendered hierarchies or privilege certain kinds of women only. In other words, they neglect gendered distributions of power that have a direct impact on access to civil society and decision-making power within it. This is in contrast to most of the women from the Kurdish, feminist and anti-capitalist feminist groups, who seek to challenge gender inequalities within civil society and identify them with male-dominance, hierarchy and as barriers to emancipation. In sum, this book highlights that we see a more complex and less idealized picture of the relation of the women's movement in Turkey to civil society than the current studies offered.

Beyond the focus on civil society, my book also makes a contribution to the broader scholarship on the women's movement in the country. One cannot assume, as analysts have tended to do, that the women's movement is fragmented along predictable and rigid ideological lines. For instance, like many others, Marshall (2009) categorizes the women's movement in Turkey in terms of political orientation such as Kemalist, Kurdish, Islamist and feminist. I too use these categorizations as my starting point, but I go on to show that there are various forms of intersections between the women's discourses originating from these different political standpoints, with for example, women activists from all political positions apart from the anti-capitalist one producing autonomy, mediation and voluntarism discourses in line with liberal and Western-based approaches. This points to the fact that discourses transcend political distinctions within the women's movement. Further, my research suggests that factors other than ideology contribute to women's civil society discourses, such as their relationship to funding, geographical location, organizational structure and framing of women's rights and feminism. This indicates the need to review the way women's organizations are typically categorized, and to question the assumption that divisions along ideological fault lines are determining of differences between groups.

Finally, my research has conceptual ramifications for feminist critique of civil society. In contrast to the strand of feminist scholarship which dismisses a focus on civil society as a strategy of little value for challenging hierarchical relations between gender and power (e.g. Jaggar, 2005; Pateman, 1988, 1989; Phillips, 1987, 1999, 2002), my findings lend weight to the alternative feminist view that engagement is unavoidable and can be positive (Arat, 1994; Eto, 2012; Hagemann, Michel and Budde, 2008; Howell, 2006, 2007; Rabo, 1996). Instead of criticizing outright the participation of women's NGOs in civil society and assuming incompatibility between civil society and feminism, we ought instead to remember that civil society is a contested terrain and pay respectful scholarly attention to ways in which women negotiate and contest the complex processes of its construction. What is more, even where some feminist and anti-capitalist feminist organizations assume an incompatibility between feminism and civil society, their critique or rejectionist approach to civil society should prompt the rethinking of the theory and practice of civil society from a feminist perspective, not its outright dismissal. Only by taking into account more substantive critiques coming from a range of specific contexts, dominant civil society discourses can be challenged in scholarship and by civil society activists.

Prospects for further research

In terms of further research, there is certainly potential for a large-scale, Turkish-specific study focusing on the civil society discourses of mixed-gender organizations with diverse agendas, ranging from environmental to youth organizations. The aim here would be to shed light on how men and women understand and practise being in civil society and to determine if they are aware of gender divisions and inequalities within civil society and within CSOs in Turkey. Exploring what activists understand by 'gender' would be a basic but essential aspect of such a study. Given what I found in my research about the rather loose ties between political standpoint and civil society discourse, it would be fruitful to examine how a wider range of organizations envision civil society in relation to the state and market, and the extent to which they reproduce and challenge gender identities and relations in Turkish society. Most obviously, this would enable a comparative analysis of how men and women understand civil society in Turkey and would contribute to existing feminist literature on gendering of civil society.

More broadly, there is also scope for further comparative research between different countries. This book focused on Turkey; however, my research provides a platform for undertaking comparative research on Turkey and other countries from the Middle East or Eastern Europe or Latin America, where the concept of civil society has also gained prominence since the 1990s. Given that Turkey has been a laboratory for Europeanization and modernization, as well as Islamization and conservatization, it would be worthwhile to compare the experiences and views of women in civil society in Turkey with those of women in other countries from different geographies experiencing similar processes. Indeed, comparative research of this sort may well enable women's organizations from different continents and regions to learn from one another; collecting and sharing such experiences and perspectives may help them better pursue their normative goals and projects. Such comparative work could also reveal the cross-border networks of solidarity and cooperation that women's organizations create in order to challenge the gendered and sexist ideas and practices of civil society.

In particular, there is great potential for up-to-date comparative work on Turkey and other countries from the Middle East, in the wake of both the so-called Arab Spring and the Gezi Park protests. The former took place throughout 2011 and has been widely perceived as an 'outcome of civil activism' and an 'awakening of civil society' (Boose, 2012; Cavatorta, 2012: 75–6; Valliatanos, 2013). The Gezi Park protests took place in late May and early June 2013 in Turkey against the demolition of a park in Istanbul and construction in its place of a shopping mall, and soon turned into massive street demonstrations against the AKP, particularly the rising authoritarianism of Prime Minister Erdoğan (Bilgiç and Kafkaslı, 2013: 8) in cities across Turkey. Although commentators were initially optimistic about the Arab Spring, critiques have been mounting in the context of counterrevolution and civil war (see Hardig, 2014), and it is still perhaps too early to know the implications of the Gezi Park protests for civil society. So political conditions in the country and across the region continue to change rapidly, pointing to the need for the continual updating of research into movements in the Middle East, including in Turkey. Overall, then, the research presented here needs to be seen as a small part of a much bigger and still ongoing conversation about the efforts of movements like the women's movement in Turkey to respond to dominant power relations and to articulate alternative possibilities.

In 2010, CEDAW Shadow Report of Turkey, women's NGOs underscored that 'the already acquired legal rights of women are subject to backlash and efforts that aim to eradicate existing discriminations are usually met with resistance' and complained about the lack of dialogue with the state institutions (CEDAW, 2010: 3). It is obvious that this point is still pertinent as expressed scholarly that the state co-opts Islamist women's NGOs in Turkey and marginalizes the others (see Doyle, 2017; Negron-Gonzales, 2016). Importantly, after the 2016 coup d'état attempt, we have seen closure of CSOs/women's CSOs, not only the ones linked to the Gülen movement but also the dissidents. At this point, there remains a lack of studies on to what extent and in what ways these current changes reflect on the area of civil society in general and women's organizations in particular. Empirical studies would be beneficial to conduct in order to take a snapshot of the current situation in Turkey in terms of women activists.

Appendix: Profile of interviewees

Name of the Group	Location	No. of Participants	Name	Education Level	Organizational Position	Employment Status	Age	Date of Interview
TKB	Ankara	4	Sevda	Bachelor	President	Lawyer	61	8 May 2012
			Lale	Bachelor	Member of executive committee	Civil servant	43	7 May 2012
			Buket	Bachelor	Member of disciplinary board	Civil servant (retired)	48	10 May 2012
			Tansu	High School	Member	Self-employment (retired)	65	4 May 2012
TÜKD	Ankara	3	Nurdan	Bachelor	President	Lawyer	46	29 June 2012
			Sevim	Bachelor	Vice president	Instructor (retired)	58	28 June 2012
			Pınar	PhD	Member of executive committee	Working in a political party	64	30 June 2012
AKDER	Istanbul	5	Perihan	MSc	General Secretary	Employee of the association	29	5 July 2012
			Birsen	Bachelor	Member	Psychological advisor	28	6 July 2012
			Hale	Bachelor	Member of executive committee	Doctor	34	9 July 2012
			Göknur	MSc	Member	Civil servant	35	11 July 2012
			Yasemin	Bachelor	Member of executive committee	Doctor	35	13 July 2012
BKP	Ankara	5	Serpil	PhD	Member of executive committee	Columnist	49	1 August 2012
			Ayşe	MSc	Vice president	Not working	47	7 August 2012

Name of the Group	Location	No. of Participants	Name	Education Level	Organizational Position	Employment Status	Age	Date of Interview
			Nurten	Bachelor	Member of executive committee	Not working	42	9 August 2012
			Cemile	High School	Member	Civil Servant (retired)	49	2 August 2012
KAMER	Diyarbakır Batman	5	Begüm	PhD	President	Lecturer (retired)	51	1 August 2012
			Tülin	University student	President of the Batman branch	Employee of the foundation	43	18 May 2012
			Nuray	Bachelor	President	Employee of the foundation	57	16 May 2012
			Sevda	Bachelor		Employee of the foundation	25	20 May 2012
			Derya	High School		Employee of the foundation	41	17 May 2012
			Seda	High school		Employee of the foundation	52	2 June 2012
SELİS	Diyarbakır	3	Ece	Bachelor	President	Lawyer	24	15 May 2012
			Gökten	Bachelor	Member	Teacher	38	24 May 2012
			Reşide	Bachelor	Member	Civil Servant	27	22 May 2012
US	Ankara	3	Didem	Bachelor	General secretary	Employee of the association	55	19 June 2012
			Fulya	Bachelor	Member of the executive committee	Employee of the association	37	21 June 2012
			Emel	MSc candidate	Member	Employee of the association	26	26 June 2012

Name of the Group	Location	No. of Participants	Name	Education Level	Organizational Position	Employment Status	Age	Date of Interview
KA-DER	Istanbul	3	Rezan	MSc	President	Translator	55	18 July 2012
			Selda	MSc	Member	Engineer (retired)	62	22 July 2012
			Çiçek	Bachelor	No membership	Employee of the association	32	21 July 2012
SFK	Istanbul	5	Burcu	Bachelor	Member	Engineer	37	30 May 2012
			Feyza	MSc candidate	Member	Student	28	31 May 2012
			Bilge	Bachelor	Member	Ceramist	56	15 June 2012
			Elçin	Bachelor	Member	Lawyer	29	23 July 2012
			Zeynep	PhD candidate	Member	Project officer in a different organization	30	26 June 2012
AMARGİ	Istanbul	5	Duygu	Bachelor	Member	Teacher	50	2 June 2012
			Burçak	Bachelor	Member	Teacher	33	2 July 2012
			Betül	Bachelor	Member	Project officer in a different organization	24	15 June 2012
			Esra	MSc	Member	Project officer (part-time)	26	16 June 2012
			Eda	High School	Member	Performer	43	3 July 2012
		41 (total)						

Notes

1 Civil society and women's NGOs: Feminist reactions

1 For critical voices to contemporary dominance of a neoliberal version of civil society, see the following: Beckman (1997); Charlton and May (1995); Carothers and Ottoway (2000); Clarke (1998); Dvoráková (2008); Encarnación (2002); Fisher (1997); Mercer (2002); Lewis (2001); van Rooy (1998) and Altan-Olcay and İçduygu (2012)

2 For further critical discussion of the gendered bias of civil society, see the following: Pateman (1988, 1989); Fraser (1992); Benhabib (1992); Howell (2006, 2007); Howell and Mulligan (2003, 2005); Hagemann, Michel and Budde (2008); Phillips (1999, 2002); Stevenson (2005); Young (2000); Weldon (2005); and Eto (2012).

3 For instance, see Krause (2008, 2012); Al-Mughni (1997); Al-Ali (2003); and Al-Ali and Pratt (2011) and Rabo (1996).

4 Some of the feminist scholars working on these topics are Arenfeldt and Golley (2012); Chatty and Rabo (1997); Jad (2004, 2007); Kandiyoti (1991, 2011a), Moghadam (1997, 2002, 2003); Göçek and Balaghi (1994).

5 Some of the studies which focus on this issue are Landig (2011); Göksel and Güneş (2005); Baç (2005); Tocci (2005); Keyman and İçduygu (2003); Ergun (2010); Sirman (2006); Üstündağ (2006); Kabasakal Arat (2006); Alemdar and Çorbacıoğlu (2010); Kuzmanovic (2012); and Bora (2011).

6 The formal enhancement of women's status was integral to the secularization process (Seçkinelgin, 2004: 175). The establishment of 'state feminism' and 'state controlled gender discourse' was the outcome of this process (Kardam, 2005: 39). State feminism aimed to promote the rights of women in public life through state policies (Tekeli, 1986; Seçkinelgin, 2004). Kabasakal Arat (1994: 74) argues that Kemalist reforms cannot be characterized as 'state feminism' since to be able to identify any movement as feminist it has to perceive 'gender inequalities and male domination' and has to act towards defeating domination. On the contrary, according to Tekeli (1981 in Tekeli, 1986: 184–5), 'the new rights given to women by the secular republicans carried a symbolic meaning in their fights against the religious authority that formed the legal basis of the previous Ottoman state'. From the state's perspective, model Republican women would 'get an education and pursue a career and were expected simultaneously to be attentive and

well-trained mothers' (White, 2003: 146; see also Sirman, 1988). In other words, the Kemalist understanding of gender equality did not lead to equality for all but rather created a group of elite women, known as Kemalist women, who got a chance to have an education and to work professionally (Kardam, 2005: 40). Thus women who were uneducated, rural and who understood Islam as a way of life were excluded from many citizenship rights. This mindset remained dominant throughout the 1950s and 1960s, although there were some initiatives to close the rift between urban and rural places for the sake of women (Çaha, 2013: 54–5).

7 It was against this backdrop that the first women's party, the Women's People Party (Kadınlar Halk Fırkası), was established in 1923 by Nezihe Muhiddin. With the closure of this party, the Turkish Women's Union was formed in 1924. In 1926, gender equality was formally guaranteed by the promulgation of the Swiss Civil Code. Practically, this meant that polygamy was abolished, women were granted equal rights of divorce, and women were given the right to vote and run in municipal elections in 1930 and in the general election in 1934 (Kandiyoti, 1989: 126; see also Arat, 1994). For Kandiyoti (1989: 126), these reforms indicated 'a new positioning of the state vis-à-vis the woman question' although they did not significantly affect the position of women in the rural areas.

8 In these years, women's and feminist groups were striving to eliminate violence against women, the oppression that women experienced in the family, 'the use of sexuality as a medium for male dominance, the misinterpretation of women in the media and the challenge against virginity tests' (Diner and Toktaş, 2010: 41). In 1987, feminists organized 'the Women's Solidarity March Against Gender-based Violence, the first major feminist rally of the second wave women's movement and the first mass political demonstration of post coup d'état Turkey' (Altınay and Arat, 2009: viii).

9 The WB has had a programme for promoting capacity building of civil society in Turkey. Similarly, the UN has had a significant influence on civil society in Turkey since the NGO and Foundations Forum organized in 1996 at the UN Habitat II Conference. This was crucial for establishing and mobilizing social actors in Turkey (Kuzmanovic, 2012: 14).

10 Examples of legislative reforms include the Civil Code (2001), the Penal Code (2004), the New Labour Law (2003), the new Social Security and General Health Insurance Law (2006), and the Law on Family Protection and Preventing Violence against Women (6284 sayılı Ailenin Korunması ve Kadına Karşı Şiddetin Önlenmesine Dair Kanun, 2012). Implementation of CEDAW, ratified in 1985, was another important outcome of the EU adaptation process for women's rights in Turkey (Çaha, 2013: 67).

11 In the Turkish context, I prefer to use women's CSO rather than women's NGO due to the women activists' preference to be called as a CSO rather than an NGO.

12 The Ergenekon and Balyoz trials, the KCK (Kurdish Democratic Confederation) operations, the silencing of the media, the imprisonment of dissenting journalists, academics, students and intellectuals, and govenment interventions in the editorial policies of newspapers and television channels are examples of AKP authoritarianism (Tolunay, 2014).

13 In October 2008, Prime Minister Erdoğan declared that 'each women should have at least three children' (Hürriyet, 2008). In May, 2012, the Erdoğan government stated that they were working on a bill to ban abortion after four weeks rather than the current ten weeks of pregnancy, apart from in emergency cases. Abortion, which became legal in 1983, was one of the most important outcomes of the women's movement in Turkey. Therefore, immediately after the AKP's declaration, the women's organizations in Turkey formed a platform called 'Abortion is a Right and the Decision Belongs to the Woman' and organized a pro-choice rally in the city centres of Istanbul, Adana, Mersin, İzmir, Diyarbakır, Çanakkale, Sinop, Antalya, Eskişehir, Van, Ankara and Sakarya to protest the ban. After the protests, even though the AKP government took a step back, they continued working on the Bill of Reproductive Health (Radikal, 2012). Today, although abortion is not banned legally, public hospitals have been implementing a de facto ban since Erdoğan's statement on abortion. As recent research conducted by Kadir Has University (2016: 5) shows, abortion has been almost banned unlawfully in Turkey.

14 For more on Gülen movement, see Walton (2013) and Seufert (2014).

15 The different approaches to democracy can be grouped into two: minimalist-complex procedural definitions (e.g. Dahl, 1989; Diamond, 1994; Schumpeter, 2003) and substantive definitions (e.g. Barber, 1984; Phillips, 1993).

16 Further, explaining why power is relational, Foucault writes, 'resistance is never in a position of exteriority in relation to power ... its existence depends on a multiplicity of points of resistance' (1978: 95).

17 Reflecting the influence of Fairclough (2001: 229), some FCDA studies have used the term 'semiosis' to define meaning-making through not only written and spoken language but also through body language and visual images.

18 I choose to use the term Islamist to label these women by following Arat (2016: 126), defining them as a 'heterogeneous group who prioritize shaping their lives according to Islamic dictates and are vocal on this choice'.

19 Women's organizations in my pilot study are ANGİKAD (Business Women Entrepreneurs and Enhancement Association), US (Flying Broom), AKDER (Women's Rights Organization against Discrimination), BKP (Capital City Women's Platform Association), ÇKD (Republican Women Association), TKB (Turkish Women's Union), GİKAP (Rainbow İstanbul Women Organizations'

Platform), Kadın Dayanışma Vakfi (Foundation for Women's Solidarity) and SFK (Socialist Feminist Collective).

20 See, for example, Esim and Cindoğlu (1999); Sancar and Bulut (2006); Coşar and Onbaşı (2008); Marshall (2009); Diner and Toktaş (2010) and Fisher Onar and Peker (2012).

21 It is important to note that Kurdish women may have different political orientations. Yet, the main reason why these women formed KAMER and SELİS is related to the struggle for establishing 'a separate women's movement out of the Kurdish movement contending with the oppression that Kurdish women face has emerged' (Diner and Toktaş, 2010: 48). Within that framework, Kurdish women's groups may vary in their ideological positions as can be seen in my research. Whereas SELİS highlights that it is a member of the Democratic Free Women's Movement (DÖKH), KAMER emphasizes that it is an independent women's group. More concretely, in the context of partnering with DÖKH, SELİS ran four campaigns, one of them titled 'Freedom to Öcalan – who is the leader of the Kurdistan Worker's Party (PKK), stop political massacre (Öcalan'a özgürlük, siyasi soykırıma son)'. However, KAMER rejects the idea that it is close to any kind of political organization. What is more, in contrast to SELİS, KAMER 'works with women of all groups, including but not limited to Kurdish, Turkish, Arab, Sunni, and Alevi' (Altınay and Arat, 2015: 16).

22 I used ideology interchangeably with political orientation, which is more in line with the approach of 'a system of collectively held normative and reputedly factual ideas and beliefs and attitudes advocating a particular pattern of social relationships and arrangements and/or aimed at justifying a particular pattern of conduct, which its proponents seek to promote, realize, pursue or maintain' (Hamilton, 1987: 38). But as depicted in FCDA, ideology and discourse are not interchangeable concepts and are not reducible to each other; however, they are relational in that discourse may be shaped by and articulated by not only political viewpoints but also other factors, and vice versa.

23 A member of SELİS explains that some feminist organizations in Turkey, such as VAKAD, openly declare that they are not representative of Kurdish women and so they seek to differentiate themselves on that basis (interview with Ece, SELİS, 15 May 2012).

24 DÖKH was founded by twenty women's organizations in 2003 as an umbrella organization with the aim of building a gender-focused, democratic, ecological and non-sexist society (Alınteri, 2009). The member organizations of DÖKH include SELİS, DİKASUM, KARDELEN Kadın Evi, KARDELEN Kadın Kooperatifi, EPİDEM, Bağlar Kadın Kooperatifi, CEREN Kadın Derneği and CEREN Danışma Merkezi. KAMER is not a member of DÖKH.

25 I am aware that some women activists in the Kemalist, Islamist and Kurdish groups may also identify themselves as feminist.

26 Social welfare organizations are tax-exempt and state support is given to promote public welfare. There are other rights and prerogatives applied to them (see Dernekler Dairesi Başkanlığı, 2013; Yalçın and Öz, 2011).

27 AKDER has not been awarded EU funding despite repeated attempts to secure EU grants (interview with Perihan, AKDER, 5 July 2012).

2 Civil society and NGOs: Theories, applications and feminist critique

1 See, for example, Carothers and Ottoway (2000); Edwards (2004); Beckman (1997); Lewis (2001); and Chandoke (2005).

2 Also see Carothers (1999); Carothers and Ottoway (2000); Comaroff and Comaroff (1999); Killingsworth (2012); and Hagemann (2008).

3 The social uprising of the so-called Arab Spring, which took place in 2011 in the Arab countries, has been perceived as an 'outcome of civil activism' and an 'awakening of civil society' (Cavatorta, 2012: 75–6; Boose, 2012; Valliatanos, 2013). It is widely accepted that the Arab Spring represents a considerable growth in grassroots activism and the formation of social movements in the region. In Tunisia, for example, informal networks of activists initiated the demonstrations but were soon joined by formal trade unions and professional associations, who played a key role in organizing the revolt. The success of these groups in overthrowing Ben Ali had an immediate knock-on effect in Egypt, inspiring civil society opposition groups to organize popular political action and demonstrations involving an unexpectedly high number of participants (Dalacoura, 2012: 64). Although the uprisings have been widely seen as a way of showing opposition to the neoliberal projects of dictatorships in Arab countries, it is still too early to judge their success or surmise their long-term consequences, particularly in the light of reaction and war in the region. Furthermore, the diversity of protests and demonstrations in different contexts across the region at the time should not be overlooked, as 'the 'Arab' world is not a unified entity' (Dalacoura, 2012: 63); nor should the 'contentious' and 'collaborative' relations between state and civil society actors be disregarded (Hardig, 2014: 1136).

4 For example, see the studies of Norton (1995); Eddin Ibrahim (1995) and Al-Sayyid (1993).

5 For a critical evaluation of Personal Status Law, see Al-Ali (1997); Zaki (1995); Abdelrahman (2004); and Wiktorowicz (2000).

6 Scholars in this camp include Abdelrahman (2004); Joseph and Slyomovics (2001); Nefissa (2005); Pratt (2005); Wiktorowicz (2000); and Zubaida (1992).

7 The Gezi Park Protests began on 27 May 2013 with a demonstration in Gezi Park near Taksim Square in İstanbul. The demonstration started as an environmentalist protest, organized under the Taksim Dayanışması (Taksim Solidarity) with 128 constituents of civil society organizations, against the felling of trees, the demolition of the park and the construction of a shopping mall in its place. However, it transformed into massive protests against the AKP over the course of a couple of days, and spread to other cities in Turkey. The rising authoritarianism of Prime Minister Erdoğan was seen as the key reason for the emergence of the protests, as well as the disproportionate force used by the police, the infringement of democratic rights and the restriction of civic freedoms (Bilgiç and Kafkaslı, 2013: 8).

8 For example, see Navaro-Yashin (1998a, 1998b); Abdelrahman (2004); Al-Ali (2004); Pratt (2005); Jad (2004); Cavatorta and Durac (2011); and Krause (2008, 2012).

9 There are two ways of reading the history of modernization in Turkey. On the one hand, the establishment of the Turkish Republic represents a discontinuity from the Ottoman legacy because of its aim to reform the political and cultural norms and codes prevalent under the rule of the Ottoman Empire. On the other hand, despite the foundation of the Republic, there was continuity from the Ottoman Empire to the Republic in terms of political, economic and ideological aims from 1908 to 1950 (Zürchrer, 1997: 3; see also Mardin, 2006). More in line with the discontinuity argument, Turkish modernizers tend to identify modernization with Westernization (Rumford, 2002: 259; see also Mardin, 1991; Lewis, 2002). Westernization via state-imposed reforms has been regarded by commentators as one of the main characteristics of Turkish history (Navaro-Yashin, 2002: 10).

10 The work of Kaliber and Tocci (2010) is interesting in drawing attention to an unresearched area, the role and impact of Turkish and Kurdish civil society actors on the Kurdish question.

11 Supporters of this approach include, among others, Keyman (2005); Keyman and İçduygu (2003); Gündüz (2004); Aydın and Keyman (2003); Heper (1985); Göle (1994); Robins (1996); and Çaha (2013).

12 Some of the scholars working on this topic are: Ketola (2010, 2011, 2013); Tocci (2005); Bayraktar (2009); Çaylak (2008); Keyman and İçduygu (2003); Alemdar and Çorbacıoğlu (2010).

13 In accordance with the legal amendments, in 2009, Committee on Equality for Women and Men was established to improve women's rights and to promote

gender equality as an authorized body of Turkey Grand National Assembly (Güneş-Ayata and Doğangün, 2017: 613).

14 See Arat (2010) for a detailed discussion on Civil Code Amendments.

15 As Squires (2003: 132) highlights, although the 'state' and the 'personal' are respectively located in 'public' and 'private' spheres, there is some confusion about where civil society ought to be placed. The classification that I employ here to discuss feminist critiques of civil society reflects this confusion. In this regard, civil society is 'cast as private when opposed to the state … and public when opposed to the personal' (Squires, 2003: 132).

16 See, for example, Arat (1994); Waylen (1994); Young (2000); Howell and Mulligan (2003, 2005); Howell (2006, 2007); Hagemann, Michel and Budde (2008); Eto (2012); Çaha (2006, 2010, 2013); Rabo (1996); Chatty and Rabo (1997); Moghadam (2002); and Leyla (2011).

17 See, for example, Krause (2008, 2012); Al-Mughni (1997); Al-Ali (2003); Al-Ali and Pratt (2011).

18 Similarly, Kandiyoti (1991: 1) engages with the category of 'Muslim women' and criticizes both Western orientalists and Muslim feminists and scholars for their 'ahistorical and ethnocentric depictions of Muslim societies', which prevent them from explaining crucial divergences in conditions for women, both within and across Muslim societies.

19 The literature on women's NGOs and civil society in CEE can be divided in two main camps: on the one hand, harsh critics demonstrate the repercussions of a 'feminism-by-design' and argue that NGOization in CEE is primarily shaped by a Western logic of neoliberalism and competitive democracy (see Ghodsee, 2011), and on the other hand, there are others suggesting a deeper analysis of women's NGOs which reveal a more political and grassroots picture of women's movement than it is claimed (see Einhorn and Sever, 2003; Helms, 2014).

20 For a discussion on NGOization in South Africa and Asia, please see the studies of Hassim (2005); Hassim and Gouws (1998) and Nagar (2011).

21 For NGOs, being autonomous has also been an important discussion beyond the Middle East (see Howell and Pearce, 2001). Howell and Mulligan (2005) highlight the necessity of being autonomous for women's organizations. In this volume, Tripp (2005) gives a general account on the African context by emphasizing the weaknesses of postcolonial states of the continent and the democratization and autonomy of women's NGOs made possible by donors. Rios-Tobar (2005) has a more critical perspective regarding autonomy in the Latin American context in that the professional NGOs, which dominate civil society after the Chilean transition to democracy, have turned feminist groups from activist social movements into interest and advocacy groups.

3 The sociopolitical context in Turkey: Official dominant civil society discourses

1 However, Çaha (2013: 29) mentions 'four potential elements of civil society in Ottoman-Turkish politics as the millet system, the guilds, the religious institutions and the system of the local notables (ayan). However, each of these institutions was overwhelmingly dependent on the state'. Women in Ottoman society also became important figures of civil society in spite of the restrictions that were placed on women in domestic life. Women were playing a leading role in the founding of religious institutions, which focus on diverse social issues (32).

2 The Republican People's Party, whose founder and chief is Mustafa Kemal Atatürk, declared itself as a political party on 29 October 1923. It can be identified as a Kemalist and social democratic party.

3 Many members of the DP were arrested during the coup, and the leader of the party, Adnan Menderes and two other party members, were executed.

4 The Justice Party was established as a right-wing party after the 1960 coup d'état by the supporters of the DP, which was disbanded by the military junta. It was also dissolved after the 1971 coup.

5 The Motherland Party is a centre-right party established in 1983 by Turgut Özal.

6 Kurdish people make up almost 20 per cent of the population in Turkey: Eleven to fifteen million out of a total population of around seventy-four million (Updegraff, 2012: 119).

7 To know more detailed discussion on Turkey's EU accession process since the Ankara Agreement, see *Fifty Years of EU–Turkey Relations: A Sisyphean Story*, edited by Armağan Emre Çakır.

8 A turban is rather different from the traditional headscarf, which is 'the style of donning of the headscarves to cover the head, neck, ears, and the shoulders of women' (Kalaycıoğlu, 2009).

9 Although they rejected this claim as 'leaders of the party have emphasized that they have broken away from the Milli Görüş' tradition of the Refah Party (Çıtak and Tür, 2008: 215), the AKP's organic links with this tradition have been obvious since the establishment of the party. This differentiates the AKP from former centre-right parties (Özman and Coşar, 2007: 455).

10 In 2013, the number of CSOs in Turkey, comprising associations, foundations, trade unions, chambers and cooperatives, reached 248,875. Of these, 99,230 are active and 149,645 are annulled which indicates that many CSOs are short lived (Dernekler Dairesi Başkanlığı, 2013). Today, as of December 2017, this number has decreased to 112,000 associations and 5,054 new foundations (established after the Republic) operating along with many informal organizations such as platforms, initiatives, and groups (ICNL, 2018).

11 It is important to emphasize that the use of civil society by EU institutions is not 'uniform'; however, it basically links to 'organised civil society'. A broad range of nongovernmental actors such as 'associations of business, trade unions, professionals, citizens organizations or cause groups' are labelled as civil society organizations (Kohler-Koch, 2010b: 1120). Additionally, at the institutional level, while the European Parliament and the Council are not so concerned about the notion of civil society, the European Commission and the Economic and Social Committee have played a key role in shaping the civil society discourse in the EU.

12 The EU grants provided to Turkey are divided into two groups: (1) pre-candidacy grants (1964–99) and (2) post-candidacy grants (1999–present). In the first period, grants called MEDA (Mediterranean Economic Development Area) (1996–9) and EUROMED (1997–9) were awarded to Turkey. In the latter period, Turkey has started to benefit from EU funding under one framework with an aim to institute political, economic, legal and administrative measures as a condition to conform to the EU acquis (ABGS, n.d.).

13 The DTP was a Kurdish political party established in 2005 after the banning of DEHAP by the Constitutional Court in 2003. BDP (Peace and Democracy Party) succeeded DTP in 2008 after its closure due to the claim of its close relationship with the PKK.

14 The KCK is Koma Civaken Kurdistan (KCK), or Kurdish Communities Union, 'an umbrella PKK organization supposedly acting as the urban arm of the PKK' (Gunter, 2013: 96).

15 In terms of social class, it should be noted that the Gezi Park uprising 'appears to be an occasionally multi-class, but predominantly middle-class movement' (Tugal, 2013: 156). It is also important to highlight that these protests were seen as 'part of a broader global movement of social solidarity and resistance', namely the so-called Arab Spring revolts and the Occupy movement originating in the United Staes as well as 'other similar forms of resistance to neo-liberal globalization in the United States, Western Europe and elsewhere' (Öniş, 2014: 8).

16 Prime Minister Erdoğan reiterated his call for three children in 2013 by stating that 'One or two children mean bankruptcy. Three children mean we are not improving but not receding either. So, I repeat, at least three children are necessary in each family, because our population risks aging' (Hürriyet Daily News, 2013).

17 HDP was established in 2012 'as the political wing of the People's Democratic Congress (Demokratik Toplum Kongresi, DTK), a platform that included a variety of mostly Kurdish left-wing parties, minority groups such as LGBTQ, and representatives of ethnic minorities' (Tekdemir, 2016: 657).

18 After the coup d'état attempt, 'the AKP government has purged hundreds of public workers in the security forces and judiciary and has seized the media enterprises linked to the Gülen movement' (Aksoy, 2016).

19 Adıyaman Kadın Yaşam Derneği, Anka Kadın Araştırmaları Derneği, Bursa Panayır Kadın Dayanışma Derneği, Ceren Kadın Derneği, Gökkuşağı Kadın Derneği, Muş Kadın Çatısı Derneği, Muş Kadın Derneği, Van Kadın Derneği and SELİS Kadın Derneği, one of the women's groups in my sampling, were the women's organization's closed down after the 2016 coup d'état attempt (Bianet, 2016).

4 Mapping civil society as a voluntaristic, autonomous and mediatory agent

1 All names used are pseudonyms.

2 Even though I did not ask which party the women voted for, they showed their sympathy with the main opposition party in Turkey, called CHP. The CHP is a centre-left Kemalist secular party. Some of the women in my sample highlighted their membership and also the administrative position they hold in the party. However, one of the women participants from TÜKD reported that 'we have some members who are members of the National Movement Party [Milliyetçi Hareket Partisi, the MHP]' (interview with Sevim, TÜKD, 18 June 2012), which is an ultra-nationalist party in Turkey.

3 Views on independence from international funding vary more widely. For example, women from the feminist group TKB are mostly highly critical of international funding, with Sevda from that organization emphasizing the need to 'tackle the bureaucracy and negative attitude of the international donors to the CSOs' (interview, 8 May 2012). In contrast, the other Kemalist organization in my sample, TÜKD, shows its strong identification with international funding through the way it uses NGO ideas and language. TÜKD thinks that international funding should be accepted, stating in the Ankara branch 2010–12 activity report that they have organized training seminars on Project Development and Ways to Reach Sources of Funding, and also that they aim to create funded projects in the field of women's studies (TÜKD, 2012). According to the women from Islamist organizations BKP and AKDER, funding does not necessarily and always endanger the independence of an association. As one of the women activists from AKDER argued, 'The EU funding lets us organize training for women and conduct field work research' (interview with Perihan, 5 July 2012). Yet even here, some women believe CSOs funded by 'invisible sources'

do not always maintain a critical or oppositional stance and 'civil society has not been always non-governmental like that and met the opposition', as Serpil from BKP articulates (interview, 12 August 2012). The Kurdish women have a more wholeheartedly pro-international funding position. All of the women in the Kurdish organization, KAMER, take a pro-EU stance and believe that projects play a key role in enhancing civil society. As stated in the book titled *Women's Problems in the Southeast (Güneydoğu'da Kadın Sorunları)*, KAMER believes that women's organizations should find their own independent resources, and it supports EU funding in this regard. Their support is not entirely uncritical, however. Like the Islamist women, they do believe that if the funding institution itself lacks independence or acts as if it were a governing agency, this can weaken the relationship between a CSO and the donor agency.

4 It is likely that the mediation discourse is so prominent among the Islamist women because of their continual organizing and struggles against the headscarf ban. In this context, lobbying and other advocacy activities are brought to the fore in several accounts, and the function of CSOs is seen to be participation in the process of decision-making and policymaking, and influencing the implementation process.

5 Reconstructing the site of civil society: Alternative voices

1 Whether this latter point, which suggests a tie between women's nature and anti-hierarchical organizing, rests on essentialist understandings of gender or a position more akin to a feminist standpoint, is not clear.

Bibliography

Abdelrahman, M. M. (2004) *Civil Society Exposed: The Politics of NGOs in Egypt*. London: Tauris Academic.

ABGS (n.d.) 'Türkiye-AB Mali İşbirliği (Turkey-EU Financial Cooperation)'. Available at: https://www.ab.gov.tr/5.html (Accessed: 18 June 2018).

Abu-Rish, Z. (2011) 'Turkish Politics, Kurdish Rights, and the KCK Operations: An Interview with Aslı Bali'. Available at: http://www.jadaliyya.com/pages/index/3047/turkish-politics-kurdish-rights-and-the-kck-operat (Accessed: 17 March 2015).

Acar, F., and Altunok, G. (2013) 'The "Politics of Intimate" at the Intersection of Neo-Liberalism and Neo-Conservatism in Contemporary Turkey'. *Women's Studies International Forum*, 41(1), pp. 14–23.

Ackerly, B., and True, J. (2010) *Doing Feminist Research in Political and Social Science*. Basingstoke: Palgrave Macmillan.

Ahmad, F. (1993) *The Making of Modern Turkey*. New York: Routledge.

Akboğa, S. (2013) 'Turkish Civil Society Divided by the Headscarf Ban'. *Democratization*, 21(4), pp. 1–24.

Akça, İ. (2014) 'Hegemonic Projects in Post-1980 Turkey and the Changing Forms of Authoritarianism'. In İ. Akça, A. Bekmen and B. Alp (eds), *Turkey Reframed: Constituting Neoliberal Hegemony*. London: Pluto Press, pp. 13–47.

AKDER (n.d.) 'Headscarf Ban in Turkey: A Unique Case of Discrimination against Women'. Pamphlet collected from AKDER office. Istanbul: AKDER.

AKDER (n.d.1) 'Başörtüsü Yasağı Açık bir Ayrımcılıktır (Headscarf Ban is an Obvious Discrimination'. Pamphlet collected from AKDER office. Istanbul: AKDER.

Akkoç, N. (2002) 'Güneydoğu'da Kadın (Woman in the Southeast)'. In İ. Y. Alyanak et al., *Güneydoğu'da Kadın Sorunları* (*Women's Problems in the Southeast*). Ankara Uçan Süpürge Yayınları.

Akman, Z. (2007) 'Gender: Painful Aspects of Change'. In: Z. Gösterişli (ed.), *Issues and Resolutions of Rights-based NGOs in Turkey*. Ankara: Odak Offset Printing, pp. 101–30.

AKP (2012) 'AK Parti 2023 Siyasi Vizyonu: Siyaset, Toplum, Dünya (2023 Political Vision of AK Party: Politics, Society, World'. Available at: https://www.akparti.org.tr/site/akparti/2023-siyasi-vizyon (Accessed: 20 January 2013).

Aksoy, H. A. (2015) 'Invigorating Democracy in Turkey: The Agency of Organized Islamist Women', *Politics & Gender*, 11(1), pp. 146–70.

Aksoy, H. A. (2016) 'Knowns and Unknowns behind Turkey's Failed Coup'. Available at: http://www.iwm.at/transit/transit-online/knowns-and-unknowns-behind-turkeys-failed-coup/ (Accessed: 10 March 2017).

Al-Ali, N. (2003) 'Gender and Civil Society in the Middle East', *International Feminist Journal of Politics*, 5(2), pp. 216–32.

Al-Ali, N. (2004) *Secularism, Gender and the State in the Middle East: The Egyptian Women's Movement*, Cambridge: Cambridge University Press.

Al-Ali, N., and Pratt, N. (2011) 'Between Nationalism and Women's Rights: The Kurdish Women's Movement in Iraq'. *Middle East Journal of Culture and Communication*, 4(3), pp. 339–55.

Al-Ali, N. S. (1997) 'Feminism and Contemporary Debates in Eygpt'. In D. Chatty and A. Rabo (eds), *Organizing Women: Formal and Informal Women's Groups in the Middle East*. Oxford: Berg Publications, pp. 173–94.

Al-Ali, N. S. (2005) 'Gender and Civil Society in the Middle East'. In J. Howell and D. Mulligan (eds) *Gender and Civil Society: Transcending Boundaries*. London: Routledge, pp. 101–17.

Alemdar, Z., and Çorbacıoğlu, R. B. (2010) 'Avrupa Birliği Sürecinde Türkiye'de Sivil Toplum: Organizasyon Düzeyine Etkiler (The European Funds' Impact on Institutional Structure of Turkish Civil Society Organizations)', CIVICUS Civil Society Index Country Report for Turkey. Istanbul: TÜSEV Publications.

Alınteri (2009) 'Tutuklu Kadınlarla Dayanışma Paneli'. Available at: http://alinteri. org/10566.id (Accessed: 21 October 2013).

Al-Mughni, H. (1997) 'From Gender Equality to Female Subjugation: The Changing Agendas of Women's Groups in Kuwait'. In D. Chatty and A. Rabo (eds), *Organizing Women: Formal and Informal Women's Groups in the Middle East*. Oxford: Berg Publications, pp. 195–209.

Al-Sayyid, M. K. (1993) 'Civil Society in Egypt?', *Middle East Journal*, 47(2), pp. 228–42.

Altan-Olcay, O., and İçduygu, A. (2012) 'Mapping Civil Society in the Middle East: The Cases of Egypt, Lebanon and Turkey', *British Journal of Middle Eastern Studies*, 39(2), pp. 157–79.

Altınay, A., and Arat, Y. (2009) *Violence against Women in Turkey: A Nationwide Survey*. İstanbul: Punto.

Alvarez, S. E. (1999) 'Advocating Feminism: The Latin American Feminist NGO "Boom"', *International Feminist Journal of Politics*, 1(2), pp. 181–209.

Alvarez, S. E. (2009) 'Beyond NGO-ization? Reflections from Latin America', *Development*, 52(2), pp. 175–84.

AMARGİ. (2012) 'Feminist Tartışmalar: AMARGİ'den Gidenlerin Ayrılık Sebepleri'. Available at: http://goo.gl/hPdhb3 (Accessed: 18 January 2013).

AMARGİ. (n.d.) 'More Organizations in Turkey'. Available at: https:// amargigroupistanbul.wordpress.com/feminism-in-turkey/more-feminist-organziations-in-istanbul/ (Accessed: 28 February 2012).

AMARGİ. (n.d.1) 'Information'. Available at: https://amargigroupistanbul.wordpress.com/about-amargi/information/ (Accessed: 15 March 2015).

Arat, Y. (1994) 'Toward a Democratic Society: The Women's Movement in Turkey in the 1980s', *Women's Studies International Forum*, 17(2–3), pp. 241–8.

Arat, Y. (1998) 'Feminists, Islamists, and Political Change in Turkey', *Political Psychology*, 19(1), pp. 117–31.

Arat, Y. (2000) 'From Emancipation to Liberation: The Changing Role of Women in Turkey's Public Realm', *Journal of International Affairs*, 54(1), pp. 107–25.

Arat, Y. (2008) 'Contestation and Collaboration: Women's Struggles for Empowerment in Turkey'. In R. Kasaba (ed.), *The Cambridge History of Turkey Volume 4: Turkey in the Modern World*. Cambridge: Cambridge University Press, pp. 388–418.

Arat, Y. (2009) 'Religion, Politics and Gender Equality in Turkey'. Available at: http:// www.unrisd.org/80256B3C005BCCF9/search/B49BF0AB76047D15C125765E004 7B1EB (Accessed: 10 January 2011).

Arat, Y. (2010) 'Women's Rights and Islam in Turkish Politics: The Civil Code Amendment', *Middle East Journal*, 64(2), pp. 235–51.

Arat, Y. (2016) 'Islamist Women and Feminist Concerns in Contemporary Turkey', *Frontiers: A Journal of Women Studies*, 37(3), pp. 125–50.

Arat, Y., and Altınay, A. (2015) 'KAMER, a Women's Center and an Experiment in Cultivating Cosmopolitan Norms', *Women's Studies International Forum*, 49, pp. 12–19.

Arenfeldt, P., and Golley, N. A. (2012) 'Introduction'. In P. Arenfeldt and N. A. Golley (eds), *Mapping Arab Women's Movement: A Century of Transformations from Within*, Cairo: American University in Cairo Press (kindle edition).

Armstrong, K. A. (2002) 'Rediscovering Civil Society: The European Union and the White Paper on Governance', *European Law Journal*, 8(1), pp. 102–32.

Aslan Akman, Canan (2008) 'Sivil Toplumun Yeni Aktörleri Olarak İslami Eğilimli Kadın Dernekleri', *Toplum ve Demokrasi*, 2(4), pp. 71–90.

Atacan, F. (2006) 'Explaining Religious Politics at the Cross-road: AKP-SP'. In A. Çarkoğlu and B. Rubin (eds), *Religion and Politics in Turkey*. New York: Routledge, pp. 45–59.

Baç, M. M. (2005) 'Turkey's Political Reforms and the Impact of the European Union', *South European Society & Politics*, 10(1), pp. 16–30.

Badran, M. (2009) *Feminism in Islam: Secular and Religious Convergences.* Oxford: Oneworld.

Barber, B. (1984) *Strong Democracy.* Los Angeles: University of California Press.

Bayraktar, D. (2009) *Crossing the Bridge: The Europeanization of Women's NGO's in Turkey.* Unpublished MSc thesis. Institut D'études Politiques de Paris.

BBC (2008) 'TBMM'den türbana onay'. Available at: http://www.bbc.co.uk/turkish/news/story/2008/02/080209_turkey_2update.shtml (Accessed: 28 September 2012).

Beckman, B. (1993) 'The Liberation of Civil Society: Neo-Liberal Ideology and Political Theory', *Review of African Political Economy,* 20(58), pp. 20–33.

Beckman, B. (1997) 'Explaining Democratization: Notes on the Concept of Civil Society'. In E. Özdalga and S. Persson (eds), *Civil Society Democracy and the Muslim World.* Istanbul: Numune Matbaasi, pp. 1–7.

Benhabib, S. (1992) 'Models of Public Space: Hannah Arendt, the Liberal Tradition, and Jurgen Habermas'. In C. Calhoun (ed.), *Habermas and the Public Sphere.* Cambridge, MA: The MIT Press, pp. 73–98.

Benhabib. S., and Cornell, D. (1987) *Feminism as Critique: Essays on the Politics of Gender in Late-Capitalist Society.* Cambridge: Polity Press.

Berktay, F. (1990) 'Türk Solu'nun Kadına Bakışı: Değişen Bir Şey Var Mı? (Perspective of Turkish Left to Woman: Is There Any Change?'. In Ş. Tekeli (ed.), *1980'ler Türkiyesi'nde Kadın Bakış Açısından Kadınlar (Women in 1980s Turkey from Women's Perspectives).* Istanbul: İletişim Yayınları, pp. 279–91.

Bernal, V., and Grewal, I. (2014) 'Introduction: The NGO Form: Feminist Struggles, States and Neoliberalism'. In V. Bernal and I. Grewal (eds), *Theorizing NGOs: States, Feminisms, and Neoliberalism.* Durham, Duke University Press, pp. 1–18.

Bianet (2008) 'Anayasa Mahkemesi Başörtüsü Düzenlemesini İptal Etti (Constitutional Court cancelled the Headscarf Arrangement'. Available at: https://m.bianet.org/bianet/siyaset/107443-anayasa-mahkemesi-basortusu-duzenlemesini-iptal-etti (Accessed: 4 February 2019).

Bianet (2010) 'Erdoğan'dan Kadınlara: Sesiniz Ölümleri Durdurabilir (From Erdogan to Women: Your Voice can Stop Death'. Available at: http://bianet.org/bianet/siyaset/123511-erdogan-dan-kadinlara-sesiniz-olumleri-durdurabilir (Accessed: 5 May 2015).

Bianet (2016) 'Kadın Dernekleri Kapatıldı, Hangi Çalışmalar Yarıda Kaldı? (Women's Associations Were Shut Down, Which Activities Were Not Finished'. Available at: http://bianet.org/bianet/toplumsal-cinsiyet/180798-kadin-dernekleri-kapatildi-hangi-calismalar-yarida-kaldi (Accessed: 3 April 2017).

Bikmen, F., and Meydanoğlu, E. (2006) 'Civil Society in Turkey: An Era of Transition', CIVICUS Civil Society Index Country Report for Turkey. Istanbul: TÜSEV Publications.

Bilgiç, E. E., and Kafkaslı, Z. (2013) 'Gencim, Özgürlükçüyüm, Ne İstiyorum? (I Am Young, Liberal, What Do I Want?', #direngeziparkı Anketi Sonuç Raporu. Available at: http://www.bilgiyay.com/Content/files/DIRENGEZI.pdf (Accessed: 6 April 2015).

BKP (2014) 'Siyasi ve Sosyal Krizlerin Çözümü Demokrasi (Democracy is the Solution for Political and Social Crises'. Available at: http://www.baskentkadin.org/ tr/?p=664 (Accessed: 1 June 2015).

BKP (n.d.). 'Başkent Kadın Platformu (The Capital City Women's Platform)'. Pamphlet collected at The Capital City Women's Platform office. Ankara: The Capital City Women's Platform.

Boose, J. (2012) 'Democratization and Civil Society: Libya, Tunisia and the Arab Spring', *International Journal of Social Science and Humanity*, 2(4), pp. 310–15.

Bora, A. (2002) 'Bir Yapabilirlik Olarak KA-DER (KA-DER as a Capability)'. In A. Bora and A. Günal. (eds), *90'larda Türkiye'de Feminizm (Feminism in Turkey in the 90s)*. İstanbul: İletisim Yayınları, pp. 109–25.

Bora, A. (2005) 'Kamu Yeniden Kurulurken Kadınlara Ne Olacak? (What Will Happen to Women When Public Is Rebuilt)', *Cogito*, 43, pp. 262–9.

Bora, A. (2011) *Feminizm Kendi Arasında (Feminism within Itself)*. Ankara: Ayizi Yayınlari.

Bora, A., and Günal, A. (2002) 'Önsöz (Introduction)'. In A. Bora and A. Günal (eds), *90'larda Türkiye'de Feminizm (Feminism in Turkey in the 90s)*. İstanbul: İletisim Yayınları, pp. 7–13.

Bora, T. (1994) 'Türkiye Sağının İdeolojik ve Siyasi Bunalımı: Oynak Merkez- "Merkez"siz Oynaklık', *Birikim*, 64, pp. 11–23.

Börzel, T. A. (2010) 'Why You Don't Always Get What You Want: EU Enlargement and Civil Society in Central and Eastern Europe', *Acta Politica*, 45(1–2), pp. 1–10.

Brysk, A. (2000) 'Democratizing Civil Society in Latin America', *Journal of Democracy*, 11(3), pp. 151–65.

Bulaç, A. (2014) 'Sivil alan, aydınlar ve STK'lar (Civil Space, Intelligentsia and CSOs)'. *Dünya Bülteni*. Available at: https://www.dunyabulteni.net/makale/amp/19490 (Accessed: 5 February 2019).

Çağlayan, H. (2007) *Analar, Yoldaşlar, Tanrıçalar: Kürt hareketinde Kadınlar ve Kadın Kimliğinin Oluşumu* (Mothers, Comrades, and Goddesses: Women in the

Kurdish Movement and the Formation of Women's Identity). Istanbul: İletişim
Yayınları.

Çaha, Ö. (2005) 'The Ideological Transformation of the Public Sphere: The Case of
Turkey'. *Turkish Journal of International Relations*, 4(1–2), pp. 1–30.

Çaha, Ö. (2006) 'Türk Kadın Hareketi: "Kadınsı" Bir Sivil Toplumun İmkanı?
(Turkish Women's Movement: The Construction of a "Feminine" Civil Society?).
Kadın Çalışmaları Dergisi, 1(3), pp. 6–15.

Çaha, Ö. (2010) *Sivil Kadin: Türkiye'de Kadın ve Sivil Toplum* (Civil Society: Women
and Civil Society in Turkey). Ankara: Savaş Yayınevi.

Çaha, Ö. (2013) *Women and Civil Society in Turkey: Women's Movements in a
Muslim Society*. Surrey: Ashgate.

Çakır, A. (2011a) 'Introduction'. In A. Çakır (ed.), *Fifty Years of EU–Turkey
Relations: A Sisyphean Story. London: Routledge*. London: Routledge, pp. 1–10.

Çakır, A. (2011b) 'Political Dimension: Always in the List of "Also-Rans": Turkey's
Rivals in EU–Turkey Relations'. In A. Çakır (ed.), *Fifty Years of EU–Turkey
Relations: A Sisyphean Story. London: Routledge*. London: Routledge,
pp. 10–46.

Carapico, S. (2002) 'Foreign Aid for Promoting Democracy in the Arab World',
Middle East Journal, 56(3), pp. 379–95.

Carothers, T. (1999) 'Civil Society', *Foreign Policy*, 117, pp. 18–29.

Carothers, T., and Ottoway, M. (2000) *Funding Virtue: Civil Society Aid
and Democracy Promotion*. Washington, DC: Carnegie Endowment for
International Peace.

Cavatorta, F. (2012) 'Arab Spring: The Awakening of Civil Society. A General
Overview'. *Dossier*, pp. 75–81. Available at: http://www.iemed.org/observatori-en/
arees-danalisi/arxius-adjunts/anuari/med.2012/Cavatorta_en.pdf (Accessed: 16
April 2013).

Cavatorta, F., and Durac, V. (2011) *Civil Society and Democratization in the Arab
World: The Dynamics of Activism*. New York: Routledge.

Çayır, K. (2000) "İslamcı Bir Sivil Toplum Örgütuü: Gökkuşağı İstanbul Kadın
Platformu (An Islamist Non-governmental Organization: Rainbow Women
Platform)". In N. Göle (ed.), *İslamın Yeni Kamusal Yüzleri (Islam in Public: New
Visibilities and New Imageries)*. Istanbul: Metis Yayınları, pp. 41–68.

Çaylak, A. (2008) 'Autocratic or Democratic? A Critical Approach to Civil Society
Movements in Turkey', *Journal of Economic and Social Research*, 10(1),
pp. 115–51.

CEDAW. (2010) 'Shadow NGO Report on Turkey's Sixth Periodic Report to the
Committee on the Elimination of Discrimination against Women', The Executive

Committee for NGO Forum on CEDAW. Available at: http://www2.ohchr. org/english/bodies/cedaw/docs/ngos/WPTPC_Turkey46.pdf (Accessed: 15 February 2017).

Çelik, A. B. (2014) 'A Holistic Approach to Violence: Women Parliamentarians' Understanding of Violence against Women and Violence in the Kurdish Issue in Turkey', *European Journal of Women's Studies*, pp. 1–17.

Chandoke, N. (2005) 'What the Hell is Civil Society?' *Open Democracy*. Available at: http://www.opendemocracy.net/democracy-open_politics/article_2375.jsp (Accessed: 25 September 2011).

Charlton, R., and May, R. (1995) 'NGOs, Politics and Probity : A Policy Implementation Perspective', *Third World Quarterly*, 16(2), pp. 237–55.

Chatty, D., and Rabo, A. (1997) 'Formal and Informal Women's Groups in the Middle East'. In D. Chatty and A. Rabo (eds), *Organizing Women: Formal and Informal Women's Groups in the Middle East*. Oxford: Berg Publications, pp. 1–22.

Chouliaraki, L., and Fairclough, N. (1999) *Discourse in Late Modernity: Rethinking Critical Discourse Analysis*. Edinburgh: Edinburgh University Press.

Çıtak, Z., and Tür, Ö. (2008) 'Women between Tradition and Change: The Justice and Development Party Experience in Turkey', *Middle Eastern Studies*, 44(3), pp. 455–69.

Clarke, G. (1998) 'Non-Governmental Organizations (NGOs) and Politics in the Developing World', *Political Studies*, 46(1), pp. 36–52.

Cohen, J., and Arato, A. (1992) *Civil Society and Political Theory*. Cambridge, MA: MIT Press.

Coşar, S., and Onbaşı, F. G. (2008) 'Women's Movement in Turkey at a Crossroads: From Women's Rights Advocacy to Feminism', *South European Society and Politics*, 13(3), pp. 325–44.

Coşar, S., and Yeğenoğlu, M. (2011) 'New Grounds for Patriarch in Turkey? Gender Policy in the Age of AKP', *South European Society and Politics*, 16(4), pp. 555–73.

Coşar, S., and Yücesan-Özdemir, G. (2012) 'Hearing the Silence of Violence: Neoliberalism and Islamist Politics under the AKP Governments'. In S. Coşar and G. Yücesan-Özdemir (eds), *Silent Violence: Neoliberalism, Islamist Politics and the AKP Years in Turkey*. Ottowa: Red Quill Books, pp. 295–327.

Comaroff, J. L., and Comaroff, J. (1999) 'Introduction'. In J. L Comaroff and J. Comaroff (eds), *Civil Society and the Political Imagination in Africa*. Chicago: University of Chicago Press, pp. 1–44.

Connelly, M. P., Parpart, J. L.and Barriteau, V. E. (2000) 'Feminism and Development: Theoretical Perspectives'. In J. L. Parpart et al. (eds), *Theoretical*

Perspectives on Gender and Development. Ottowa: International Development Research Centre, pp. 51–161.

Cox, R. (1999) 'Civil Society at the Turn of the Millennium: Prospects for an Alternative World Order', *Review of International Studies*, 25(1), pp. 3–28.

Craig, J. (2007) 'Development'. In G. Blakeley and V. Bryson (eds), *The Impacts of Feminism on Political Concepts and Debates*, Manchester: Manchester University Press, pp. 110–26.

Çubukçu, S. U. (2004) 'Contribution to Substantial Democracy: Women's Non-Governmental Organisations'. In F. Berktay et al. (eds), *The Position of Women in Turkey and in The European Union: Achievements, Problems, Prospects*. Istanbul: KA-DER, pp. 99–120.

Dağı, İ. (2012) 'Post modern otoriterlik'. *Türkiye Yazarlar Birliği*. Available at: http://www.tyb.org.tr/ihsan-dagidan-post-modern-otoriterlik-9153h.htm (Accessed: 5 February 2019).

Dahl, R. (1989) *Democracy and Its Critics*. New Haven: Yale University Press.

Dalacoura, K. (2012) 'The 2011 Uprising in the Arab Middle East: Political Change and Geopolitical Implications', *International Affairs*, 88(I), pp. 63–79.

Delibaş, K. (2009) 'Conceptualizing Islamic Movements: The Case of Turkey', *International Political Science Review*, 30(1), pp. 89–103.

Dernekler Dairesi Başkanlığı (2013) 'Dernek Sayıları (Numbers of Associations)'. Available at: https://www.dernekler.gov.tr/tr/anasayfalinkler/yillara-gore-faal-dernek.aspx (Accessed: 5 February 2013).

De Tocqueville, A. (1971) *Democracy in America*. London: Oxford University Press.

Diamond, L. (1994) 'Rethinking Civil Society: Toward Democratic Consolidation', *Journal of Democracy*, 5(3), pp. 4–17.

Diken (2014) 'Erdoğan'dan 'inci'ler: Kadınla erkeğin fıtratı farklıdır, feministler anneliği kabul etmiyor ("Pearls" of Erdoğan: Disposition of Woman and Man is different, feminists reject accept motherhood)'. Available at: http://www.diken.com.tr/erdogandan-inciler-kadinla-erkegin-fitratlari-farklidir-feministler-anneligi-kabul-etmiyor/ (Accessed: 9 March 2015).

Dikici-Bilgin, H. (2009) 'Civil Society and State in Turkey: A Gramscian Perspective'. In M. McNally and J. Schwarzmantel (eds), *Gramsci and Global Politics: Hegemony and Resistance*. London: Routledge, pp. 107–19.

Diner, C., and Toktaş, Ş. (2010) 'Waves of Feminism in Turkey: Kemalist, Islamist and Kurdish Women's Movements in an Era of Globalization', *Journal of Balkan and Near Eastern Studies*, 12(1), pp. 41–57.

Doyle, J. D. (2017a) 'Government Co-option of Civil Society: Exploring the AKP's Role within Turkish Women's CSOs', *Democratization*, 25(3), pp. 1–19.

Doyle, J. D. (2017b) 'State Control of Civil Society Organizations: The Case of Turkey', *Democratization*, 24(2), pp. 244–64.

Draft Treaty Establishing a Constitution for Europe (2003) 'Title III – Union Competences', Official Journal (C 169/01).

Donoghue, F. (2001) 'Women and Volunteering – a Feminised Space?' Available at: https://ssrn.com/abstract=952670 or http://dx.doi.org/10.2139/ssrn.952670 (Accessed: 7 June 2018).

Dvoráková, V. (2008) 'Civil Society in Latin America and Eastern Europe: Reinvention or Imposition?', *International Political Science Review*, 29(5), pp. 579–94.

EC (2005) 'Communication from the Commission to the Council, the European Parliament, the European Economic and Social Committee and the Committee of Regions: Civil Society Dialogue between the EU and Candidate Countries'. Brussels: Commission of the European Communities.

Eddin Ibrahim, S. (1995) 'Civil Society and Prospects of Democratization in the Arab World'. In A. R. Norton (ed.), *Civil Society in the Middle East*, Vol. 1. Leiden: E. J. Brill, pp. 27–54.

Edwards, M. (2004) *Civil Society*. UK: Polity Press.

Einhorn, B., and Sever, C. (2003) 'Gender and Civil Society in Central and Eastern Europe', *International Feminist Journal of Politics*, 5(2), pp. 163–90.

Encarnación, O. G. (2002) 'On Bowling Leagues and NGOs: A Critique of Civil Society's Revival', *Studies in Comparative International Development*, 36(4), pp. 116–31.

Erdoğan, N. (2000) 'Kemalist Non-Governmental Organisations: Troubled Elites in Defence of a Sacred Heritage'. In S. Yerasimos, G. Seufert and K. Vorhoff (eds), *Civil Society in the Grip of Nationalism*. Istanbul: Orient-Institute, pp. 251–81.

Erdoğan-Tosun, G. (2008) 'Sivillik, Karşılıklılık ve Diğerkamlık Eğilimlerinin Gözlenebildiği Sivil Toplum Demokratikleşme Sürecinin Tamamlayıcısı Olacaktır (Civil Society in which Civility, Reciprocity and Alturism are Observed Will Be Complementary to Democratization Process)'. In M. Şentürk and A. Erdoğan (eds), *Sivil Toplum Kavramı Tartışmaları: Makaleler*. Istanbul: Kaktüs Yayınları, pp. 123–39.

Ergun, A. (2010) 'Civil Society in Turkey and Local Dimensions of Europeanization', *Journal of European Integration*, 32(5), pp. 507–22.

Eschle, C., and Maiguashca, B. (2011) *Making Feminist Sense of the Global Justice Movement*. Lanham: Rowman & Littlefield.

Esim, S., and Cindoğlu, E. (1999) 'Women's Organizations in 1990s Turkey: Predicaments and Prospects', *Middle Eastern Studies*, 35(1), pp. 178–88.

Eto, M. (2012) 'Reframing Civil Society from Gender Perspectives: A Model of a
    Multi-layered Seamless World', *Journal of Civil Society*, 8(2), pp. 1–21.

Ewig, C. (1999) 'The Strengths and the Limits of the Women's Movement
    Model: Shaping Nicaragua's Democratic Institutions', *Latin American Research
    Review*, 34(3), pp. 75–102.

Fairclough, N. (1992) *Discourse and Social Change*. Cambridge: Polity Press.

Fairclough, N. (1995) *Critical Discourse Analysis: The Critical Study of Language*.
    London: Longman.

Fairclough, N. (2001) 'The Discourse of New Labour: Critical Discourse Analysis'. In
    S. Wetherell, S. Taylor and S. Yates (eds), *Discourse as Data: A Guide for Analysis*.
    London: Sage and the Open University, pp. 229–66.

Fairclough, N. (2003) *Analysing Discourse: Textual Analysis for Social Research*.
    London: Routledge.

Ferree, M. M., and Tripp, A. M. (2006) 'Preface'. In M. M. Ferree and A. M. Tripp
    (eds), *Global Feminism: Transnational Women's Activism, Organizing, and
    Human Rights*. New York: New York University Press.

Fisher Onar, N., and Paker, H. (2012) 'Towards Cosmopolitan Citizenship? Women's
    Rights in Divided Turkey', *Theory and Society*, 41(4), pp. 375–39.

Fisher, W. (1997) 'Doing Good? The Politics and Antipolitics of NGO Practices',
    Annual Review of Anthropology, 26, pp. 439–64.

Flying Broom (2011) *Who We Are?*. Available at: http://ucansupurge.org.tr/en/?page_
    id=56 (Accessed: 15 June 2012).

Foucault, M. (1978) *The History of Sexuality, Volume I: An Introduction*.
    New York: Pantheon Books.

Foucault, M. (1984) 'Truth and Power'. In P. Rainbov (ed.), *The Foucault Reader: An
    Introduction to Foucault's Thought*. London: Penguin Books.

Fraser, N. (1992) 'Rethinking the Public Sphere: A Contribution to the Critique of
    Actually Existing Democracy'. In C. Calhoun (ed.), *Habermas and the Public
    Sphere*. Cambridge, MA: MIT Press, pp. 109–42.

Gal, S. (1997) 'Feminism and Civil Society'. In J. W. Scott, C. Kaplan and D. Keates
    (eds), *Transitions, Environments, Translations: Feminisms in International
    Politics*. London: Routledge, pp. 30–46.

Gazioğlu, E. (2010) *Mobilizing for Women's Organisations: Women Activists'
    Perception of Activism and Women's Organisation in Turkey*. Unpublished PhD
    thesis. University of York.

Gellner, E. (1994) *Conditions of Liberty: Civil Society and Its Rivals*.
    London: Penguin Group.

Ghodsee, K. R. (2011) 'Civil Society-by-design: Emerging Capitalism, Essentialist
    Feminism and Women's Nongovernmental Organizations in Postsocialist Eastern

Europe'. In K. Hageman, S. Michel and G. Budde (eds), *Civil Society and Gender Justice: Historical and Comparative Perspectives*. New York: Berghahn Books, pp. 224–42.

Göçek, F. M., and Balaghi, S., *Reconstructing Gender in the Middle East*, New York: Columbia University Press.

Göçmen, İ. (2014) 'Religion, Politics and Social Assistance in Turkey: The Rise of Religiously Motivated Associations', *Journal of European Social Policy*, 24(1), pp. 92–103.

Göksel, D. N., and Güneş, R. B. (2005) 'The Role of NGOs in the European Integration Process: The Turkish Experience', *South European Society and Politics*, 10(1), pp. 57–72.

Göle, N. (1996) 'Authoritarian Secularism and Islamist Politics: The Case of Turkey'. In A. R. Norton (ed.), *Civil Society in the Middle East. Vol. 2*. Leiden: E. J. Brill, pp. 17–43.

Göle, N. (1997) 'Secularism and Islamism in Turkey: The Making of Elites and Counter-Elites', *The Middle East Journal*, 51(1), pp. 46–58.

Göle, N. (2003) 'Contemporary Islamist Movements and New Sources for Religious Tolerance', *Journal of Human Rights*, 2(1), pp. 17–30.

Gramsci, A. (1971) 'Selections from the Prison Notebooks of Antonio Gramsci'. In Q. Hoare and G. N. Smith (eds), New York: International Publishers.

Guardian (2012) 'Turkish Women Join Pro-Choice Rally as Fears Grow of Abortion Ban'. Available at: http://www.guardian.co.uk/world/2012/jun/03/turkish-women-rally-abortion-ban (Accessed: 7 September 2012).

Güler, H. (2007) 'Uzun Yılların Kısa Hikayesi (Short Story of Long Years)'. In C. Aydın et al. (eds), *Dünden Bugüne Başkent Kadın Platformu* (From Yesterday to Today Başkent Kadın Platformu). Ankara: Ayban Matbaacılık.

Gültekin, Ö. (2007) 'Dün, Bugün ve Gelecek: Bir Yolculuk var tanıklık ettiğim … '. In C. Aydın et al. (eds) *Dünden Bugüne Başkent Kadın Platformu* (From Yesterday to Today Başkent Kadın Platformu). Ankara: Ayban Matbaacılık.

Güneş-Ayata, A., and Doğangün, G. (2017) 'Gender Politics of the AKP: Restoration of a Religio-conservative Gender Climate', *Journal of Balkan and Near Eastern Studies*, 19(6), pp. 610–27.

Gunter, M. (2013) 'Reopening Turkey's Closed Kurdish Opening', *Middle East Journal*, 20 (2), pp. 88–98.

Habermas, J. (1989) *The Structural Transformation of the Public Sphere*. Cambridge: Polity Press.

Habermas, J. (1996) *Between Facts and Norms: Contributions to a Discourse Theory of Law and Democracy*. Cambridge: Polity Press. (Original work published in 1992.)

Hacıvelioğlu, F. (2009) 'Kadın Kurtuluş Hareketini Sınırlayan Bir Dinamik: "Projecilik" (A Dynamic that Limits Women's Emancipation Movement: "Projectism")', *Feminist Politika*, 1, pp. 16–17.

Hagemann, K. (2008) 'Civil Society Gendered: Rethinking Theories and Practices'. In K. Hagemann, S. Michel and G. Budde (eds), *Civil Society and Gender Justice: Historical and Comparative Perspectives*. New York: Berghahn Books, pp. 17–43.

Hagemann, K., Michel, S., and Budde, G. (2008) *Civil Society and Gender Justice: Historical and Comparative Perspectives*. New York: Berghahn Books.

Hall, J. A. (1995) *Civil Society: Theory, History, Comparison*. Cambridge: Polity Press.

Hamilton, M. B. (1987) 'The Elements of the Concept of Ideology', *Political Studies*, 35, pp. 18–38.

Hardig, A. C. (2014) 'Beyond the Arab Revolts: Conceptualizing Civil Society in the Middle East and North Africa', *Democratization*, pp. 1131–53.

Hassim, S. (2005) 'Voices, Hierarchies and Spaces: Reconfiguring the Women's Movement in Democratic South Africa', *Politikon: South African Journal of Political Studies*, 32(2), pp. 175–93.

Hassim, S., and Gouws, A. (1998) 'Redefining the Public Space : Women's Organisations, Gender Consciousness and Civil Society in South Africa', *South African Journal of Political Studies*, 25(2), pp. 53–76.

Hawkesworth, M. E. (2001) 'Democratization: Reflections on Gendered Dislocations in the Public Sphere'. In R. M. Kelly, J. H. Bayes, M. Hawkesworth and B. Young (eds), *Gender, Globalization and Democratization*. Lanham: Rowman & Littlefield, pp. 223–36.

Hegel, G. W. F. (1998) 'Philosophy of Objective Spirit'. In S. Houlgate (ed.), *The Hegel Reader*. Oxford: Blackwell.

Helms, E. L. (2014) 'The Movement-ization of NGOs? Women's Organizing in Post-war Bosnia-Herzegovina'. In V. Bernal and I. Grewal (eds), *Theorizing NGOs: States, Feminisms, and Neoliberalism*. Durham: Duke University Press, pp. 21–49.

Hemment, J. (2004) 'The Riddle of the Third Sector : Civil Society, International Aid, and NGOs in Russia', *Spring*, 77(2), pp. 215–41.

Hemment, J. (2007) *Empowering Women in Russia: Activism, Aid and NGOs*. Bloomington: Indiana University Press.

Heper, M. (1985) *The State Tradition in Turkey*. Walkington: Eothen Press.

Howell, J. (2005) 'Introduction'. In J. Howell and D. Mulligan (eds), *Gender and Civil Society: Transcending Boundaries*. London: Routledge, pp. 1–23.

Howell, J. (2006) 'Gender and Civil Society'. In M. Glasius, M. Kaldor and H. Anheir (eds), *Global Civil Society Yearbook 2005/6*. London: Sage, pp. 2–27.

Howell, J. (2007) 'Gender and Civil Society: Time for Cross-Border Dialogue', *Social Politics*, 14(4), pp. 415–36.

Howell, J., and Mulligan, D. (2003) 'Editorial', *International Feminist Journal of Politics*, 5(2), pp. 157–61.

Howell, J., and Mulligan, D. (eds) (2005) *Gender and Civil Society: Transcending Boundaries*. London: Routledge.

Howell, J., and Pearce, J. (2001) *Civil Society and Development: A Critical Exploration*. London: Lynne Rienner.

Hughes, K. (2004) 'Turkey and the European Union: Just another Enlargement'. A Friends of European Working Paper. Available at: www.cdu.de/en/doc/Friends_ of_Europe_Turkey.pdf (Accessed: 2 November 2010).

Hughes, E. (2015) 'Resolution of Turkey's Kurdish Question a Process in Crisis'. Available at: http://www.democraticprogress.org/wp-content/uploads/2016/06/ DPI-A-Process-in-Crisis-Edel-Hughes.pdf (Accessed: 20 June 2016).

Hürriyet (2008) 'Erdoğan: En az üç çocuk doğurun (Erdoğan: Give Birth to at Least Three Children)'. Available at: http://www.hurriyet.com.tr/gundem/8401981.asp (Accessed: 20 August 2012).

Hürriyet (2018) '7 OHAL KHK'sı Meclis'te kabul edildi'. Available at: http://www. hurriyet.com.tr/7-ohal-khksi-mecliste-kabul-edildi-40728607 (Accessed: 20 January 2018).

Hürriyet Daily News (2013) 'Turkish PM Erdoğan Reiterates His Call for Three Children'. Available at: http://www.hurriyetdailynews.com/turkish-pm-erdogan-reiterates-his-call-for-three-children.aspx?pageID=238&nid=38235 (Accessed: 18 April 2015).

Hürriyet Daily News (2013) 'Turkish PM Erdoğan Reiterates His Call for Three Children'. Available at: http://www.hurriyetdailynews.com/turkish-pm-erdogan-reiterates-his-call-for-three-children.aspx?pageID=238&nid=38235 (Accessed: 18 April 2015).

İbrahim, F., and Wedel, H. (1997) 'Giriş (Introduction)'. In F. Ibrahim and H. Wedel (eds), *Ortadoğu'da Sivil Toplumun Sorunları (Problems of Civil Society in the Middle East)*. İstanbul: İletişim Yayınları, pp. 11–29.

ICNL (2018) 'Civic Freedom Monitor: Turkey'. Available at: http://www.icnl.org/ research/monitor/turkey.html (Accessed: 15 January 2018).

Ishkanian, A. (2009) '(Re)claiming the Emancipatory Potential of Civil Society: A Critical Examination of Civil Society and Democracy Building Programs in Armenia since 1991', *Armenian Review*, 51(1–4), pp. 9–34.

Jad, I. (2004) 'The NGOisation of Arab Women's Movements', *IDS Bulletin*, 35(4), pp. 34–42.

Jad, I. (2007) 'NGOs: Between Buzzwords and Social Movements', *Development in Practice*, 17 (4–5), pp. 622–9.

Jaggar, A. (2005) 'Arenas of Citizenship'. *International Feminist Journal of Politics*, 7(1), pp. 3–25.

Jorgensen, M., and Philips, L. (2002) *Discourse Analysis as Theory and Method*. London: Sage Publications.

Joseph, S. (1997) 'The Reproduction of Political Process among Women Activists in Lebanon: "Shopkeepers" and Feminists'. In D. Chatty and A. Rabo (eds), *Organizing Women: Formal and Informal Women's Groups in the Middle East*. Oxford: Berg Publications, pp. 57–80.

Joseph, S., and Slyomovics, S. (2001) 'Introduction'. In S. Joseph and S. Slyomovics (eds), *Women and Power in the Middle East*. Philadelphia: University of Pennsylvania Press.

Kabasakal Arat, Z. F. (1994) 'Turkish Women and the Republican Reconstruction of Tradition'. In F. M. Göçek and S. Balaghi (eds), *Reconstructing Gender in the Middle East*. New York: Columbia University Press, pp. 57–78.

Kabasakal Arat, Z. F. (2006) 'Feminist Proje Girişimleri: Genel Sorunlar ve Türkiye icin Değerlendirmeler (Feminist Project Initiatives: General Problems and Evaluations for Turkey)'. *AMARGİ*, 3, pp. 30–1.

KA-DER (2010) *About Us*. Available at: http://ka-der.org.tr/en/about-us/ (Accessed: 26 August 2012).

KA-DER (2012) 'Tüzük (By-law)'. Available at: http://ka-der.org.tr/tuzuk/ (Accessed: 5 May 2015).

KA-DER (n.d.) 'Kadın Yurttaşların ve Aktivistlerin Seçmenler ve Aktif Yurttaşlar Olarak Güçlendirilmesi Projesi (2013–2015) (Empowerment of Women Citizens Project)'. Available at: http://ka-der.org.tr/kadin-yurttaslarin-ve-aktivistlerin-secmenler-ve-aktif-yurttaslar-olarak-guclendirilmesi-projesi-2013-2015/ (Accessed: 5 May 2015).

Kadıoğlu, A. (1994) 'Women's Subordination in Turkey: Is Islam Really the Villian', *The Middle East Journal*, 48(4), pp. 645–61.

Kadıoğlu, A. (1998) 'The Paradox of Turkish Nationalism and the Construction of Official Identity', *Middle Eastern Studies*, 32(2), pp. 177–93.

Kadıoğlu, A. (2005) 'Civil Society, Islam and Democracy in Turkey: A Study of Three Islamic Non-Governmental Organizations', *The Muslim World*, 95(1), pp. 23–41.

Kadir Has University Gender and Women's Studies Research Centre (2016) 'Yasal Ancak Ulaşılabilir Değil: Türkiye'deki Devlet Hastanelerinde Kürtaj Hizmetleri (Legal but not Accessible: Abortion Services at States Hospitals in Turkey)'.

Available at: http://www.khas.edu.tr/w243/files/documents/abortion-tr.pdf (Accessed: 11 January 2017).

Kalaycıoğlu, E. (1998) 'Sivil Toplum ve Neopatrimonyal Siyaset (Civil Society and Neopatrimonial Politics)'. In E. F. Keyman and A. Y. Sarıbay (eds), *Küreselleşme, Sivil Toplum ve İslam* (Globalization, Civil Society and Islam). Ankara: Vadi Yayınlari, pp. 111–36.

Kalaycıoğlu, M. E. (2009) 'Hicab, Turban, and Democracy: Religious Freedom versus Political Protest', *Studies in Public Policy*, 459, pp. 1–25.

Kaldor, M. (2003) *Global Civil Society: An Answer to War*. Cambridge: Polity Press.

Kaliber, A., and Tocci, N. (2010) 'Civil Society and the Transformation of Turkey's Kurdish Question', *Security Dialogue*, 41(2), pp. 191–215.

KAMER (n.d.) 'Nebahat Akkoç, KAMER Foundation'. Available at: http://www.europarl.europa.eu/document/activities/cont/200905/20090508ATT55488/200905 08ATT55488EN.pdf (Accessed: 1 September 2012).

KAMER (2011) *İstersek Biter (We can Stop it)*. İstanbul: Berdan Matbaacılık.

Kandiyoti, D. (1989) 'Women and the Turkish State: Political Actors or Symbolic Pawns?'. In N. Yuval-Davis and F. Anthias (eds), *Woman-Nation-State*. London: Macmillan, pp. 126–49.

Kandiyoti, D. (1991) 'Introduction'. In D. Kandiyoti (ed.), *Women, Islam and the State*. London: Macmillan, pp. 1–21.

Kandiyoti, D. (2011a) 'Disentangling Religion and Politics: Whither Gender Equality', *IDS Bulletin*, 42(1), pp. 10–14.

Kandiyoti, D. (2011b) 'A Tangled Web: The Politics of Gender in Turkey'. Available at: https://www.opendemocracy.net/5050/deniz-kandiyoti/tangled-web-politics-of-gender-in-turkey (Accessed: 15 January, 2015).

Kardam, F. (2005) *Turkey's Engagement with Global Women's Human Rights*. London: Ashgate.

Karns, M. P., and Mingst, P. K. (2010) *International Organizations: The Politics and Processes of Global Governance*, 2nd edition. Boulder: Lynee Rienner.

Karpat, K. H. (1959) *Turkey's Politics: The Transition to a Multi-party System*. Princeton: Princeton University Press.

Kaviraj, S., and Khilnani, S. (2001) 'Introduction: Ideas of Civil Society'. In S. Khilnani and S. Kaviraj (eds), *Civil Society: History and Possibilities*. Cambridge: Cambridge University Press, pp. 1–7.

Kaya, A. (2015) 'Islamisation of Turkey under the AKP Rule: Empowering Family, Faith and Charity', *South European Society and Politics*, 20(1), pp. 47–69.

Keane, J. (1988) 'Despotism and Democracy'. In J. Keane (ed.), *Civil Society and the State: New European Perspectives*. London: Verso, pp. 35–71.

KEİG (2019) 'Selis Kadın Danışmanlık Merkezi (SELİS Women's Counselling Centre)'. http://www.keig.org/selis-kadin-danismanlik-merkezi-diyarbakir/ Available at: (Accessed: 1 February 2019).

KESK (2012) 'Kadın ve Aile Bireylerinin Şiddetten Korunmasına Dair Yasa Taslağı'nda Kadının Adı Yok! (Woman's Name is not in the Draft Law on Protection of the Woman and Family from Violence!)'. Available at: http://www. kesk.org.tr/node/838 (Accessed: 8 August 2013).

Ketola, M. (2009) 'Politics of Civil Society: The Early Impact of EU Funding on Turkish Civil Society Organisations'. *LSE Contemporary Turkish Studies 2nd Annual Doctoral Dissertation Conference*, pp. 1–14. 6 May 2011. Available at: http://lse.academia.edu/MarkusKetola/Papers/253440/Politics_of_Civil_Society_the_Early_Impact_of_EU_Funding_on_Turkish_Civil_Society_Organisations (Accessed: 1 December 2010).

Ketola, M. (2010) 'Europeanisation and Civil Society: The Early Impact of EU Pre-Accession Policies on Turkish NGOs'. Unpublished PhD thesis. The London School of Economics.

Ketola, M. (2013) *Europeanization and Civil Society: Turkish NGOs as Instruments of Change*. London: Palgrave Macmillan.

Ketola, M. (2011) '"A Gap in the Bridge?": European Union Civil Society Assistance in Turkey', *European Journal of Development Research*, 24(1), pp. 89–104.

Keyman, F. (2005) 'Modernity, Democracy and Civil Society'. In F. Adaman and M. Arsel (eds), *Environmentalism in Turkey: Between Democracy and Development?*. London: Ashgate, pp. 35–50.

Keyman, F. (1995) 'On the Relation between Global Modernity and Nationalism: The Crisis of Hegemony and The Rise of (Islamic) Identity in Turkey', *New Perspectives in Turkey*, 8(13), pp. 93–120.

Keyman, F., and İçduygu, A. (2003) 'Globalization, Civil Society and Citizenship in Turkey: Actors, Boundaries and Discourses', *Citizenship Studies*, 7(2), pp. 219–34.

Khilnani, S. (2001) 'The Development of Civil Society'. In S. Khilnani and S. Kaviraj (eds), *Civil Society: History and Possibilities*. Cambridge: Cambridge University Press, pp. 11–32.

Kili, S. (1980) 'Kemalism in Contemporary Turkey', *International Political Science Review*, 1(3), pp. 381–404.

Killingsworth, M. (2012) *Civil Society in Communist Eastern Europe: Opposition and Dissent in Totalitarian Regimes*, Chelmsford: European Consortium of Political Research Press.

Klees, S. (2002) 'NGOs: Progressive Force or Neo-Liberal Tool?', *Current Issues in Comparative Education*, 1(1), pp. 49–54.

Kohler-Koch, B. (2010a) 'Civil Society and EU Democracy: 'Astroturf' Representation?', *Journal of European Public Policy*, 17(1), pp. 100–16.

Kohler-Koch, B. (2010b) 'How to Put Matters Right? Assessing the Role of Civil Society in EU Accountability', *West European Politics*, 33(5), pp. 1117–41.

Koldiska, K. (2009) 'Institutionalizing Intersectionality', *International Feminist Journal of Politics*, 11(4), pp. 547–63.

Konings, P. (2009) *Neoliberal Bandwagonism: Civil Society and the Politics of Belonging in Anglophone Cameroon*. Manko: Langaa.

Krause, W. (2008) *Women in Civil Society*. New York: Palgrave Macmillan.

Krause, W. (2012) *Civil Society and Women Activists in the Middle East: Islamic and secular organizations in Egypt*. London: I.B. Tauris.

Kubicek, P. (2005) 'The European Union and Grassroots Democratization in Turkey', *Turkish Studies*, 6(3), pp. 361–77.

Kumar, K. (1993) 'Civil Society: An Inquiry into the Usefulness of an Historical Term', *The British Journal of Sociology*, 44(3), pp. 375–95.

Kutter, A., and Trappmann, V. (2010) 'Civil Society in Central and Eastern Europe: The Ambivalent Legacy of Accession', *Acta Politica*, 45(1–2), pp. 41–69.

Kuzmanovic, D. (2010) 'Project Culture and Turkish Civil Society', *Turkish Studies*, 11(33), pp. 429–44.

Kuzmanovic, D. (2012) *Refractions of Civil Society in Turkey*. Hampshire: Palgrave Macmillan.

Landig, J. (2011) 'Bringing Women to the Table: European Union Funding for Women's Empowerment Projects in Turkey', *Women's Studies International Forum*, 34(3), pp. 206–19.

Lang, S. (1997) 'The NGOization of Feminism: Institutionalization and Institution Building within the German Women's Movements'. In J. W. Scott, C. Kaplan and D. Keates (eds), *Transitions, Environments, Translations: Feminisms in International Politics*. New York: Routledge, pp. 101–21.

Lazar, M. M. (2005) 'Politicizing Gender in Discourse: Feminist Critical Discourse Analysis as Political Perspectives and Praxis'. In M. M. Lazar (ed.), *Feminist Critical Discourse Analysis*. New York: Palgrave Macmillan, pp. 1–31.

Lazar, M. M. (2007) 'Feminist Critical Discourse Analysis: Articulating a Feminist Discourse Praxis', *Critical Discourse Studies*, 4(2), pp. 141–64.

Lewis, D. (2001) 'Civil Society in Non-Western Contexts : Reflections on the "Usefulness" of a Concept'. Civil Society Working Paper series No: 13. London: Centre for Civil Society, London School of Economics and Political Science.

Lewis, B. (2002) *The Emergence of Modern Turkey*, 3rd edition. New York: Oxford University Press.

Lewis, L. (2012) 'Convergence and Divergences: Egyptian Women's Activism over the Last Century'. In P. Arenfeldt and N. A. Golley (eds), *Mapping Arab Women's Movement: A Century of Transformations from Within*. Cairo: American University in Cairo Press (kindle edition).

Leyla Kuzu, Ş. (2010) 'Türkiye'de Sivil Toplum Kuruluşlarinin Değişen İşlevi ve Kadin STK'lar: KAGİDER ve KAMER Ornekleri (The Changing Functions of Civil Society Organizations and Women's CSOs in Turkey: Cases of KAGİDER and KAMER)'. Unpublished PhD thesis. Ege University, Izmir, Turkey.

Leyla, Ş. (2011) 'The New Actors of Women's Movement : Women's NGOs and Their Potentials', *Eurasian Journal of Anthropology*, 2(1), pp. 1–14.

Mardin, Ş. (1969) 'Power, Civil Society and Culture in the Ottoman Empire', *Comparative Studies in Society and History*, 11, pp. 258–81.

Mardin, Ş. (1971) 'Ideology and Religion in the Turkish Revolution', *International Journal of Middle East Studies*, 2(3), pp. 197–211.

Mardin, Ş. (2006) *Religion, Society and Modernity in Turkey*. New York: Syracuse University Press.

Marshall, G. A. (2005) 'Ideology, Progress, and Dialogue: A Comparison of Feminist and Islamist Women's Approaches to the Issues of Head Covering and Work in Turkey', *Gender & Society*, 19(1), pp. 104–20.

Marshall, G. A. (2009) 'Authenticating Gender Policies through Sustained-Pressure: The Strategy behind the Success of Turkish Feminists', *Social Politics: International Studies in Gender, State & Society*, 16(3), pp. 358–78.

Marshall, G. A. (2013) *Shaping Gender Policy in Turkey: Grassroots Women Activists, the European Union and the Turkish State*. Albany: State University of New York Press.

Martin, P. Y. (1990) 'Rethinking Feminist Organizations', *Gender & Society*, 4(2), pp. 182–206.

Marx, K. (1994) 'German Ideology, Part I'. In L. H. Simon (ed.), *Selected Writings*. Indianapolis: Hackett Publishing.

Mercer, C. (2002) 'NGOs, Civil Society and Democratization: A Critical Review of the Literature', *Progress in Development Studies*, 2(5), pp. 5–22.

Mert, N. (2007) 'DP'den AKP'ye Merkez Sagin Kisa Tarihi (7) (A Short History of Centre Right from DP to AKP)'. Available at: http://www.radikal.com.tr/haber.php?haberno=224309 (Accessed: 24 April 2012).

Milan, F. (2013) 'Two Ideals of Democracy Clashing in Turkey', *Changing Turkey*. Available at: https://changingturkey.wordpress.com/2013/06/07/two-ideals-of-democracy-clashing-in-turkey-by-francesco-f-milan/ (Accessed: 8 June 2013).

Ministry of EU Affairs (2017) 'Turkey and EU Civil Society Dialogue II Project'.
Available at: https://www.ab.gov.tr/turkey-and-eu-civil-society-dialogue-ii-
project_45649_en.html (Accessed: 10 June 2018).

Moghadam, V. M. (1997) 'Women's NGOs in the Middle East and North
Africa: Constraints, Opportunities, and Priorities'. In D. Chatty and A. Rabo (eds),
Organizing Women: Formal and Informal Women's Groups in the Middle East.
Oxford: Berg Publications, pp. 23–55.

Moghadam, V. M. (2002) 'Citizenship, Civil Society and Women in the Arab Region',
Al-Raida, 19(97–8), pp. 12–22.

Moghadam, V. M. (2003) 'Engendering Citizenship, Feminizing Civil Society',
Women and Politics, 25(1–2), pp. 63–87.

Mousseau, D. (2006) 'Democracy, Human Rights and Market Development in
Turkey: Are They Related?', *Government and Opposition*, 41(2), pp. 298–326.

Murdock, D. (2003) 'That Stubborn "Doing Good" Question: Ethical/Epistemological
Concerns in the Study of NGOs', *Ethnos*, 68(4), pp. 507–32.

Nagar, R. (2011) *Ateşle Oynamak* (Playing with Fire). Ankara: Ayizi Yayinlari.

Narlı, N. (1999) 'The Rise of the Islamist Movement in Turkey', *Middle East Review of
International Affairs*, 3(3), pp. 38–48.

Navaro-Yashin, Y. (1998a) 'Uses and Abuses of "State and Society" in Contemporary
Turkey', *New Perspectives on Turkey*, 18, pp. 1–22.

Navaro-Yashin, Y. (1998b) 'Bir iktidar soylemi olarak sivil toplum (Civil Society as a
Discourse of Power)'. *Birikim*, 105–6, pp. 57–62.

Navaro-Yashin, Y. (2002) *Faces of the State: Secularism and Public Life in Turkey.*
Princeton: Princeton University Press.

Nefissa, S. B. (2005) 'Introduction: NGOs and Governance in the Arab World: A
Question of Democarcy'. In S. B. Nefissa et al. (eds), *NGOs and Governance in the
Arab World*. Cairo: American University in Cairo Press, pp. 1–16.

Negron-Gonzales, M. (2016) 'The Feminist Movement during the AKP Era in
Turkey: Challenges and Opportunities', *Middle Eastern Studies*, 52(2), pp. 198–214.

Norton, A. R. (1995) 'Introduction'. In A. R. Norton (ed.) *Civil Society in the Middle
East*, Vol. I. Leiden: E. J. Brill, pp. 1–16.

NTV (2009) 'HEP, DEP ve HADEP de kapatılmıştı (HEP, DEP and HADEP Have
Also Been Shut Down)'. Available at: http://www.ntvmsnbc.com/id/25029246/
(Accessed: 26 April 2012).

NTV (n.d.) 'Ergenekon Davasında Sona Gelindi (Coming to the End of Ergenekon
Trial)'. Available at: http://interaktif.ntv.com.tr/ergenekon/ (Accessed: 1
March 2015).

Oakley, A. (1981) 'Interviewing Women: A Contradiction in Terms'. In H. Roberts (ed.) *Doing Feminist Research*. London: Routledge & Kegan Paul, pp. 30–62.

Okin, S. M. (1998) 'Gender, the Public, and the Private'. In A. Phillips (ed.), *Feminism and Politics*. New York: Oxford University Press, pp. 116–42.

Öktem, K. (2011) *Angry Nation: Turkey since 1989*. London: Zed Books.

Onbaşı, F. (2008) 'Civil Society Debate in Turkey: A Critical Analysis'. Unpublished PhD thesis. Middle East Technical University.

Öniş, Z. (2007) 'Conservative Globalists versus Defensive Nationalists: Political Parties and Paradoxes of Europeanization in Turkey', *Journal of Balkan and Near Eastern Studies*, 9(3), pp. 247–61.

Öniş, Z. (2014) 'Monopolizing the Center: The AKP and the Uncertain Path of Turkish Democracy'. Available at: http://www.suits.su.se/polopoly_fs/1.200640.1408970851!/menu/standard/file/Onis%20Monopolizing%20the%20center-Final%20Draft%2019%20August%202014.pdf (Accessed: 17 April 2015).

Orakçı, N. (2007) 'Sivil Toplum Kuruluşlarına Yönelik Kadınların İnsan Hakları Semineri'. Available at: http://www.baskentkadin.org/tr/?p=5 (Accessed: 8 April 2015).

Özbudun, E. (2014) 'AKP at the Crossroads: Erdoğan's Majoritarian Drift', *South European Society and Politics*, 19(2), pp. 155–67.

Özçetin, H. (2009) 'Breaking the Silence': The Religious Muslim Women's Movement in Turkey', *Journal of International Women's Studies*, 11(1), pp. 106–19.

Özçetin, B., and Özer, M. (2015) 'The Current Environment for Civil Society in Turkey', *Comparative Nonprofit Sector Working Paper*, no.53.

Özdalga, E. (1997) 'Civil Society and Its Enemies: Reflections on a Debate in the Light of Recent Developments within the Islamic Student Movement in Turkey'. In E. Özdalga and S. Persson (eds), *Civil Society Democracy and the Muslim World*. Istanbul: Numune Matbaasi, pp. 1–7.

Özman, A., and Coşar, S. (2007) 'Reconceptualizing Center Politics in Post-1980 Turkey: Transformation or Continuity?'. In F. Keyman (ed.), *Remaking Turkey: Globalization, Alternative Modernities, and Democracy*. Lanham: Lexington Books, pp. 201–22.

Paker, H., Özoğuz, S., and Baykan, B. G. (2008) 'Türkiye'de kadın ve sivil toplum: örgütlenme ve son eğilimler (Woman and Civil Society in Turkey: Organising and Last Tendencies'. Betam Araştırma Notu 08/15. Available at: http://betam.bahcesehir.edu.tr/2008/11/turkiyede-kadin-ve-sivil-toplum-orgutlenme-ve-son-egilimler/ (Accessed: 28 April 2015).

Pankhurst, D., and Pearce, J. (1996) 'Feminist Perspectives on Democratisation in the South: Engendering or Adding Women In?'. In H. Afshar (ed.), *Women and Politics in the Third World*. London: Routledge, pp. 41–50.

Pateman, C. (1988) *Sexual Contract*. Cambridge: Polity Press.

Pateman, C. (1989) *The Disorder of Women*. Cambridge: Polity Press.

Pelczynski, Z. A. (1984a) 'Introduction: The Significance of Hegel's Separation of the State and Civil Society'. In Z. A. Pelczynski (ed.), *The State and Civil Society: Studies in Hegel's Political Philosophy*. Cambridge: Cambridge University Press, pp. 1–14.

Pelczynski, Z. A. (1984b) 'Nation, Civil Society, State: Hegelian Sources of the Marxian Non-Theory of Nationality'. In Z. A. Pelczynski (ed.), *The State and Civil Society: Studies in Hegel's Political Philosophy*. Cambridge: Cambridge University Press, pp. 262–79.

Petras, J. (1997) 'Imperialism and NGOs in Latin America', *Monthly Review*, 49(7), pp. 10–27.

Phillips, A. (1987) 'Introduction'. In A. Phillips (ed.), *Feminism and Equality*. Oxford: Basil Blackwell.

Phillips, A. (1993) *Democracy and Difference*. Cambridge: Polity Press.

Phillips, A. (1999) 'Who Needs Civil Society? A Feminist Perspective', *Dissent*, 46(1), pp. 56–61.

Phillips, A. (2002) 'Does Feminism Needs a Conception of Civil Society?'. In S. Chambers and W. Kymlicka (eds), *Alternative Conceptions of Civil Society*. Princeton: Princeton University Press, pp. 71–90.

Pratt, N. (2005) 'Hegemony and Counter-hegemony in Egypt: Advocacy NGOs, Civil Society and the State'. In S. B. Nefissa et al. (eds), *NGOs and Governance in the Arab World*. Cairo: American University in Cairo Press, pp. 123–50.

Prinsloo, J. (2007) 'News Constructs of Customary Identity versus Democratic Practice: The Case of Lindiwe Dlamini and Mswati III of Swaziland', *Communication*, 33(1), pp. 77–95.

Pusane, Ö. K. (2014) 'Turkey's Kurdish Opening: Long awaited Achievements and Failed Expectations', *Turkish Studies*, 15(1), pp. 81–99.

Pusch, B. (2000) 'Stepping into the Public Sphere: The Rise of Islamist and Religious-Conservative Women's Non-Governmental Organisations'. In S. Yerasimos, G. Seufert and K. Vorhoff (eds), *Civil Society in the Grip of Nationalism*. Istanbul: Orient-Institut, pp. 475–505.

Putnam, R. D. (1995) 'Bowling Alone: America's Declining Social Capital', *Journal of Democracy*, 6(1), pp. 65–78.

Rabo, A. (1996) 'Gender, State and Civil Society in Jordan and Syria'. In C. Hann and E. Dunn (eds), *Civil Society: Challenging Western Models*. London: Routledge, pp. 153–75.

Radikal (2012) 'İzinsiz kürtaja hapis cezası geliyor (Unauthorizes Abortion Will Be punished)'. Available at: http://www.radikal.com.tr/Radikal.aspxaType=RadikalDe tayV3&ArticleID=1094502&CategoryID=77 (Accessed: 25 August 2012).

Radikal (2013) 'Hakim, savcı, asker ve poliste başörtü yok (There Is No Headscarf for Judge, Attorney General, Military Officer and Police)'. Available at: http://www. radikal.com.tr/turkiye/hakim_savci_asker_ve_poliste_basortu_yok-1153218 (Accessed: 12 May 2014).

Radikal (2014) 'Arınç: Kadın Herkesin İçinde Kahkaha Atmayacak (Arınç: Woman Should Not Laugh Publicly)'. Available at: http://www.radikal.com.tr/turkiye/ hakim-savci-asker-ve-poliste-basortu-yok-1153218/ (Accessed: 25 March 2015).

Rai, S. (2012) 'Women and the State in the Third World'. In H. Afshar (ed.), *Women and Politics in the Third World*. London: Routledge. pp. 26–41.

Raik, K. (2006) 'Promoting Democracy through Civil Society'. *CEPS Working Document*, No. 237.

Reinharz, S. (1992) *Feminist Methods in Social Research*. Oxford: Oxford University Press.

Reinharz, S., and Chase, S. (2003) 'Interviewing Women'. In J. Holstein and J. Gubrium (eds), *Inside Interviewing: New Lenses, New Concerns*. Thousand Oaks, CA: Sage.

Riessman, C. K. (1987) 'When Gender Is Not Enough: Women Interviewing Women'. *Gender and Society*, 1(2), pp. 172–207.

Rios-Tobar, M. (2005) 'Chilean Feminism(s) in the 1990s: Paradox of an unfinished transition'. In J. Howell and D. Mulligan (eds), *Gender and Civil Society: Transcending Boundaries*, London: Routledge, pp. 139–63.

Rose, G. (1997) 'Situating Knowledges: Positionality, Reflexivities and Other Tactics', *Progress in Human Geography*, 21, pp. 305–20.

Rumford, C. (2002) 'Placing Democratization within the Global Frame: Sociological Approaches to Universalism, and Democratic Contestation in Contemporary Turkey', *The Sociological Review*, 50(2), pp. 258–77.

Sadurski, W. (2004) 'Accession's Democracy Dividend : The Impact of the EU Enlargement upon Democracy in the New Member States of Central and Eastern Europe', *European Law Journal*, 10(4), pp. 371–401.

Sancar, S., and Bulut, A. (2006) 'Turkey: Country Gender Profile', Final Report. Available at: http://www.jica.go.jp/english/operations/thematic_issues/gender/ background/pdf/e06tur.pdf (Accessed: 5 May 2011).

Sarıbay, A. Y. (1998) 'Türkiye'de Demokrasi ve Sivil Toplum (Democracy and Civil Society in Turkey)'. In E. F. Keyman and A. Y. Sarıbay (eds), *Küreselleşme Sivil Toplum ve İslam (Globalization, Civil Society and Islam)*. Ankara: Vadi Yayınları, pp. 88–111.

Sariolghalam, M. (1997) 'Prospects for Civil Society in the Middle East: An Analysis of Cultural Impediments'. In E. Özdalga and S. Persson (eds), *Civil*

Society Democracy and the Muslim World. Istanbul: Numune Matbaasi, pp. 55–61.

Schippers, B. (2005) 'Civil Society'. In I. Mackenzie (ed.), *Political Concepts: A Reader and Guide*. Edinburgh: Edinburgh University Press, pp. 343–54.

Schumpeter, J. (2003) *Capitalism, Socialism and Democracy*. London: Routledge.

Seçkinelgin, H. (2004) 'Contradictions of a Sociocultural reflex: Civil Society in Turkey'. In M. Glasius, D. Lewis and H. Seçkinelgin (eds), *Exploring Civil Society: Political and Cultural Contexts*. London: Routledge, pp. 173–81.

Seufert, G. (2000) 'The Impact of National Discourses on Civil Society'. In S. Yerasimos, G. Seufert and K. Vorhoff (eds), *Civil Society in the Grip of Nationalism*. Istanbul: Orient-Institut, pp. 25–49.

Seufert, G. (2014) 'Is the Fethullah Gülen Movement Overstretching Itself? A Turkish Religious Community as a National and International Player', *SWP Research Paper*, pp. 1–31.

Seungsook, M. (2002) 'Carving Out Space : Civil Society and the Women's Movement in South Korea', *The Journal of Asian Studies*, 61(2), pp. 473–500.

SFK (2008) 'Başlarken (When Beginning)'. Available at: http://sosyalist feministkolektif.org/biz-kimiz/178-baslarken.html (Accessed: 28 February 2012).

SFK (2013) 'Beyoğlu'na Feminist Sözümüz Var (We have a Feminist Word to Beyoğlu)'. Available at: http://www.sosyalistfeministkolektif.org/feminizm/ tarihimizden/755-bey-oglu-na-feminist-soezuemuez-var-kampanyas-brosuerue. html (Accessed: 19 April 2015).

Stephan, R. (2012) 'Women's Rights Activism in Lebanon'. In P. Arenfeldt and N. A. Golley (eds), *Mapping Arab Women's Movement: A Century of Transformations from Within*. Cairo: The American Univetsity in Cairo Press (kindle edition).

Silliman, J. (1999a) 'Expanding Civil Society, Shrinking Political Spaces: The Case of Women's Nongovernmental Organisations'. In J. Silliman and Y. King (eds), *Dangerous Intersections: Feminism, Population and the Environment*. London: Zed Books, pp. 133–62.

Silliman, J. (1999b) 'Expanding Civil Society: Shrinking Political Spaces – The Case of Women's Nongovernmental Organizations'. *Social Politics*, 6(2), pp. 23–53.

Şimşek, S. (2004) 'The Transformation of Civil Society in Turkey: From Quantity to Quality', *Turkish Studies*, 5(3), pp. 46–74.

Sirman, N. (1988) 'Turkish Feminism: A Short History', *WLUML Dossier*, 5/6, pp. 1–12.

Sirman, N. (2006) 'Proje Toplumunda Sanal Kadınlar (Virtual Women in Project Society)'. *AMARGI*, 3, p. 22.

Sloat, A. (2005) 'The Rebirth of Civil Society: The Growth of Women's NGOs in Central and Eastern Europe', *European Journal of Women's Studies*, 12(4), pp. 437–52.

Smith, L. M. (1975) 'Women as Volunteers: The Double Subsidy', *Journal of Voluntary Action Research*, 4(3–4), pp. 119–36.

Somer, M., and Liaras, E. (2010) 'Turkey's New Kurdish Opening: Religious Versus Secular Values', *Middle East Policy*, 17(2), pp. 152–65.

Sprague, J. (2005) *Feminist Methodologies for Critical Researchers*. Lanham: Rowman & Littlefield.

Squires, J. (2003) 'Public and Private'. In R. Bellamy and A. Mason (eds), *Political Concepts*. Manchester: Manchester University Press, pp. 131–45.

Stevenson, L. S. (2005) 'The Impact of Feminist Civil Society and Political Alliances on Gender Policies in Mexico'. In J. Howell and D. Mulligan (eds), *Gender and Civil Society: Transcending Boundaries*. London: Routledge, pp. 163–96.

STGM (2018) 'STÖ Veri Tabanı (NGO Database)'. Available at: http://www.stgm.org.tr/tr/stoveritabani (Accessed: 1 June 2018).

Sunderland, J. (2004) *Gendered Discourses*. New York: Palgrave Macmillan.

Sunderland, J., and Litosseliti, L. (2002) 'Gender Identity and Discourse Analysis: Theoretical and Emprical Considerations'. In L. Litosseliti and J. Sunderland (eds), *Gender Identity and Discourse*. Amsterdam: John Benjamins Publishing, pp. 3–43.

Sunderland, J., and Litosseliti, L. (2008) 'Current Research Methodologies in Gender and Language Study: Key Issues'. In K. Harrington, L. Litosseliti, H. Sauntson and J. Sunderland (eds), *Gender and Language Research Methodologies*. Basingstoke: Palgrave Macmillan, pp. 1–21.

T24 (2017) 'AKP'li Tunç: 98 bin kamu çalışanı ihraç edildi, 1401 dernek kapatıldı'. Available at: http://t24.com.tr/haber/akpli-tunc-98-bin-kamu-calisani-ihrac-edildi-1401-dernek-kapatildi,387851 (Accessed: 1 March 2017).

Taniguchi, H. (2006) 'Men's and Women's Volunteering: Gender Differences in the Effects of Employment and Family Characteristics', *Nonprofit and Voluntary Sector Quarterly*, 35 (1), pp. 83–101.

Tank, P. (2005) 'Political Islam in Turkey: A State of Controlled Secularity', *Turkish Studies*, 6(1), pp. 3–19.

Tekdemir, Ö. (2016) 'Conflict and Reconciliation between Turks and Kurds: The HDP as an Agonistic Actor', *Southeast European and Black Sea Studies*, 16(4), pp. 651–69.

Tekeli, Ş. (1981) 'Women in Turkish Politics'. In N. Abadan-Unat (ed.), *Women in Turkish Society*. Leiden: E. J. Brill, pp. 293–311.

Tekeli, Ş. (1986) 'The Emergence of the Feminist Movement in Turkey'. In D. Dahlerup (ed.), *The New Women's Movement*. London: Sage Publications, pp. 179–99.

Tekeli, Ş. (1989) '80'lerde Turkiye'de Kadinlarin Kurtulus Hareketinin Gelismesi (Development of Women Emancipation Movement in Turkey in the 80s)', *Birikim*, No.3, pp. 34–41.

Tekeli, Ş. (1990) 'Women in the Changing Political Associations of the 1980s'. In A Finkel and N. Sirman (eds), *Turkish State, Turkish Society*, New York: Routledge, pp. 259–89.

Tekeli, Ş. (2010), 'The *Turkish Women's Movement: A Brief History of Success*', *Quaderns de la. Mediterrània*, 14(1), pp. 119–23.

Tiehen, L. (2000) 'Has Working More Caused Married Women to Volunteer Less? Evidence from Time Diary Data, 1965 to 1993', *Non-profit and Voluntary Sector Quarterly*, 29(4), pp. 505–29.

Tinker, I. (1999) 'NGOs: An Alternative Power Base for Women?'. In E. Prugl and M. Mayer (eds), *Gender Politics in Global Governance*. Lanham: Rowman & Littlefield, pp. 1–39.

TKB (2007) 'Tüzük (By-law)'. Available at: http://www.turkkadinlarbirligi.org/tuzuk/T%C3%BCz%C3%BCk (Accessed: 1 May 2015).

TKB (2015) 'Tarihçe (History)'. Available at: http://www.turkkadinlarbirligi.org/kurumsal/Tarih%C3%A7e (Accessed: 1 May 2015).

Tocci, N. (2005) 'Europeanization in Turkey: Trigger or Anchor for Reform?', *South European Society and Politics*, 10(1), pp. 73–83.

Tolunay, Ö. İ. (2014) 'Women in Erdoğan's Turkey', *New Politics*, XIV(4). Available at: http://newpol.org/content/women-erdo%C4%9Fan%E2%80%99s-turkey (Accessed: 4 April 2015).

Toprak, B. (1996) 'Civil Society in Turkey'. In A. R. Norton (ed.), *Civil Society in the Middle East*. Vol. 2. Leiden: E. J. Brill, pp. 87–118.

Toprak, B. (2005) 'Islam and Democracy in Turkey', *Turkish Studies*, 6(2), pp. 167–86.

Townsend, J. G., Zapata, E., Rowlands, J., Alberti, P., and Mercado, M. (1999) *Women and Power: Fighting Patriarchies and Poverty*. London: Zed Books.

Treleaven, L. (2004) 'A Knowledge-Sharing Approach to Organisational Change: A Critical Discourse Analysis'. In H. Tsoukas and N. Mylonopoulos (eds), *Organizations as knowledge-Systems: Knowledge, Learning and Dynamic Capabilities*. New York: Palgrave Macmillan, pp. 154–80.

Tripp, A. M. (2005) 'Women in Movement: Transformations in African Political Landscapes'. In J. Howell and D. Mulligan (eds), *Gender and Civil Society: Transcending Boundaries*. London: Routledge, pp. 78–101.

Tugal, C. (2013) '"Resistance Everywhere": The Gezi Revolt in Global Perspective', *New Perspectives on Turkey*, 49, pp. 147–62.

TÜKD (n.d.) 'Mission'. Available at: https://www.tukd.org.tr/?page_id=107 (Accessed: 19 September 2012).

TÜKD (2010) 'Tüzük (By-law)'. Available at: http://www.tukd.org.tr/tukd-eski-site/ tuzuk.asp.html (Accessed: 21 May 2015).

TÜKD (2012) '2010–2012 Faaliyet Raporu (2010–2012 Activity Report)'. Available at: http://www.tukd.org.tr/tukd-eski-site/yonetim_donemi_etkinlikleri_2012.asp. html (Accessed: 21 May 2015).

TÜKD (2012) 'Dünya Kadınlar Gün Etkinlikleri (International Women's Day Activities)', Pamphlet collected from TÜKD office. Ankara: TÜKD.

TÜİK (2013) 'Yıllara Göre İl Nüfusları, 2007–2013 (Population of Provinces by Years, 2007–2013)'. Available at: www.tuik.gov.tr/PreIstatistikTablo.do?istab_id=1590 (Accessed: 5 July 2013).

Uçar, H. (2009) 'Women's Rights in Turkey: Interaction of State and Non-State Actors in the Implementation of Judicial Equality', *Friedrich-Ebert-Stiftung Fokus Türkei* 15.

Updegraff, R. (2012) 'The Kurdish Question', *Journal of Democracy*, 23(1), pp. 119–28.

US (n.d.) 'Gölge Meclisi Projesi (Watch Your Shadow Project)'. Available at: http:// ucansupurge.org/yazdir?6A0EAD26C8B12963D7ACD863D10636C9 (Accessed: 28 May 2015).

US (2011) *Demokraside Kadin İzleri Projesi: Yasama El Kitabi* (The Route of Women in Democracy: Legislation Guide). Ankara: Ziraat Gurup Matbaa.

Uslu, E. (2008) 'Ulusalcılık: The Neo-nationalist Resurgence in Turkey', *Turkish Studies*, 9(1), pp. 73–97.

Üstündağ, N. (2006) 'Türkiye'de Projecilik Üzerine Eleştrel Bir Değerlendirme (A Critical Evaluation of Projectism in Turkey)', *AMARGİ*, 3, pp. 23–4.

Usul, A. R. (2011) *Democracy in Turkey: The Impact of EU Political Conditionality*. London: Routledge.

Walton, J. F. (2013) 'Confessional Pluralism and the Civil Society Effect: Liberal Mediations of Islam and Secularims and Secularism in Contemporary Turkey', *Journal of the American Ethnological Society*, 40(1), pp. 182–200.

Watson, P. (1997) 'Civil Society and the Politics of Difference in Eastern Europe'. In J. W. Scott, C. Kaplan and D. Keates (eds), *Transitions, Environments, Translations: Feminisms in International Politics*. London: Routledge, pp. 21–30.

Waylen, G. (1994) 'Women and Democratization: Conceptualizing Gender Relations in Transition Politics', *World Politics*, 46(3), pp. 327–54.

Weldon, S. L. (2005) 'The Dimensions and Policy Impacts of Feminist Civil Society: Democratic Policy-making on violence against women in the fifty US States'. In J. Howell and D. Mulligan (eds), *Gender and Civil Society: Transcending Boundaries*. London: Routledge, pp. 196–222.

White, J. B. (1996) 'Civic Culture and Islam in urban Turkey'. In C. Hann and E. Dunn (eds), *Civil Society: Challenging Western Models*. London: Routledge, pp. 141–52.

White, J. B. (2002) *Islamist Mobilization in Turkey: A Study in Vernacular Politics*. Seattle: University of Washington Press.

White, J. B. (2003) 'State Feminism, Modernization, and the Turkish Republican Woman', *Feminist Formations*, 15(3), pp. 145–59.

White, G. (2004) 'Civil Society, Democratization and Development: Clearing the Analytic Ground'. In P. Burnell and P. Calvert (eds), *Civil Society in Democratization*. London: Frank Cass, pp. 6–22.

Wiktorowicz, Q. (2000) 'Civil Society as Social Control: State Power in Jordan', *Comparative Politics*, 33(1), pp. 43–61.

Wodak, R., and Meyer, M. (2009) 'Critical Discourse Analysis: History, Agenda, Theory, Methodology'. In R. Wodak and M. Meyer (eds), *Methods of Critical Discourse Analysis*. London: Sage Publications, pp. 1–33.

Wood, L. A., and Kroger, R. O. (2000) *Doing Discourse Analysis: Methods for Studying Action in Text and Talk*. London: Sage Publications.

Valliatanos, S. (2013) 'Arab Civil Society at the Crossroad of Democratization: The Arab Spring Impact'. Neighbourhood Policy Paper No: 10. Istanbul: Kadir Has University.

Van Rooy, A. (1998) 'Civil Society as Idea: An Analytic Hatstand?' In A. Van Rooy (ed.), *Civil Society and the Aid Industry: The Politics and Promise*. London: Earthscan, pp. 6–27.

Yalçın, A., and Öz, Y. (2011) *Sivil Toplum Örgütleri İçin Hukuk Rehberi (Law Guide for Civil Society Organisations)*. Ankara: Odak Ofset Matbaacılık.

Yerasimos, S. (2000) 'Civil Society, Europe and Turkey'. In S. Yerasimos, G. Seufert and K. Vorhoff (eds), *Civil Society in the Grip of Nationalism*. Istanbul: Orient-Institut, pp. 11–25.

Yılmaz, Z. (2015) 'The AKP and Its Family Policy in the Re-establishment Process of Authoritativeness in Turkey'. In J. Karakoç (ed.), *Authoritarianism in the Middle East: Before and After the Arab Uprising*. Hampshire: Palgrave Macmillan, pp. 150–72.

Yılmaz, E. S. A. (2015) 'A New Momentum: Gender Justice in the Women's Movement', *Turkish Policy Quarterly*, 13(4), pp. 107–15.

Yıldız, A. (2008) 'Problematizing the Intellectual and Political Vestiges'. In Ü. Cizre (ed.), *Secular and Islamic Politics in Turkey: The Making of the Justice and Development Party*, Oxon: Routledge, pp. 41–62.

Young, I. M. (2000) *Inclusion and Democracy*. New York: Oxford University Press.

Zaki, M. (1995) *Civil Society and Democratization: 1981–1994*, Cairo: Ibn Khaldaun Centre.

Zubaida, S. (1992) 'Islam, the State and Democracy: Contrasting Conceptions of Society in Egypt', *Middle East Report*, 179, pp. 2–10.

Zürcher, E. J. (1997) *Turkey: A Modern History*. London: I.B. Tauris.

Index

www.ingramcontent.com/pod-product-compliance
Lightning Source LLC
Chambersburg PA
CBHW050433280326
41932CB00013BA/2100